HARD WOMEN, HARD WAR

UNCIVIL WARS

Series Editors

Stephen Berry, University of Georgia
Amy Murrell Taylor, University of Kentucky
Fay Yarbrough, Rice University

Advisory Board

Joseph Belein, Pennsylvania State University, Behrand
Brandi Brimmer, University of North Carolina at Chapel Hill
Maria Angela Diaz, University of Illinois Urbana-Champaign
Gregory Downs, University of California, Davis
Megan Kate Nelson, megankatenelson.com
Kristen Oertel, University of Tulsa
Joshua D. Rothman, University of Alabama
KT Shively, Virginia Commonwealth University
David Silkenat, University of Florida

Hard Women, Hard War

How Southern Women Shaped U.S. Policy During the Civil War

Laura Mammina

THE UNIVERSITY OF GEORGIA PRESS

ATHENS

© 2026 by the University of Georgia Press
Athens, Georgia 30602
www.ugapress.org
All rights reserved

Set in Garamond by Westchester Publishing Services

Use of any part of this book in training for any artificial intelligence (AI), large language model (LLM), machine learning technologies, or similar generative language system without license is expressly prohibited.

Printed digitally

EU Authorized Representative

Easy Access System Europe—Mustamäe tee 50, 10621 Tallinn, Estonia, gpsr.requests@easproject.com

Library of Congress Cataloging-in-Publication Data

Names: Mammina, Laura author
Title: Hard women, hard war : how southern women shaped U.S. policy during the Civil War / Laura Mammina.
Other titles: Uncivil wars
Description: Athens : The University of Georgia Press, [2026] | Series: Uncivil wars | Includes bibliographical references and index.
Identifiers: LCCN 2026017263 | ISBN 9780820380599 hardback | ISBN 9780820380605 paperback | ISBN 9780820380612 epub | ISBN 9780820380629 pdf
Subjects: LCSH: Women—Political activity—Southern States—History—19th century | African American women—Political activity—Southern States—History—19th century | United States—History—Civil War, 1861–1865—Women
Classification: LCC E628 .M28 2026 | DDC 973.7082—dc23/eng/20260416
LC record available at https://lccn.loc.gov/2026017263

For Stephen, always

CONTENTS

ILLUSTRATIONS

Figures

Tables

HARD WOMEN, HARD WAR

Introduction

THE FACTS SEEMED quite plain: On June 11, 1863, Union soldiers burned the small town of Darien, Georgia, to the ground. Whether it deserved to burn was another matter. The details appeared damning: African American soldiers, commanded by abolitionist officers, attacked a city inhabited largely by civilians. Although Federals "landed without resistance," the commanding officer issued "express orders" that Darien be burned, arguing that "Southerners must be made to feel that this was a real war." At least one subordinate officer vehemently disagreed, characterizing the town as "deserted" and calling incendiarism a "barbarous sort of warfare" that descended into "wanton destruction."[1]

Enlisted men embraced bringing the war to rebels' doors. Fifty-Fourth Massachusetts Sgt. George E. Stephens declared that the attack had "sprea[d] terror to the hearts of the rebels throughout this region." Ordinary soldiers celebrated that they had deprived the enemy of valuable resources, remarking that the army secured "cattle, sheep, pigs, [and] poultry" and noting that "the plunder acquired afforded many comforts and even luxuries." The enlisted men even questioned whether the raid had traumatized Darien residents. Stephens recalled that given the chance to come with the Union army, the two white women they met "requested to be left behind."[2]

Focusing on commanders' and soldiers' experiences of the Darien attack leads us to believe that the incident was a disagreement between Federals about how to wage war.[3] But the story changes dramatically by including Southern women. The two working-class white women who requested to be left behind—Mary J. Russell and Mary C. Hazzard—made their Confederate sympathies clear when they declined the U.S. Army's offer of protection. Their defiantly rebellious behavior might have spurred the military to further destruction, because after that, Federals burned the town. They burned the businesses that lined the docks, which had readied rice and salt to evade Union gunboats. They burned the schooner *Pet*, loaded with cotton and bound for Nassau. They burned the Methodist, Presbyterian, and Episcopalian churches, which prayed every Sunday for the success of Confederate armies and wisdom for Jefferson Davis. And they burned private dwelling houses, perhaps even the homes of Russell and Hazzard, who may have contributed to driving one of Darien's only Unionist families out of their home.[4]

That family was headed by freeborn Black woman Elizabeth Garey. She and her family had resided in Darien their entire lives. It was Garey who provided the Federals with the intelligence leading to the attack. She did so because, as she recounted in postwar testimony to the Southern Claims Commission, she hoped "that the South should be conquered." And so she kept up connections with childhood friends, people who had self-emancipated at Federal headquarters in Beaufort. The grapevine telegraph made it possible for Garey, living behind enemy lines, to relay information about Confederate forces to the men of the First South Carolina Regiment.[5] These connections led to Darien's burning. And when the aftermath of the attack placed her and her family in a vulnerable position, she struck another blow at the Confederacy. A few weeks after Darien burned, Garey recounted that "the Rebels found we were in communication with the Yankees and . . . gave us four hours to get away." The USS *Wamsutta* carried them to safety but not before Garey's husband "directed [Capt. John W. Kittredge] to where the Rebel camp was, & the captain shelled them from the steamer."[6] Elizabeth Garey and Federal soldiers waged a successful, collaborative raid on a strategic location full of Confederate sympathizers.

This project restores Southern women to their central place negotiating and collaborating with the Federal army, particularly over military policies that affected civilians. Drawing on the stories of women like Garey, *Hard Women, Hard War: How Southern Women Shaped U.S. Policy During the Civil War* demonstrates that Southern women forced Federal soldiers to adjust and sometimes change their civilian policies. As Elizabeth Garey demonstrates, Southern women had their own ideas about how the Civil War should be fought. To Garey, Darien was not the undefended, deserted town that some Union commanders made it out to be but instead a rich plantation region brimming with enslaved people. It was home to blockade runners who sought to sell cotton to European buyers. It was an unabashedly rebel town, one that had persecuted Garey and her family for their Union loyalties. It had welcomed the Confederate army and Confederate militia. And so one of its own, tired of being "threatened with death & injury" because of her "Union sentiments," turned the town into a battlefield. Because of Elizabeth Garey's actions, Darien became what historian Thavolia Glymph has termed an "archiv[e] of slavery's destruction," as the enslaved men and women who remained in Darien used the Federal army's arrival to self-emancipate.[7] Garey knowingly sacrificed her home and her family's safety by sharing vital information with the Federal army, leading white officers and Black enlisted men to seize valuable resources from staunch Confederates. Rather than protecting her home, Garey invited the Federals to destroy it. Her home—and her town—were necessary sacrifices to ensure the Confederacy's defeat.

Hard Women, Hard War argues that Southern women forced a reckoning over the Federal army's policies toward civilians from the very beginning of the war until the bitter end of the conflict. Free and enslaved Black women encouraged Federals to make hard war on unrepentant rebels, white Unionist enslavers advocated protection of their human property, and elite Confederate ladies' defiance spurred the army to bring the war to Southern women's homes. These women put themselves in the midst of the army, and the war, to defend their homes. Enslavers sought to protect slavery, which might mean working for or against the Union, and Black women sought to prove their loyalty in order to destroy slavery and establish homes in freedom. In making this argument, the book advances the insights of scholars who study military policy toward civilians, including William Blair, Mark Grimsley, Chandra Manning, Erik Mathisen, Mark Neely, and Charles Royster. While Neely and Royster emphasize the role of enemy commanders and battlefield defeats in pushing the war's destructiveness, Blair and Grimsley note the key role of civilians in pushing the Federals toward hard war. Manning and Mathisen meanwhile show how formerly enslaved men and women pushed the Federal government to appreciate their loyalty in exchange for support.[8] This study builds on previous work by arguing that white and Black Southern women forced Federals to change their policies. Initially, the U.S. Army was not concerned about Southern women, focusing instead on keeping white male civilians out of the rebel army. Steeped in the rhetoric of domesticity and drawing on hagiography of the American Revolution, commanders expected white Southern women to provide the emotional and material support expected of women during a time of war.[9] These attitudes and the vague policy of conciliation required extensive revision in the face of duplicitous

Confederate ladies, demanding white Unionist women and freedom-seeking Black women. Elite Confederate women demanded civilian status but refused to forgo their rebel loyalties, defying the U.S. Army in ways both large and small. Conversely, enslaved Black women's actions proved their loyalty to the Union even though the army did not consider them civilians. As many of their male kin served in the United States Colored Troops (USCT) to demonstrate their loyalty and forge bonds with the Federal government, Black women advocated that their loyalty entitled them to civilian status, and their actions forced the issue as they made their way to Federal lines or brought complaints against Union soldiers who had wronged them.[10] The presence of the Federal army motivated Black and white Southern women to make bold and surprising demands, causing the military to recalculate its policies and recalibrate its treatment of them. Rather than pursuing a strategy to encourage white Southerners back into the Union, the actions of white and Black Southern women motivated the army to pursue policies of confiscation, foraging, emancipation, and, eventually, raiding. This book argues that the onslaught from Southern women was one of the crucial factors spurring the U.S. military toward hard war as it collaborated with loyal Black women while visiting destruction on disloyal enslaving women.

The book also contributes to the growing scholarship on the decisive impact of guerrillas. As scholars of the guerrilla conflict, including Donald Sutherland, have demonstrated, Southern women were one part of a much larger population pushing the U.S. Army toward hard war. To Sutherland, the widespread nature of the guerrilla conflict—combined with the loyalty of enslaved people and hostile Southern civilians—pushed the Federal military in multiple theaters of the war to enact harsher policies.[11] Although Sutherland does not devote his entire attention to Southern women, he notes their contributions, particularly in Missouri and during the Atlanta campaign. Other scholars view the conflict as inherently local and personal, seeing guerrilla warfare as a break with normal social and cultural conventions. In his study of wartime Missouri, Michael Fellman finds Missouri's women "compelled to be full participants in the war" in order to survive. While Sutherland and Fellman tend to focus on women as either guerrillas themselves or victims of guerrilla violence, more recent scholarship adds nuance. LeeAnn Whites, Kristen L. Streater, and Joseph M. Beilein Jr. argue that Confederate women played instrumental roles in the origination and continuation of guerrilla warfare.[12] This manuscript adds important insights to this growing literature. At the very beginning of the conflict, rebel women vocally and materially supported the Confederacy, attracting the attention of Federal commanders and soldiers. And even in areas rife with guerrilla violence, military men fixated on rebel women's displays of disloyalty, insisting that action be taken to neutralize the threat posed by Confederate women. From there it took little time at all for some, particularly Western armies, to insist that the army act against these women in order to curtail the threat they posed to its success.

It was not only the disloyalty of Confederate women that spurred the army to abandon conciliation and move toward hard war policies. The loyalty of free and enslaved Black women also encouraged a change in tactics. Historians have noted the effect of harsh war policies on Southern women. Scholars LeeAnn Whites, Alecia P. Long, Jacqueline Glass Campbell, and Lisa Tendrich Frank argue that Southern women reacted and responded to Federal military policy.[13] By examining white and Black Southern women's interactions with the Federal military over the course of the entire war, this book demonstrates that women's actions created concrete changes in Federal policy. In particular, the defiance of elite rebel women moved the army to institute harsher war policies. Rather than remaining in the domestic sphere, wealthy rebel women weaponized their households to materially support the Confederate project and used their significant social and political capital to provide outspoken, defiant support for the rebel government. The Federal army realized that these women unrepentantly opposed the Union and interpreted the conciliation policy as a sign of weakness. Harsher war policies aimed, in part, to neutralize the threat posed by elite Confederate women. By seizing their enslaved people and their agricultural products, the Union command signaled its recognition of women's homes as places of military significance. Rebel women's actions thus precipitated sweeping changes in the military's orientation toward Southern civilians.

Harsher war policies also recognized the groundswell of support from enslaved and free Black women. Women held in bondage put themselves on the military's radar by self-emancipating within Federal lines, where they provided the material support the army had initially expected of white women. Confiscation was a small but crucial move toward recognizing Black women's important contributions to the war effort, and these women made clear that they preferred to labor for the U.S. Army because of their loyalty to the Union. In return, Black women insisted that the army expand its definition of civilians to include them. Free and enslaved women outside of army lines also stressed their civilian status when they demanded redress from Federal soldiers who sexually assaulted them. African American women worked throughout the war to establish themselves as autonomous individuals in control of their bodies and homes.

The U.S. Army had hoped that harsher war policies would sideline white Southern women, but women continued their attempts to negotiate military policy.[14] Policies of emancipation pulled Unionist enslavers further into the conflict. They joined elite Confederate women in accusing the army of waging war on women and children, creating a powerful front that set enlisted men and commanders on the defensive. Women enslavers' support for the Union or Confederacy arose out of their conviction that one or the other was best suited to protect slavery, the very basis of their homes. In the wake of emancipation, enslaving women strategically employed the rhetoric of home to de-emphasize plantation households as spaces of economic and political importance.[15] When enslaving women invoked their actions as defending their homes, they appealed to notions of domesticity grounded in white supremacy, insisting that white women and girls were the only women and children who mattered.[16]

While enslaving women sought to protect the plantation household, free and enslaved Black women sought to destroy it. These women advocated strategies that would bring war to plantations to punish rebels and eradicate slavery. Free Black women, including Harriet Tubman and Elizabeth Garey, planned targeted raids, relying on white Federal commanders and African American Union soldiers to emancipate the loyal and destroy Confederate resources. But these collaborative raids proved controversial, and by the end of the war, commanders refused to cooperate with African American women or readjust their policies based on Southern women's reactions. Scholars Jacqueline Glass Campbell and Lisa Tendrich Frank note that Confederate women reacted and responded to Sherman's soldiers who invaded their domestic sanctuaries, arguing that the experience increased elite rebel women's support for the Confederate nation.[17] A very different picture emerges when we place Sherman's March in the context of the collaborative, emancipatory raids of the Department of the South. Sherman's rejection of collaboration with civilians and his insistence that all Southern civilians be made to feel hard war policies resulted in some of his men targeting free and enslaved Black women for particular and often egregious property destruction. Beginning in the Atlanta campaign and continuing into the Carolinas, Sherman rejected African American loyalty and the emancipatory potential of raiding in favor of policies that sought to subdue all Southern women. The postwar years continued to sideline free and enslaved Black women's wartime contributions. Elizabeth Garey's instrumental role in the Darien raid is buried in her Southern Claims Commission file, and she has not received credit for her involvement in that battle until now.

This book argues that slavery's centrality to Southern homes motivated Southern women in their wartime negotiations with the Federal military.[18] In doing so, it brings together the insights of scholars of slavery. Some scholars demonstrate that enslaved people used the U.S. military to advance freedom struggles, pushing it toward emancipation.[19] Others emphasize enslaved women's actions on the home front as undermining the Confederacy from within.[20] By framing this story around white and Black Southern women's competing ideas of home, we can see that they sought to use the Federal military to gain the advantage. Enslaving women strategically stressed the importance of home because it drew on nationwide ideas of domesticity and cast their struggles as personal rather than political or economic.[21] Women enslavers weaponized the power of home to motivate the Federal army to help them keep slavery intact, and they often found a sympathetic audience. Soldiers who might be troubled by human chattel bondage in the abstract found arguments of Black inferiority and slavery's role in civilizing African Americans to be convincing.[22] Conversely, enslaved and free Black women stressed the importance of home precisely because the Southern household denied them legal protections over their domestic spaces.[23] Black women had to convince the U.S. military that, although Southern law categorized them as human chattel, the army should recategorize them as civilians who could provide vital support to win the war. In exchange for their wartime service, Black women sought recognition as free women who could then build homes in freedom.[24] Unraveling Southern women's wartime invocation of home reveals that slavery lay at the center of Southern women's battles over Federal military policy.

Southern women insisted that their defense of home informed their political allegiances. Enslaving women had much at stake during the Civil War since their wealth and privilege rested on the continuance of human chattel bondage. These considerations might lead them to become rebels or Unionists; they supported whichever side seemed best able to protect slavery.[25]

The political loyalties of non-enslaving white women had more variation. Some advocated for the maintenance of slavery, while others came to recognize that "one group of white people outranked the other precisely because it was in a position to oppress and exploit black people."[26] Free and enslaved Black women supported the Union because it proved malleable to their antislavery politics.[27] Enslaved women knew that their and their family's vulnerability rested on the fact that they were legal dependents within their enslavers' households. Restrictive legislation undermined free Black women's ability to control their homes, families, and bodies. Black women insisted that free homes would only be possible with the destruction of slavery. Like the women of the revolutionary generation, Southern women "articulate[d] a political ideology that blended the domestic and public spheres," grounding their support for rebels or Unionists in their desire to defend their homes.[28]

Southern women's political allegiances motivated them to actively engage with the Federal military. Because the army functioned as an arm of the state, it had the ability to either protect or destroy their homes. Building on the work of Kristen Brill, Angela Esco Elder, Judith Giesburg, Thavolia Glymph, and Stephanie McCurry, this book echoes their findings that Civil War women "constructed a new relationship with the state that was not mediated through their husbands."[29] Part of the reason Southern women forged relationships with the Federal military was because of the absence or impotence of male relatives. War took Southern men away from home, whether they served in armies, evaded draft boards, worked as government officials, or languished under arrest. Wartime gave women more freedom of action and made them seem less threatening. Thus we find women confronting the army in their yards and gardens, on roads, and within military lines, refugee camps, and the offices of military officials. Women seized on the war to advocate for their interests, justifying their relationships with the Federal military as advancing home front concerns.[30] Civilian women insisted that war compelled them to move outside of their homes to defend their homes.

Hard Women, Hard War establishes a new interpretation of Southern women's wartime behavior by examining their interactions with the Federal army. The book studies white and Black women, both elite and poor, although some appear more frequently than others. Enslaving women and free and enslaved Black women appear in nearly every chapter, while the voices of poor farming women are highlighted when available, particularly as they engaged with hard war policies toward the end of the conflict. The project also takes a broad geographic focus rather than examining a particular region or a particular campaign.[31] By spanning all four years of the conflict and incorporating every slaveholding state with a significant record of military-civilian contact, the book argues that concerted pressure from Southern women forced the army to change its policies. Even with a broad geographic focus, the book remains sensitive to regional variation. Since it follows Federals and Southern civilians wherever they met, certain geographic locations are more important than others: Texas is barely mentioned, while Virginia appears in nearly every chapter. Focusing on a diverse group of people throughout the slaveholding South reveals the near constant pressure Southern women applied on the Federal army as they advocated for their political interests grounded in the defense of their homes.

Reconstructing interactions necessitates using a wide variety of sources and reading those sources against the grain. Some are obvious and familiar: literate soldiers' and Southern women's letters, diaries, and memoirs culled from eight archives in six states as well as fifty microfilmed, digitized, or published volumes. These accounts provide excellent firsthand detail, but they are overwhelmingly white and elite. Testimonies from 173 Black Southern women about their experiences with the Federal army come from nine volumes of the WPA Ex-Slave Narratives. With the caveat that many interviewers were white (and sometimes even relatives of former enslavers), these sources are invaluable testimonies to African Americans' experiences with Federals.[32] Southern Claims Commission files from 180 individual women in six states bring in diverse voices from those who otherwise might not have left records. Although recorded after the war, depositions from free and enslaved Black women and poor farming women, as well as corroboration by family, friends, and neighbors, reveal how economically disadvantaged women experienced the war. Official government sources include 319 court-martial cases and 512 accounts of Southern women's interactions with the Federal army in the *Official Records*. Military sources are used extensively but approached with care since they are biased toward their white and male authors. By reading them against the grain, we gain valuable insight into Southern women's demands that the army respond to their concerns. This extensive research allows for a multiplicity of voices from people who had very different opinions about the war's prosecution and the place of civilians within the conflict. My goal has been to preserve this rich texture in order to tease out what can be learned by placing military records into conversation with civilian voices.[33] As a result, we learn something new and exciting about the Civil War: that civilians successfully pressured the Federal military to adjust its policies toward Southern women.

The story begins at the war's outset with the hazy policy of conciliation. Chapter 1, "Southern Women and the Chaos of Conciliation," argues that conciliation was less of a policy than a mentality enjoining the army to treat civilians not as potential enemies but as fellow members of the United States. This idea flowed from the logic that secession was an illegal overreaction to Lincoln's presidential election.[34] If the army could prove to Southern civilians that it simply desired to restore the Union, then the military could win hearts and minds on the home front while whipping rebels on the battlefield. But the military's idea contained several flaws. It assumed that civilians would remain on the sidelines, and it equated "civilians" with white men while ignoring white and Black women. Chapter 1 argues that Southern women refused to abide by these categories and instead demanded that the U.S. Army address their concerns. Elite Confederate women emphasized their status as "true women," weaponizing their gender to secure civilian status even as they materially supported the rebel military. White Unionist women emphasized their loyalty to the nation and demanded protection from Confederates and the safeguarding of their human property. Black women insisted that, during a civil war, loyalty trumped race, and that the army benefited when it treated them as people rather than as property. Conciliation crumbled in the face of this onslaught from civilians, because the army could not remain neutral when faced with white Unionists who feared reprisals from rebels, Black women who supported the war's cause, and elite rebels doing everything they could to ensure the Union's demise.

As the war progressed, soldiers and civilians' social interactions further highlighted these tensions. Chapter 2 argues that wartime social interactions created a crisis for the Federal army. When officers and soldiers began occupying Confederate territory and spending time with middle-class and elite women—their social peers—they began to realize the depth of women's treachery. Rather than "true women" who conducted themselves with purity, piety, and sincerity, rebels behaved duplicitously.[35] They appeared kind and conciliatory to gain soldiers' trust and then sent supplies and intelligence along to the Confederate army. Close associations with rebel women led officers and soldiers to advocate for harsher policies toward civilians. Unimpressed with white Unionists, who made demands of the army, and contemptuous of enslaved and free Black women, whom white soldiers did not believe to be women, traitorous Confederate women came to stand in for all Southern women. While Federals would continue to distinguish between loyal and disloyal and white and Black, they found female Southern civilians to be lacking. Thus, they did not feel any compunction to continue to spare them from war's hardships. By mid-1862, wealthy Confederate women's actions encouraged the army to assert their dominion over the Southern home front through harsher war policies.

With conciliation largely abandoned, the Federal army turned to hard war. Chapter 3 argues that while confiscation, foraging, and emancipation were in theory separate policies, Federals often implemented them and civilians experienced them at the same time. Confiscation appeared first in the Eastern theater, as Federals in Virginia encouraged rebels' enslaved people to make their way to Union army lines. Confederate women understood that Federals intended this policy to punish them for their rebellion, and they sought to move enslaved people out of the way of the army. These actions motivated even more enslaved people to self-emancipate to prevent family separation, and Black women behind military lines continued to advocate that they be treated as loyal civilians in need of aid. In the Western theater, enslaved women's struggles for freedom faced a hostile Federal army resistant to waging war on slavery. Confederate and Unionist women enslavers influenced these attitudes, condemning confiscation and arguing that emancipation was "making war on women and children." These wealthy women forged direct relationships with the military in the hopes of influencing policy, using traditionally feminine tactics such as pleading and petitioning alongside more masculine tactics of demanding protection and engaging in subterfuge. Throughout the Southern slaveholding states, women responded to hard war policies by advocating the military to redress their concerns, forging relationships with this branch of the federal government independent of male relatives.

Chapter 4, "Wartime Sexual Assault and the Progress of Emancipation," considers Black women's accusations of rape against white Federals and white women's accusations of rape against Black Federals in the context of the destruction of slavery. Just a few months into the war, enslaved and free Black women and girls complained to Federal authorities of sexual assault by U.S. soldiers. They insisted that even if Southern law did not recognize the rape of an enslaved woman as a crime, the Federal military must make redress.

While progress was slow and halting, and white Federals continually objected to Black testimony, eventually the military began trying and convicting white soldiers for the rape or attempted rape of Black women and girls. On the other hand, rebel rumors that Black Federals would unleash widespread sexual violence against virtuous white Southern women never materialized. Only a few white women and girls, most of them poor, accused Black Federals of sexual assault. And their claims were often not credible. Instead, their accusations reveal that in the wake of emancipation, white women interpreted the presence of Black soldiers in their home as a violation, leading to spurious charges of rape. While some officers refused to convict African American soldiers on flimsy evidence, others allowed long-standing racist ideas of Black men's hypersexuality to influence them, resulting in higher rates of conviction and harsher punishments for Black defendants. The evidence from wartime trials for sexual assault indicates a break with the past. Southern Black women accused white men of sexual assault, sometimes obtaining a conviction. On the other hand, Black men had now lost some of the protections that slavery had provided them when accused of rape by poor white women.

Emancipation's reach even extended to a new wartime policy, that of raiding. The fifth chapter, "From Collaborative to Noncooperative Raiding," begins in 1863, as abolitionist commanders, Black Federals, and Black female civilians on the Sea Islands engaged in liberatory raids that sought to destroy Confederate resources and plantations while striking fear into the hearts of rebels. Criticism from the Northern press, Confederate officials, and even Federal commanders resulted in the army abandoning the practice. As Western commanders came east, however, they instituted raiding practices of their own. While these raids also intended to destroy Confederate resources and strike fear in the hearts of rebels, their intention was not to liberate African Americans. Instead, Western commanders and enlisted men focused on "living off the country," language that disappeared civilians from the land, and insisted that political loyalties no longer mattered. Using these strategies, the army attempted to take charge of military policy and refuse women's attempts to negotiate or collaborate. But Southern women continued to try to set the boundaries of raiding by establishing their loyalty, demanding guards, or pleading with enlisted men. At times they succeeded, but at others—and this was particularly true for African American women—their pleas fell on deaf ears. In the postwar period, however, loyal Southern women made clear their active involvement in raiding through their testimony before the Southern Claims Commission, demonstrating that the army's attempt to treat them as war's passive victims was unsuccessful.

Civilian women pushed the Federal army, from individual enlisted men to commanders of battalions, to respond to their concerns. They were often successful.[36] The book's title illuminates these struggles. Southern women's actions reveal a dynamic conflict in which women's loyalty or disloyalty pushed the Federal army to adjust its policies. Confederate and Unionist enslavers insisted on protection of their domestic spaces while enslaved women sought to carve homes for themselves in freedom.[37] Their actions pushed the U.S. Army toward hard war. Foraging, emancipation, and raiding caused soldiers and commanders to become more fully enmeshed in Southern women's homes. *Hard Women, Hard War* uncovers the strategies white and Black Southern women used to advance individual and collective struggles, revealing that war was present within the South even before Federals ever arrived.

CHAPTER ONE

Southern Women and the Chaos of Conciliation

During a bitter December 1862 in Cincinnati, Ohio, the U.S. Army conducted an inquiry into one of its own: Gen. Don Carlos Buell. Reflecting back on the first year and a half of the war, there was no doubt that the general had lost precious territory in Kentucky and failed to subdue Confederates in East Tennessee. But the commission also argued over non-battlefield matters: Had Buell's conciliatory policy toward white Southern civilians—his attempt to "secur[e] the neutrality if not the friendship of the population . . . by just and mild treatment"—contributed to his army's lack of success?[1] The final report brought little closure. Commissioners declared that Buell deserved "neither blame nor applause" for his treatment of civilians because he was merely following government policy. But the commission acknowledged the Federal civilian policy's many flaws. Chief among them was that Buell "could violate no orders on the subject, because there were none." In the commission's estimation, the lack of guidelines, not the conciliatory policy itself, was the problem.[2] The result, just one and a half years into the war, was chaos.

But conciliation did not turn into chaos because of a lack of guidelines. The larger problem was that the unofficial policy did not factor Southern women into the equation. And although several prominent military figures espoused conciliation, including the first two generals-in-chief, Winfield Scott and George B. McClellan, its meaning and implementation varied from commander to commander and theater to theater.[3] While the specifics of the policy varied, it rested on three main principles. Conciliation's first principle was that the only foe the United States would need to subdue would be men in arms. This idea assumed that only white men who had been inducted into the rebel army would participate in the conflict.[4] Conciliation's second principle was that the military would respect the rights and privileges of citizens not in arms, and military records demonstrate that the army equated "citizens" with Southern white men.[5] Conciliation's third principle held that commanders could convince citizens to remain neutral, if not friendly, by respecting their rights and privileges. This third principle assumed that secession was unpopular with white male Southerners and that the military's good treatment would draw them back to the Union.[6] Preoccupied with white Southern men, military policy paid scant attention to white women, who according to the laws of war were "enemies who make no resistance."[7] As for Black women and children? President Lincoln himself was quite clear that "the fugitive slave clause of the constitution ought to be enforced." In the opinion of the commander in chief, enslaved people were not civilians or citizens. The army ought to consider them property.[8]

The three-part definition of conciliation that guided Federal policy during the first year of the war had little to say about women. Guided by these principles, military commanders, officers, and enlisted men initially believed they could offer white female civilians a nebulous concept of "protection," and that these women would make no demands of them.[9] The Lincoln administration and its generals believed that the war would be fought on the battlefield, so they prepared for a conflict that would have little to do with Southern white women and their homes.[10] Black women's needs were immaterial. When the Union was restored, they would remain in bondage. The military's task seemed straightforward and clear. Win on the battlefield. "Protect" white women and children. And prevent servile insurrection.[11]

There was only one problem. Southern women insisted that war concerned them and refused to remain on the sidelines. Elite Confederate women insisted there was no contradiction between being a rebel and being a "true woman," and they weaponized their gender to secure civilian status even as they materially supported the Confederate military. White Unionist women emphasized their loyalty to the nation and demanded protection from Confederates and the safeguarding of their human property. Black women insisted that their loyalty to the Union and not their status as enslaved individuals should define them, giving them access to civilian status. When white and Black Southern women demanded that the army address their concerns, they reshaped military policy.

Conciliation did not crumble because of a lack of guidelines; it failed because Southern women refused to abide it. White and Black women insisted that their political sympathies, grounded in their defense of their homes, compelled them to actively engage with the U.S. Army. Long before Federals arrived on Southern soil, Southern civilians decided how they would behave toward the army and what they would ask of it. Over the next year and a half, the U.S. Army contended with elite rebel women who sought to ensure the Union's demise, with white Unionists who desired protection from Confederate reprisals, and with Black women who demanded safety and freedom in exchange for their loyalty. All told, white Unionists' demands, rebel women's subterfuge, and African Americans' persistence forced the U.S. military to adapt its policies and acknowledge that Southern women would play a central role in the conflict.

Defining Citizens Before Fort Sumter

Even before the firing on Fort Sumter, President Lincoln and General-in-Chief Scott preoccupied themselves with keeping white Southern men out of the Confederate army. Both men worried that aggressive action would lead to a flood of enlistments if not the secession of additional slaveholding states. However, they disagreed over which actions were aggressive. In October 1860, Scott urged then President Buchanan to garrison Southern forts. Less than two months later, Lincoln directed Francis Blair to instruct Scott that "if the forts shall be given up before the inauguration, the General must retake them afterwards." By March, Scott believed that retaking federal property would be foolhardy, entailing a two- or three-year conflict resulting in enormous loss of life and property. He urged Lincoln toward three other possibilities: accept the Crittenden Compromise, collect duties outside of Confederate-occupied forts, or let the seceded states "*depart in peace*!" Lincoln's response was a letter, by way of Secretary of War Simon Cameron, instructing the general to "exercise all possible vigilance for the maintenance of all the places within the military department of the United States."[12] One way or another, the forts would be held.

Lincoln's delicate balancing act—holding Federal forts while not antagonizing white Southern men—filtered down to the commanders of those forts. Officers at Fort Taylor, near the sizable city of Key West, Florida, worked to remain on good terms with the city's elite men. In March, Capt. J. M. Brannan assured Assistant Adjutant General Lorenzo Thomas that "we are on terms of friendship with the best portion of the citizens," even though a number of them had raised "flags of the Southern Confederacy" over their stores.[13] Brannan's reference to "citizens" who operated businesses seems to indicate that he was primarily concerned with Key West's white men. Even though these men passively showed support for rebels by displaying Confederate emblems, Brannan's concern was to keep them from actively supporting the rebellion through military service. Maintaining good relationships, he believed, was key.

Even when the aftermath of Fort Sumter required harsher policies, commanders in Key West continued to stress the importance of good relationships. In language similar to that used by President Lincoln in his proclamation calling up the militia, Brevet Col. Harvey Brown, the newly minted commander of the Department of Florida, instructed the fort's new commander to use his forces to "protec[t] . . . citizens . . . [in] the pursuit of their legitimate private occupations." Since the commencement of hostilities might turn white men into troublemakers, Brown authorized "suspending the writ of habeas corpus, and . . . immediately remov[ing] from the island all dangerous or suspected persons" if rebellion or insurrection occurred. One month later, the fort's commander found it necessary to suspend the writ and declare martial law. Even after taking these stringent measures, Brown ordered his subordinate to "uphol[d] the laws and suppres[s the] rebellion" in a "spirit of kindness and conciliation, so that if possible [all citizens] may be led from error rather than be driven into it by an undue exercise of authority."[14] In these early months in a strategic location along the Gulf Coast, civilian policy focused on treating white men with kindness in order to keep them out of the rebel army—and maintaining a crucial fort.

While Federals focused their efforts on white men, Black men attempted to escape the clutches of the rebellion. In early March, four enslaved men in Pensacola, Florida, made the trek to Federal lines at Fort Pickens. Once they arrived, they argued that Federal commanders should grant them asylum, asserting that the U.S. Army garrison owed them protection and should "grant them their freedom." The fort's commander, First Lt. A. J. Slemmer, knew that President Lincoln was unequivocal about enforcing the Fugitive Slave Act. Recounting the incident to Adjutant General Thomas, he relayed that he "did what [he] could to teach them the contrary." That afternoon, he acted as a slave catcher and turned the refugees over to Pensacola's city marshal. But the city's enslaved people would not be deterred. That same evening, four more enslaved men made their way to Fort Pickens seeking refuge and freedom.[15] While Federals hoped that white Southern men would only passively support the Confederacy, they spurned active Union support from Black men. In the weeks before

Fort Sumter, encouraging loyalty among enslaved people would only antagonize Southerners. And so at first, protecting the loyal only extended to white men. Before the firing on Fort Sumter and the commencement of hostilities, President Lincoln, General-in-Chief Scott, and commanders on the ground had decided which civilians to conciliate and who counted as loyal.

Even Northern Black men found their support for the Union spurned. Philadelphian George E. Stephens, a skilled craftsman and correspondent for the prominent Black newspaper *The Weekly Anglo-African*, rightly anticipated white America's attitude toward the conflict. Given the Supreme Court's *Dred Scott* decision and President Lincoln's appeasement of proslavery Democrats, Stephens reasoned that politicians and commanders would embrace narrow war aims that would not prioritize ending slavery. Even so, Stephens urged his male readers to enlist, believing that if Black men joined en masse, they could turn the conflict into a war over slavery. Stephens encouraged his readers, "Remember that ten thousand men under the unfurled banner of insurrection can sweep away the slaves' shackles like a tornado does chaff." And Stephens followed his own advice. When Pennsylvania refused to organize Black regiments, he became an officer's cook and personal servant, a post that allowed him to wave the "banner of insurrection" by "run[ning] off slaves . . . from [Maryland] down to Washington." Similar to the men in Pensacola, Stephens took matters into his own hands to demonstrate Black men's loyalty to the Union and their insistence that the Civil War must also take aim at slavery.[16]

Individual commanders brought policies of conciliation with them as they marched their armies to meet Confederates on the battlefield in early summer. Just before the First Battle of Bull Run, Robert Patterson, commanding the Department of Pennsylvania, issued orders to his men that made clear the racial and gender implications of military policy toward civilians. Patterson instructed his soldiers, "You are not the aggressors," characterizing Confederates as "insurgents . . . misled by ambitious rulers." Federals were not enemy invaders but fellow Americans, whose duty was to "sustain the civil power, to relieve the oppressed, and to retake that which is unlawfully held." Patterson characterized the conflict as the business of men: Rebel politicians instigated the conflict. Rebel militias seized control of Federal property and imprisoned Unionist men. Confederate governments spread illegitimate control over "loyal citizens," people who had a duty to support the U.S. government—and those people were white and male.[17] In contrast, Federals entered Virginia to "punish sedition[,] . . . protect the loyal, and . . . suppress servile insurrection."[18] In keeping with Patterson's racialized and gendered interpretation of the conflict, white male Federals would restore the Unionist (white and male) political order and release white male Unionist political prisoners. While doing so, they would keep a close eye on Black men in order to prevent them from revolt.[19] The war, then, was a conflict between white men, one in which Black men and especially women had no legitimate place.

Thus, as hostilities commenced, soldiers lacked clear guidelines for how they should respond to white Southern women. But white Southern women had definite ideas about what they expected from Federals. White Unionist women eagerly anticipated the U.S. Army's arrival, believing that the country's long-standing wartime policy of protecting civilian property, particularly enslaved people, would prove a boon to them and their families. As the elite, well-educated Josie Underwood of Bowling Green, Kentucky, observed, "It is the South against the established government based upon the Constitution . . . which sound-thinking men throughout the South deplore *most* because it will ruin the South." Underwood, the daughter of a lawyer and former Whig politician, believed firmly that staying in the Union was the best way to ensure the survival of chattel slavery, while disunion and war threatened the very basis of Southern society. Massachusetts-born Louisa Brown Pearl of Nashville noted with disdain that "one of my best negro women was taken from me by her master thro' fear of Federals." These women expected that the Federal army's commitment to "protecting the loyal" would benefit them because it would uphold slavery, the basis of the Southern social order. One of their primary reasons for supporting the Union was that its preservation would protect the institution of slavery, an institution from which they derived much benefit.[20]

White Unionist women remained confident that the Federal army would eventually be successful and regarded occupation by Confederates as a temporary setback. In Bowling Green, Josie Underwood referred to rebel troops as "Philistines" and watched helplessly as a "whole brigade of infantry marched straight through our yard to pitch their tents. . . . They are camped for God only knows how long." Just sixty miles away in Hopkinsville, Ellen Wallace lamented the end of Kentucky's neutrality. "After a noble struggle for peace," she recorded in her diary, "our beloved Kentucky . . . is . . . about to be engulfed in the fearful strife." Ever the pragmatist, however, Wallace made sure to send Confederate pickets baskets of apples and other bounty from her farm. Julia Chase of Winchester, Virginia, anxiously awaited the Federal army. "How long must it be before their arms are crowned with success?" she lamented in

August 1861. Unionist women felt certain that Federals would eventually prevail on the battlefield, and they waited expectantly for the U.S. Army to restore the order and harmony of the old union.[21]

Confederate women had no reason to rejoice as Federals inched closer. Many believed that the soldiers their men characterized as "barbarian[s]" and "hired Dutch cut-throats" intended to murder, rape, and pillage their way through the South. Elite Virginian Helen Struan Bernard maintained that Federals' "sole object is to subjugate & plunder the South." Subjugation and plunder were not abstractions to elite rebel women, who well knew what it meant to exercise mastery over human beings.[22] Bernard conjured images of subservience to reflect what a loss of power, authority, and possessions meant to Confederates. Rebel women felt certain that Federals intended to dominate them and reduce them to poverty. Conjuring gendered and racialized images of civil war, elite rebel women indicated that the arrival of Federals meant the utter destruction of their elite status through the destruction of slavery.

While reality was not nearly as dire, declarations of loyalty did have ramifications for Confederate women. When they aligned themselves with Confederate male relatives, rebel women encountered suspicion and not the preferential treatment from powerful men to which they were accustomed. Native Virginian Betty Herndon Maury, daughter of former U.S. Navy Commodore Matthew Fontaine Maury, felt anxious to leave Washington, D.C., after her father resigned his commission and joined the Confederacy. Before the war, Maury's status as a wealthy white woman, as well as her father's position of power and influence, would have granted her a sympathetic hearing from government officials. Now that she was a professed rebel with male relatives in the Confederate government, the War Department denied her application for a pass. But Maury was determined to leave. Only by using her mother's maiden name to hide her identity did Maury obtain permission to go south.[23] When ardent Confederate women aligned themselves with male relatives and rejected their loyalty and obligation to the U.S. government, they knew that they could no longer petition the government or expect protection. Maury's actions demonstrate that she did not want conciliation from Federals, which would have necessitated that she reject her and her family's rebel allegiances. Rather than face this prospect, she turned to deception to escape from further interactions with the Federals.

While white Unionists waited and Confederates worried, Black women intervened with the Almighty. While they felt certain that a war over slavery would end the peculiar institution, they refused to leave it to chance. Jane Ferguson, mother of Booker T. Washington, expressed her Union loyalty by praying over her children that the Federal army would be successful so that they would all be free. Dora Franks of Mississippi heard her enslavers talking about a "bloody war" that would take away all the slaves. "From dat minute I started praying for freedom. All de res' o' de women done de same." As the faith of these women demonstrates, war would provide opportunities for individuals to seek their freedom, but in order for slavery to end, the Federal army needed to be successful. And for that to happen, Federals required divine intervention.[24]

Southern Black women prayed that the war would bring freedom, but they also had a healthy skepticism of an all-white invading army. Enslavers exacerbated these fears. Jennie Small of Pocahontas County, West Virginia, recalled her enslavers teaching her "to fear the Yankees," telling tall tales of soldiers with horns or that soldiers would force them to pull carts and wagons like cattle. In Savannah, Georgia, the "Yankees" dominated the thoughts of twelve-year-old Susie Baker. Would they be friend or foe? Her grandmother instructed her not to listen to enslavers, whose greatest fear was that their enslaved people would "go over to the Yankees." Baker was determined to see them with her own eyes, trusting that she alone could make the right decision about whether African Americans like her could trust them.[25] Unlike white Unionist women, Black women had no reason to expect that white Federal soldiers would treat them well. They remained wary of individual soldiers, certain that the men could uphold slavery just as surely as they could dismantle it.

In the months between secession and first battles, Federals and Southern women acted on their ideas of the conflict and what they expected of each other. While Federals remained preoccupied with preventing white Southern men from joining the rebels, white Unionist women expected protection of themselves and their animate and inanimate property, white Confederate women awaited vengeful Federal soldiers who would lay waste to their society, and Black women took steps to ensure that the war would bring freedom.

Initial Encounters in Virginia and Maryland

As the Army of Northeastern Virginia marched south, its commander, Brig. Gen. Irvin McDowell, insisted that the army conciliate Southern civilians.

But disagreement within the ranks soon appeared, as enlisted men attacked rebel property and insisted that retribution and not kindness was what secessionists deserved. Soon after their arrival in Alexandria, Virginia, the Washington, D.C.–based Georgetown Volunteers decided to teach the town's secessionists a lesson by seizing the property of wealthy Confederates who fled the area before the army's arrival. McDowell would have none of it. He termed the soldiers' behavior as "trespass, depredations, and attempts at burglary." While McDowell understood that these men from the nation's capital might feel antipathy toward secessionists, he argued that feelings should not get in the way of policy. To make an example out of these men for defying the conciliation policy, he sought approval to try the men using military commissions. The incident in Alexandria demonstrates rifts in the conciliation policy once Federals arrived on Confederate soil. Enlisted men believed that rebels required punishment for sedition, not conciliation.[26]

What was perhaps most distressing about the Georgetown Volunteers' behavior was that it confirmed reports spread by Confederates that Federals would steal, plunder, and even rape white Southern women. While conducting an expedition to Rockville, Maryland, in Patterson's Department of Virginia, Lt. Charles Stone encountered these very perceptions. In his reports to General-in-Chief Scott, Stone faulted "Virginians and active secessionists" for teaching "women and children . . . to expect every species of outrage and horror" when the Federals arrived. In accordance with conciliationist views, Stone believed that Federals' good behavior won over female civilians. The women of Poolesville, Stone noted approvingly, "seem to gain confidence in the Government day by day." Military men like Stone agreed with Scott and Patterson that Federals' orderly behavior would counter rebels' malicious gossip, gossip that had terrified impressionable women and children. All that Federals needed to do was to protect women from harm and refrain from dastardly deeds.[27]

Conciliationist officers in Gen. George McClellan's Department of the Ohio confronted similar perceptions in western Virginia. And since they did not intend to occupy portions of the territory as they did in Baltimore, they had to embrace new strategies. Leading an expedition that cut through the city of Charleston, Brig. Gen. J. D. Cox dealt with rebel allegations that he and his men were "robbers and murderers of women and children" through strict orders to his men: They were not to stop when they passed through towns inhabited by civilians. Instead, they "march[ed] through in soldierly order, no man leaving the ranks or shouting or making any unnecessary noise."[28] Through orderly behavior, Cox sought to reassure the white women of western Virginia that Federals posed them no threat.

Federals also countered rebel rumors by positioning themselves as liberators of innocent white women subject to Confederate depredations. Elsewhere in western Virginia, Gen. George McClellan discovered that a local woman had been imprisoned by Confederate officials for three weeks merely because of her Union sentiments. McClellan insisted on meeting with the woman, penning a letter to his wife about the "affecting interview" and crediting Federals with "liberat[ing] . . . [her] . . . from prison." Later that summer, men in McClellan's newly formed Army of the Potomac also recognized the need to shield civilians from harm. In Loudoun County, Virginia, Ohioan John H. Shober credited much of civilians' "union feeling" to Confederate confiscation policies. The rebel government, which had taken civilians' "cattle, horses, wagons, or . . . grain . . . with out leave or remuneration," had turned the people against them.[29] Early in the conflict, conciliationist commanders and soldiers realized that they not only needed to treat white Southern women with respect, they also needed to protect women by liberating them from Confederate persecution.

White Unionist women responded to Federals with gratitude and displays of loyalty. Through public ceremonies, these women sought to unite the two sides through their support for the Union. Soon after Federals' arrival, loyal white women in Harpers Ferry held a flag-raising ceremony for the soldiers. Soldiers and civilian women gathered on a warm summer evening in the town square, exulting as the Stars and Stripes once again flew over the town. Through public expressions of their patriotic devotion and their appreciation of Federal forces, loyal women positioned themselves as Federals' true friends and allies, as civilians who could be counted on to firmly support the Union cause.[30]

But the Federal defeat at First Bull Run strained the relationship between Federal soldiers and white Unionist women. These women counted on U.S. soldiers to deliver them from Confederates. They had not expected battlefield reverses and Federal retreats. As U.S. forces withdrew from Harpers Ferry, Col. Wilder Dwight remarked that "panic stricken women and children pursued us . . . not daring to remain without our protection." Loyal white women, stranded for months in enemy territory, hoped Federal soldiers would actively protect them from hostile Confederates by maintaining garrisons in

FIG 1.1. Alfred Waud, "Sharpsburg Citizens Leaving for Fear of the Rebels"—Loyal white civilians dreaded returning to rebel rule after experiencing life within Federal lines. This sketch by war correspondent Waud depicts Sharpsburg, Maryland, residents fleeing the Confederate army. (Library of Congress)

their towns. For women who had very publicly declared their loyalty to the Union, Federal retreat spelled disaster, so these women desperately attempted to remain within U.S. army lines. The reaction of the women of Harpers Ferry to the Federal army's withdrawal signified that white Unionist women expected active protection from the United States, a pattern that would repeat itself throughout the war.[31]

Federals appreciated support from white Unionist women, but they expected support from all civilian women, even rebels. Erstwhile commander of the Department of Annapolis Benjamin Butler treated Baltimore residents with a firm hand, and officers and enlisted men continued to reap the benefits for months to come. New Yorker James L. Rea noted that even though he and his comrades camped in the "strongest secession neighborhood in Balt[imore]," he was "well treated by the citizens, who brought us bread and butter and supplied us with all the milk we could use." Federals treated elite rebel women with civility and expected women of this class to return the favor. And they also expected that kind treatment would result in civilians changing their allegiances. New Englander Wilder Dwight anthropomorphized the entire city, noting that "Repentant Baltimore seems now to be trimming her cap anew."[32] Dwight used gendered imagery and a nod to women's supposedly mercurial nature to describe Federals' expectations of individual women and entire Southern cities. Once these groups encountered well-behaved Federals, they would be persuaded back into the Union.

As white Federals worked on Maryland rebels, Black men sought to extend Benjamin Butler's confiscation policy in loyal states in order to encourage a groundswell of Unionism among enslaved people. In Bladensburg, Maryland, under conciliationist McClellan's Army of the Potomac, George Stephens attempted to shelter "a little boy about 15 years of age, a fugitive from *slavery*." The young man, Frank, attempted to find shelter from his violent enslaver within Federal lines, and Stephens tried to aid him in his quest for freedom. Both men's efforts were in vain. An army sergeant worked with the local sheriff to re-enslave young Frank. Stephens wrote scathingly to his readers in the *Afro-American* about nonsensical Federal policy. While the military refused to give passes to people from Maryland to visit friends in the Virginia camps, it issued passes "to Maryland slave-holders to cross over to the Virginia side to search for runaway slaves." Federals deprived themselves of support from young men like Frank while allowing Maryland enslavers to consort with rebels in Virginia. Rather than embracing Union sentiment no matter its origins, the United States protected Maryland rebels' human property.[33]

Across the border in Virginia, Black men and women pushed the issue of freedom by fleeing to Union lines to seek recognition as loyal civilians. Once Secretary of War Simon Cameron authorized Gen. Benjamin F. Butler to accept people enslaved by rebels within his lines, entire families arrived at Fort Monroe, Virginia. They acted in order to avoid family separation: The nearness of the Federal army caused enslavers to put able-bodied men to work on Confederate fortifications even as they sent women and children south. Military policy soon caught up with Black Southerners' plans: The army's interpretation of the First Confiscation Act instructed commanders to "refrain from surrendering" to enslavers anyone who came to Union lines. And so, even though the army forced all able-bodied men into difficult physical labor and only gave rations (and not pay) to workers and their families, some women decided that Fort Monroe was their best option. Two months after the policy went into effect, nearly nine hundred African Americans claimed the Union army's protection at the fort.[34] More than half of them were women and children.

But at Fort Monroe, General Butler did not treat Black women the same way his fellow commanders treated white female civilians. Butler saw no need to reassure these women of the army's intentions and offered them only the bare minimum of protection. Able-bodied Black women could remain within Federal lines only if they provided labor to the army. By the end of July,

FIG 1.2. *Harper's Weekly*, "Stampede of Slaves from Hampton to Fortress Monroe"—This illustration from the popular New York periodical depicts Black men and women leaving enslavers for Federal lines. Note the large numbers of women and children. (Library of Congress)

Butler required Black women to labor for the army as laundresses, seamstresses, and cooks. While Butler maintained that he would "take the same care of these men, women, and children . . . as I would of the same number of [white] men, women, and children," his requirement that they work and his paying them only with rations belied this assertion. Butler continued to view Black women through the lens of the antebellum racialized gender order. Even though these women were loyal to the Union and sought freedom within Federal lines, he did not treat them like white women, people his fellow commanders considered to be "innocents" in need of protection. Instead, Butler viewed Black women as laborers.[35]

Even though the contraband policy had its limits, it provided opportunities to advance the cause of freedom. Still stationed in Maryland, where the Army of the Potomac continued to return Unionist enslaved people to their Confederate enslavers, George Stephens decided to engage in smuggling. In late summer, he and his comrades began helping Maryland enslaved people seek shelter within Federal lines in Virginia. One of their first operations was to help a married couple, Washington and Diana, who feared wartime separation and the insecurity of "let[ting] [a] strange man own [them]." The couple sought refuge with Stephens's company but would hardly be safe if they remained in the Old Line State. And so Stephens, who had learned his lesson from the ordeal with Frank, "hurr[ied] the[m] . . . to the Virginia side," where Washington and Diana hid their Maryland origins to claim contraband status.[36] African Americans within and outside of the Confederacy pushed the issue of freedom. Political leaders and military commanders might have had narrow war aims, but Black people like Stephens, Washington, and Diana focused on ending slavery by any means necessary.

As the Federal army moved south, conciliationist commanders and soldiers began to realize that their conception of civilians was too narrow. White Southern women terrified of U.S. soldiers and enslaved people seeking recognition of their loyalty broadened the definition of who was a civilian. As Federals spread deeper into the Confederacy and farther west into the Border States, they would contend with recalcitrant rebels who forced a reckoning over conciliation.

Insufficient Unionism in Virginia and the Border States

After the significant loss at the Battle of Wilson's Creek in Missouri, John C. Frémont's Department of the West dug in for a much longer conflict than they had anticipated. For enlisted men, this meant extended contact with a population that seemed overwhelmingly and disturbingly secessionist, particularly in light of Confederate attacks and guerrilla machinations. In Fredericktown, Seventeenth Illinois Pvt. George A. Wilson focused not on guerrillas but on the townsfolk, noting, "The people here are nearly all rebels." Even so, Wilson found that the U.S. Army's occupation of the town had some effect, because the population was "disposed to be quite civil now in fact some of the loudest 'Secesh' are regular Union. . . . Its [*sic*] good policy for them to be." But Wilson also observed that many residents had fled south, "believing that the d——d abolitionists (*as they call us*) would murder them all whether in arms or not."[37] Wilson seemed bitter and frustrated because President Lincoln and General-in-Chief Scott insisted on mild policies to encourage Unionism in Missouri. Reality proved quite different. Instead of widespread Unionism, Wilson found rabid secessionism and a tendency toward prevarication.

Perhaps most distressing for Wilson and other enlisted men was how Fredericktown's female civilians treated U.S. soldiers. Convinced that Federals would commit depredations, the women would "ru[n] like the very devil" with "their children in their arms" if Federals approached a house simply to ask for a drink of water. Based on this behavior, Wilson dismissed Fredericktown civilians as "a set of fools."[38] Enlisted men like Wilson expected to find innocent Southern women who required protection from Confederates. Instead they found gullible, foolish females more inclined to believe rebel lies than to depend on Federals for protection. The strength of rebel sentiment among female civilians caused Federals to resent and malign white Southern women.

Although Federals continued to look for Unionism in Missouri, they struggled to find it. On a two-hundred-mile expedition west of St. Louis, Brig. Gen. Chester Harding Jr. reported to Major General Frémont that the "whole region" was "thoroughly disloyal." Similar to Wilson in Fredericktown, Harding discovered that Missouri civilians placed "no faith . . . in anything but the fears of the rebels." A frustrated Harding found it difficult even to punish Missouri secessionists for collaborating with the Confederate army, since he did not have enough men to leave a garrison that would ensure protection of "loyal citizens" from the "vengeance . . . [of] secessionists." All that Harding could do was focus on the behavior of his soldiers. He praised his men to Frémont, writing that "although we passed through a country where we found few but enemies, there was no interference with private property and no irregularities of any kind were committed."[39] The declaration of martial law, and provision of harsh punishments for guerrillas, had not resulted in masses of white civilians loyal to the Union. Instead, the population remained staunchly Confederate. The behavior of individual Federals seemed to have no material impact on the political sympathies of civilians.

Commanders like Harding could not find much Unionism in Missouri because they looked for it among white civilians. The glaring oversight—combined with President Lincoln's reversal of Frémont's intention to liberate enslaved people belonging to aiders of the rebellion—made it difficult for Missouri's African Americans to find recognition of their loyalty—and an escape from slavery—within Federal lines. As a result, enslaved people headed not for the Union army but for free states. West of Fulton in Saline County, enslaved young man Richard Bruner seized on wartime chaos to make a bid for freedom. Bruner recounted his dissatisfaction with slavery and the brutal beatings he received owing to his "terrible temper." Forced into the tobacco fields at a young age, he carried water to field hands before joining them to hoe the crop. War provided a chance for a different life. Bruner knew he would find no security within Federal lines, so he made his way to Kansas. There he bided his time until the Federal army would finally allow Black men to serve. He waited several years.[40]

While Federals had found nothing but disappointment in Missouri, they held out hope that another border state, Kentucky, would be more fertile ground for the cultivation of Unionism. In Louisville under command of Maj. Gen. Robert Anderson's Department of the Cumberland, James Birney Shaw of the Tenth Indiana was pleased to find that "the female sex" was "most ardent and effusive in their welcome" of Federal troops. Kentuckian Alfred Pirtle, a member of the Home Guards of Louisville, also remembered the exuberant welcome that the women of his city gave to the arrival of Federal soldiers. Here was the display of Unionism from white Southern women that Federals had been expecting for months: loyal women who knew that U.S. soldiers intended to deliver them from Confederates, not subject them to depredations.[41]

While Louisville women celebrated the arrival of Federals, the women of Paducah, close to Missouri, were a different story entirely. Illinoisan Charles Wright Wills found much to admire about the city and its white female residents, recording that he "never saw so many pretty women in my life," expounding on how all of them were "fat, smooth-skinned, small boned, highbred looking women." Wills had expected all white Southern women to be uneducated and slovenly. The white women of Paducah defied expectations, coming across as genteel ladies. But while the women looked elite, their actions told a different story. Wills was surprised that some of the ladies "hollered 'Hurrah for Jeff' at us." Even so, he excused their behavior. This early in the war, enlisted men like Wills were unconcerned by elite white women's displays of support for the Confederacy, which could be excused as the excitement of a moment.[42] At least initially, Federals did not read more significance into such displays.

While Federals held out hope for Unionism among Kentucky's white women, familiarity between Federals and Black women in Virginia bred nothing but contempt. U.S. commanders had grown tired of caring for Black women and children at Fort Monroe. That fall, the new commander of the Department of Virginia, Maj. Gen. John E. Wool, complained to Secretary of War Simon Cameron that women and children were a drain on the army's resources. "Am I to find food and shelter for the women and children," he questioned, "who can do nothing for themselves?" Wool characterized Black women and children as dependent, perhaps in hope of putting them outside his lines. Yet in the next breath, Wool admitted that his statements were not true. Those women who could work did so, and he acknowledged that "thus far we have been able to employ in various ways most of the adults."[43] By characterizing Black women and children as a drain on military resources, the commander of the department overseeing Fort Monroe signified that caring for Black women and children was not a priority. Rather than a group that could support the Federal military effort, Wool indicated that Black women and children were a distraction.

Elsewhere in Virginia, the men of McClellan's Army of the Potomac began to show contempt for white civilians. In Fairfax, New Jersey native David Samson declared, "Our men place no more Confidence in the protestations of Virginia Unionists." Samson and other enlisted men had wearied of civilians trying to save their resources by claiming fealty to the Union. These soldiers believed that, as soon as the army required resources from the populace, the loyal population grew exponentially. Samson and his fellow soldiers paid civilians no mind. The men took what they needed in order to make life comfortable, and as a result northern Virginians' "Barn yards hen roosts Corn fields and Ancient and once peaceful Village have to suffer a scourge of which Old Virginia, will never recover." Samson and his fellow enlisted men did so in defiance of orders McClellan issued just one month earlier, which prohibited "depredating upon the property of citizens," warning that those who did so would be "arrested and brought to trial."[44] The general's orders to the contrary, enlisted men in the Army of the Potomac began to question the wisdom of conciliation. With their own eyes they could see the unreliability of Unionism. Civilians could no longer be trusted and so should be punished by experiencing the harshness of war.

As enlisted men grew jaded, officers beginning new campaigns continued to be optimistic. During the South Carolina Expedition, Brig. Gen. Thomas W. Sherman believed his operation would result in hundreds of elite rebels finding themselves within Federal lines. On his arrival in Beaufort, South Carolina, Sherman issued a proclamation to the region's white population, assuring them that he and his men had come with "no feelings of personal animosity; no desire to harm your citizens, destroy your property, or interfere with any of your lawful rights or your social and local institutions."[45] Sherman hoped to signal that elite Carolinian planters had nothing to fear from Federals, who would harm neither their extensive landholdings nor their extensive slaveholdings. Sherman's proclamation adhered to the logic of conciliation, believing that kind treatment would return rebels to the Union or at least mitigate their disloyal leanings.

Sherman's proclamation did not reach its intended recipients, because Confederates had not waited to see how the Federal army would behave. Instead, they had taken off whatever property, human and otherwise, they could carry and fled to the Carolina upcountry. Days after his arrival, Sherman was still in a state of disbelief: "Every white inhabitant has left the island," he wrote in his report to Adj. Gen. Lorenzo Thomas. "The wealthy islands of Saint Helena, Ladies, and most of Port Royal are abandoned by the whites." Rather than conciliating rebels and protecting their property, Sherman faced "hordes of apparently disaffected blacks" engaged in the "pillage" of the "beautiful estates of the planters."[46] Federals would not be able to enact conciliation along the Sea Islands, for there were no white civilians to conciliate. Instead, they would deal with a Black population intent on the destruction of the plantation system and on their freedom.

As the campaign season of 1861 drew to a close, enlisted Federals' hopes for widespread Unionism among the white population faded like the shortening days. Their jaded outlook contrasted with the views of the new general-in-chief, George B. McClellan. A frequent interlocutor of Winfield Scott, McClellan remained certain that conciliating the Southern white population was a key element to winning the war. The men on the ground in the Army of the Potomac felt quite differently. While out foraging in Leesburg, Virginia, Stinson P. Everill of the First Pennsylvania went into what he thought was a "secesh house" and struck up a conversation with an eighteen-year-old female resident. When Everill asked the young lady about her political sympathies, she demurred, stating that "under the existing circumstances she did not like to answer the question." The young woman refused because she was fearful of reprisals from Confederate neighbors. Once Everill assured her that he would keep her reply confidential, she responded that "her father was a Union man and that she was satisfied that the north was right and the South wrong." Rather than the presence of the Federal army inspiring loyal women to publicly display their support for the union, Unionist families worried about declaring their political sympathies. Unionists would always be surrounded by Confederates. And the Federal army would not always be there to protect them.[47]

For their part, living under Confederate rule made elite white Unionist women form concrete expectations of the Federal army. These women came to expect that the U.S. Army would personally deliver them and their families from Confederates and would devote itself to protecting their families and their property. These white Unionists despaired over the depredations perpetrated by Confederate soldiers. Unionist Louisa Brown Pearl worried over how rebels conducted themselves, as cavalry "brok[e] open stores & helped themselves to whatever they like." The soldiers behaved so erratically that she worried "they may take it into their heads to burn us out when they get ready to go," so she hoped "the Northern army will come & take possession soon, or we shall all be in danger." In Bowling Green, the Confederate army occupied Josie Underwood's home for months. The family returned only to find that their "home was burned—the night before—by the soldiers who occupied the place." "Only the gable end of the house was standing," Underwood recalled, "and as we drove up . . . the last standing wall fell in with a crash and we arrived only in time to witness this final catastrophe." Similar to Pearl, mistreatment by Confederates caused Underwood to place her hope in Federals. Even though the army shelled the city before entering, Underwood "rejoiced . . . to learn that a Union army was just across the river." After suffering under rebel rule, white Unionists women felt sure that Federals intended to not only whip the rebels on the battlefield but also restore the rule of law and protect their personal property.[48]

Although white Unionist women hoped to be delivered from Confederates, in reality Federals could not completely displace either the rebel army or Confederate guerrillas. Particularly in southern Kentucky, Federal forces struggled to control Confederate raids, and thus loyal women remained vulnerable. In contested territory near the Cumberland River, rebels raided Jamestown, where they robbed houses and "made the women give up the shirts and other clothing of their husbands." Publicly embracing the Union in contested territory was dangerous business, for Confederate neighbors worked closely with the rebel army to identify Unionists so that they would be the target of rebel raids. For these reasons, some women remained quiet about their loyal sympathies.

Federals under the command of Henry Halleck's Department of the Missouri did not connect their failure to protect white Unionist civilians to the dearth of Unionist sentiment. Instead, soldiers blamed loyal Kentuckians for the army's inability to protect against rebel raids. Brig. Gen. J. T. Boyle complained to Halleck that "the people, even the good Union people, circulate the most devilish lies in regard to the enemy" and thus "our own scouts . . .

are not reliable." Not only did loyal civilians bear the brunt of Confederate raids, but Federals also blamed them for not providing reliable information about the enemy.[49]

By the end of 1861, Federals had seen enough of the behavior of white civilians in Kentucky and Missouri. They had hoped for widespread Unionism, for reliable information about rebels, or at least for civilians who appreciated their stabilizing influence. Since they had not found what they wanted, some believed it was time for a new civilian policy. The Department of the Missouri's new commander, Maj. Gen. Henry W. Halleck, concluded one and a half months after assuming command that it was not "armed and open enemies" who engaged in bridge and railroad burning but those who "pretended [to be] quiet citizens, living on their farms." "Our army here," he argued, "is almost as much in a hostile country as it was when in Mexico." Halleck despaired of finding Unionism among Missouri's white men. Instead of continuing to look for it, he proposed a new tack, declaring that "the time for conciliation, I am sorry to say, has passed. Nothing but the military power can now put down the rebellion and save the Union men in this State. It is useless now to try any other remedy."[50] In Kentucky and Missouri, civilians' blatant Confederate sympathies and behavior as guerrillas convinced the army to forgo kindness in favor of military might.

In fall of 1861, Federals spent more time in Virginia and spread into new areas in Missouri, Kentucky, and the Carolinas. But instead of their presence inspiring an outpouring of Unionism, soldiers encountered mistrust and prevarication. Even the truly loyal worried about voicing their sympathies, more concerned about Confederate reprisals than aiding the U.S. army. Even so, some within the army held out hope that winter and spring would bring a rebirth. As Federals launched a river assault into Kentucky and Tennessee, they eagerly anticipated Unionism in the Volunteer State.

The Rebellious Ladies of Nashville

Rumors about Federals' arrival in central Tennessee spread like wildfire. And elite Confederates expected little good to come of it. Some women were convinced that U.S. soldiers would engage in depredations, even going so far as to sexually assault them. Alice Ready, a sixteen-year-old from Murfreesboro, Tennessee, was convinced that Federal soldiers would try to enter her bedroom. Ready envisioned defending her chastity by shooting Union soldiers and "pil[ing] their dead bodies at the door." In Ready's imaginings, Federal "subjugation" took on a personal, intimate meaning, one in which U.S. soldiers would dominate the Confederate home front by sexually exploiting elite women. Wartime chaos meant elite women might be deprived of the protection of their family, and so Ready envisioned having to defend her honor herself.[51]

Rumors about dastardly Federals gave way to panic when Nashville Confederates faced the imminent arrival of the U.S. military. Merchants threw open their stores, encouraging passersby to help themselves. Grocers forced customers to take all they could carry. Carriages, carts, wagons, and buggies lined the streets of the city as families raced to pack up their belongings. Elizabeth Pendleton Hardin recorded the chaos, describing how "men, women, and children, the rich, the poor, white and black, mingled together in one struggling mass" in their haste to leave the city, giving way only long enough for retreating Confederate soldiers to pass. The city's civilians—at least those who could afford to leave—refused to wait to see how the Federal army would behave. For some, fleeing the city was preferable to living under an occupying army.[52]

Days later, Federal soldiers under command of conciliationist Don Carlos Buell marched into Nashville to find the city nearly deserted. Buell himself held out hope of encouraging Unionism, writing to General-in-Chief McClellan, "Though the mass of people appear to look upon us as invaders, . . . I have seen several strong indications of loyalty in individuals." His orders to his soldiers emphasized his belief in latent loyalty, declaring that "thousands of hearts in every part of the State will swell with joy to see that honored flag reinstated. . . . The voice of her own people will soon proclaim its welcome." His men had an important part to play in inculcating Unionism, and so his next words reminded them of appropriate conduct. "We are in arms, not for the purpose of invading the rights of our fellow-countrymen, but to maintain the integrity of the Union and protect the Constitution," Buell enjoined. The commander made no mention of the First Confiscation Act, instead hinting at the fugitive slave clause and the preservation of the Union. His next words made his focus on white men quite clear: "Peaceable citizens are not to be molested in their persons or property."[53] Buell expected that his army's occupation of Nashville would concentrate on encouraging Unionism and protecting property.

While Buell focused on latent loyalty, officers and enlisted men focused on those who had fled. "All who could go had skedaddled," observed Federal officer James Birney Shaw. Soldiers wondered at the inhabitants' hasty exit: Beautiful residences sat empty. Fields lay idle. The city's poor residents had appropriated the lavish furnishings of the wealthy, using them to adorn their dwellings. Nashville's Black residents took the opportunity to make friendly overtures toward the U.S. Army, explaining to soldiers how the strange sights came to be. Hundreds of wealthy white civilians, they recounted, had been whipped into frenzy by rumors of Yankee brutality. Certain that Federals would rob, murder, and rape them, they fled. Incredulous Federals could scarcely comprehend Confederates' naivete. "The fools believed [the exaggerated stories]," Shaw remarked incredulously, "and left the city."[54] Federals had to wonder how rebel lies had once again been more successful than the truth of Federal policy. Nashville posed the question of how Federals could win over white civilians with kind treatment if those civilians refused to live under Federal authority.

Not everyone, of course, had left Nashville. A significant portion of white civilians remained, most of them female, and these women did not cheer the arrival of Federals. Ohioan William Babcock Hazen noted that Nashville civilians "showed great bitterness" toward U.S. soldiers. One civilian in particular stood out, "a lady in handsome toilet," for as soon as she saw Hazen she "stamped vigorously upon the sidewalk and cheered for Jeff Davis." Directly after her display, the entire brigade rounded the corner with its "splendidly cadenced step, and glistening arms." The lady fled to the nearest house. Hazen's encounter with the elite woman in Nashville demonstrated to him that rebel sympathies had addled the senses of wealthy women. Instead of remaining ensconced in their homes where they belonged, these ladies made fools of themselves through public displays of sympathy for the rebel government. But when presented with the military might of the U.S. Army, they retreated to their proper sphere. For Hazen, this incident reassured him that the Federal army was now in control, and even if elite women did sympathize with rebels, their displays would be dealt with easily.[55]

Nashville's wealthy white women recalled their first meetings with Federals quite differently. Instead of being awed by military might, they remained unmoved. Elizabeth Pendleton Hardin found the U.S. Army's display quite ludicrous, noting soldiers' "magnificent uniforms" and "bands which made the city echo to hostile airs." Even with all of this pageantry, Hardin asserted that the men "fail[ed] to make any impression on the contemptuous Southerners," a fact that "tormented and enraged" Federal troops. Elite women either refused to look at the army or stared at them with "silent malediction."[56] Hardin and other elite women were not cowed by the arrival of Yankees. Instead, Federal occupation strengthened their commitment to the rebel cause and hardened their resolve to display their Confederate sympathies in every way available to them.

Southern-born Federals quickly realized that elite women's public displays of Confederate sentiment signaled trouble. Kentuckian Alfred Pirtle wrote his family that "no welcome cheers greeted Federals" in Nashville. Instead, "frowns and clouded brows and secesh talk is poured in our faces." Pirtle saw "a young lady with a minature [*sic*] rebel flag pinned on her dress" and an even younger one who "grit[ted] her teeth and stamp[ed] her feet" at Federals. From all of these displays, Pirtle concluded, "I do not think there is any Union feeling that I can see or hear of in Nashville," a fact he attributed to the people being "so thoroughly drilled by Secesh politicians and the Southern heart thoroughly fired."[57] Pirtle was more realistic about the dearth of Unionism, but he could not attribute women's behavior to their own rational choices. Instead, these wealthy ladies had been duped by male politicians, who had inflamed women's emotions to the point that they could not think clearly. The result was that young ladies behaved more like animals than well-bred women.

East of Nashville in Edgefield, Pennsylvanian Joseph Gibson also found much rebel sentiment among female civilians. While stationed as a provost guard, Gibson "had a good opportunity of observing the citizens" and thus "obtained some insight into the character of the southern people." Gibson focused on female civilians, however, noting that "some of the women of the city sought to show their contempt for Union soldiers in many ways not creditable to themselves," meaning that these women were behaving not like women but like male partisans. But Gibson felt that these virulent secessionists could not be "true representatives of Southern womanhood," noting that he and other Federals had difficulty distinguishing between different socioeconomic classes of white female civilians. He maintained that "the insults to the soldiers" came not from "true Southern wom[en]" but from lower-class women.[58] To men like Gibson, it was inconceivable that elite women would engage in public displays against Federals. The only way he could make sense of the women of Edgefield's behavior was to blame poor farming women for disrespectful behavior toward the men of the U.S. Army.

It was indeed elite rebel women who behaved like partisans, and they gloried in their unladylike behavior. Elizabeth Hardin found the first days of Federal occupation to be depressing. The only bright spot for her and other ladies lay in "insulting our oppressors." Hardin and her fellow elites took pleasure in "refus[ing] to let even the hem of [our] garments touch [Union soldiers]" and by returning soldiers' "most polite bows . . . with a stony gaze." Confederate ladies showed their support of secession through one of the most powerful tools they had: determining which men were fit for polite society. These women banded together to label all Federals, even officers and commanders, as ruffians unfit for refined ladies to look at, much less acknowledge. In doing so, these women maintained that they did not transgress ideals of ladylike behavior but instead fulfilled them to the highest degree. A woman's ultimate role was to serve her family and preserve patriotic sentiment. In Nashville, Confederate women established that ladies had a wartime duty to ostracize their country's sworn enemies.

Middle Tennessee women stayed the course even after the Confederate reversal at the Battle of Shiloh. On arriving in the city in April, Minnesotan James Madison Bowler wrote his wife that "the people here are as vividly *secesh* as the most ardent could desire" and that "they avoid, as far as possible, all communication with Union men." Bowler was not referring to the behavior of male civilians. He noted with distaste that "some are very saucy and impudent, as can be seen by . . . the disdainful faces and pouting lips of some of the ladies." In all his time in the city, Bowler had neither met nor heard of Union ladies. The behavior of Confederate women defied the Federal army's expectations of white civilians and also flouted their ideas of appropriate female behavior. Rather than remaining on the sidelines, elite rebels were acting as partisans in the conflict. They actively supported the Confederate government, sought to damage Federal morale, and remained undeterred by the increasing presence and size of the U.S. Army.[59]

Nashville's Confederate women had to wonder at U.S. soldiers' expectations that the protection and kindness they offered would be either welcomed or wanted. Rebel women regarded Federal soldiers not as liberators but as oppressors, despots, and cutthroats, and they found it laughable that Yankees expected Confederate women to either remain on the sidelines or switch their allegiance. Kate Carney of Murfreesboro seemed incredulous when the

Federals complained to her that they had not received a single kind word since arriving in the town. "How can they look for kindness," she marveled, "when they have come to take every thing away . . . [and] ruin every thing, we hold dear." To women like Carney, Federals who waged a war on slavery and intended to subjugate the Confederacy did not deserve kindness, even from ladies.[60]

Elite women continued their displays of rebel sentiment in both public and private. As they shunned Federal soldiers on the street, in private they reproved Southern-born male friends and acquaintances who joined the Federal army. Even United States soldiers recognized that rebel women's antics proved effective. Federal soldiers stationed in Murfreesboro, Tennessee, declared to Alice Ready that Confederate women deserved "the credit for the number of men the South has in the field." By ignoring, scolding, glaring, and goading—behaviors all considered unladylike—rebel women sought to punish invading Union soldiers and embolden Confederate troops.[61]

Nashville proved a turning point for the officers and enlisted men in the Department of the Ohio. Not only had white civilians fled before their arrival, but others engaged in open hostility. And the hostility was not coming from white male civilians. Instead it was elite white women who scorned and ostracized them, treating U.S. soldiers as though they were lawless ruffians. While some Federals attempted to find excuses for elite white women's behavior, others began to connect wealthy women's partisan displays to the depth of secessionist sentiment.

Conclusion: The Chaos of Conciliation

As 1862 wore on, Federals in Banks's Division of the Army of the Potomac arrived in the Shenandoah Valley. In Winchester, Federals finally received what they had been hoping for since they arrived in the Old Dominion. Officer Julian Wisner Hinkley of the Third Wisconsin had pleasant reflections of Winchester, noting that as Federals "marched in with colors flying and band playing, the citizens were rejoicing everywhere over their deliverance from the Confederates." Hinkley singled out Winchester's female civilians, who waved "innumerable handkerchiefs" to "welcome us." From these displays, Hinkley concluded that "strong Union sentiment" existed in the town.[62]

And Unionism did exist in Winchester. Women like Julia Chase, single and in her late thirties, cheered the arrival of Federals, calling it "glorious news" and exulting that the national flag "is waving over our town." Her only regret was that the soldiers had not arrived sooner, because in the days preceding the Federals' arrival, the Confederate army had engaged in much mischief.[63] Chase, as an elite white woman of significant property, did not flood the streets to welcome U.S. soldiers. Nevertheless, she celebrated their arrival and hoped for their success.

But Chase knew that Federals had much to prove to her fellow townspeople, many of whom were staunch secessionists. Some of them had even refused to stay in Winchester when they heard that Federals intended to take possession. Just a week before Wisconsinite Hinkley and other soldiers marched through the town, Chase recorded in her diary that "quite a number of our people are leaving town, frightened almost to death of the Yankees." And those who remained were no better. In fact, once Federal soldiers arrived, Chase hoped that the soldiers would "show by their conduct . . . that they are not all monsters and have not come for the purpose of cutting [civilians'] throats & destroying their homes."[64] Chase, like Hinkley, believed that the conduct of the U.S. Army would persuade secessionists from their rebellion. If the rumors could simply be disproved, and if Federals would do the bare minimum of protecting civilians and their property, then Winchester's rebellion might melt away.

Winchester's Confederate civilians—at least those who remained—did not fear bodily harm at the hands of Federals. Instead, townspeople like elite white woman Laura Lee and her sister remained defiant. In the days leading up to the arrival of U.S. soldiers, the Lee sisters did not cower in fear but instead systematically put "into place[s] of safety . . . everything contraband," including Confederate flags, "military clothes, [and] war letters."[65] The arrival of Federals signaled to the Lee sisters that they would soon be living in occupied territory. Rather than submitting to U.S. rule, the Lee sisters resolved to go underground and support the Confederacy through duplicity.

Soldiers on the ground soon realized that they had been deceived by Winchester civilians' initial displays of hospitality. Although Major General Banks encouraged conciliation, strictly limiting soldiers' ability to leave camp and forbidding them from interfering with private or public property, enlisted men felt these attempts did little good. Massachusetts soldier John Viles believed that Unionism only seemed to predominate, and that was because "many of the prominent Secesh decamped before the Union troops come [*sic*] in." This was a troubling sign for Federals who had once again hoped to encourage loyal sentiment among civilians. Even more alarming was that disloyalty rather than Unionism flourished with Federal occupation. Viles observed that while Winchester's men kept to themselves, "some of the women thinking their sex is sufficient protection say many very insulting remarks though not directly to the soldiers."[66] In Winchester as in Nashville, outright opposition to Federal occupation came not from white men but from elite white women. The question was, would the Federal army allow these women to continue to engage in disunion?

Laura Lee certainly felt emboldened. While Federal occupation at first "overwhelmed" her "with feelings of degradation and humiliation, (but never a particle of fear)," she soon recovered. "Indignation got the mastery," she seethed, "and now we feel nerved for all that may come." Lee drew strength from the predominance of secessionist feeling among Winchester civilians. She reported that Federals had learned after only a few days in the town that "the Union feelings which they boasted prevailed here . . . had no more real existence then the rest of their fabrications." Lee asserted that Federals had only hoped for loyalty among the civilians, but hoping could not make it so. And Lee characterized the entire conciliation policy as mere manipulation. "They say private property shall be respected and that any soldiers who insult a lady shall be shot," she reported. "That sounds well, but I do not trust them. I believe it is only . . . in hope of making us Union people."[67] An unrepentant rebel, Lee believed everything that Federals did was a cunning and calculated trick, insinuating that U.S. soldiers were confidence men, hoping to trick Southern civilians into switching their loyalties through good treatment.

Federals soon found that Union feeling did not even predominate in Union-leaning areas. Just north of Winchester in Charles Town, in what would soon be West Virginia, Massachusetts officer Wilder Dwight had taken on the duties of a provost marshal. While western Virginia had left the Old Dominion during the secession crisis, rebel feeling predominated enough in Charles Town for Dwight to refer to it as "this hot secession town." Dwight's rank and position did not shield him from rebel insults. In the process of securing rooms from an elite townswoman, the "good lady" informed Dwight that he could have the rooms but that she "hop[ed] you'll be beaten in your next battle." Dwight found such instances to be "amusing" rather than threatening. Even so, he reflected, "I think we under-estimate the strength of the secession sentiment and overestimate the Union feeling." The presence of

Federals had not, as they assumed, inspired Unionism among white Southern civilians. Instead, it had inflamed rebellion, and in the least-expected quarter: among elite white women. In spring of 1862, the U.S. Army confronted the question of whether elite rebel women posed a significant threat, and if they did, what should be done about it.[68]

Rebel women's defiance of Federal occupation—and their knowledge of the First Confiscation Act—had consequences for enslaved people. When Laura Lee of Winchester spirited away her "contraband" to places of safety, she lamented that "the servants . . . could not conveniently be stored away." While Lee did not have the resources to take refuge with her enslaved people, many enslavers did. Their actions devastated families. Early in the Peninsula Campaign, George Stephens remarked on the effects while campaigning with Hooker's Division in spring of 1862. As Federals advanced, rebel enslavers had run off "wives, husbands, children, and parents" in order to "aid the cause of slavery." Enslaved people in Virginia who had remained with enslavers to keep their families together had now been cruelly separated. With less to lose, they made their way to Federal lines. "Scores of freedmen are coming in," Stephens recorded in the *Anglo-African*. But this freedom was bittersweet. "Some come in wifeless and childless; some husbandless and fatherless."[69] For some enslaved people in the Old Dominion, the presence of Federals had not been enough of a reason to seek freedom. Instead, family ties proved more important. Only when enslavers ruptured these ties did Black men and women relocate to Federal lines.

What became clear to enslaved people that spring was that the rewards of leaving for Federal lines outnumbered the risks. But seizing these rewards meant moving quickly. Dennis Bland, a formerly enslaved man from Virginia, made his way to Federal lines at Budds Ferry, Maryland. Soon after, he hired two enslaved men to build his wife and children a boat so that they could cross the Potomac and be reunited. At the last minute, Mrs. Bland's escape route evaporated when the men who had made the boat used it themselves. Dennis Bland had no choice but to return to Virginia to spirit them away to safety. Miraculously, the family defied the odds, arriving within Federal lines to experience freedom together as a family. The actions of the Blands demonstrate how much Black men and women prioritized their familial bonds and the lengths to which they would go to keep their families together in the midst of war.[70]

Whether they left for U.S. Army lines or remained with enslavers, Black men and women made clear that they were more than "contraband," more than property: They were mothers, fathers, husbands, wives, sons, and daughters. Nowhere is this more clear than in the actions of an enslaved Black mother just outside of Athens, Alabama. When Col. John Basil Turchin's Eighth Brigade of Buell's Army of the Ohio invaded the state in May 1862, soldiers ransacked stores and houses throughout the county. A squad of soldiers arrived on the plantation of Charlotte Hine, where three Federals surrounded a fourteen-year-old Black girl. Two of the men sexually assaulted the young woman while the third looked on. The girl's mother ran to Hine, begging her "to save her daughter," as Hine later recalled. Hine ran out into her yard to confront the soldiers, but merely ended up witnessing the "horrid outrage[s]." Hine did lock up the mother in a closet, because Federals had made clear that they would "have her next," and while the soldiers tried to hunt her down, she eluded them.[71]

The enslaved mother was determined to hold the Federal soldiers who had assaulted her daughter accountable. Alabama law considered the rape of an enslaved child to be a crime against an enslaver's property, but this mother reasoned that civil war and the presence of the U.S. Army had suspended the status quo. Besides, the mother's enslaver would not be holding Federals to account, as she had tucked her tail and run to Tennessee.[72] Intent upon justice, the enslaved mother sent her daughter to camp to make a complaint and identify the soldiers who had raped her. The young girl identified one man, Myer Bowers of the Thirty-Seventh Indiana, and "charged him with committing a rape on her."[73]

Rather than responding to and investigating the allegations, some officers insisted on applying the discriminatory laws of their home states. For Bowers's commanding officer, Col. Carter Gazlay, it was enough that Bowers "denied positively having committed any rape." Gazlay refused to arrest Bowers when pressed, insisting that he would not arrest one of his men on "negro testimony." The only ally that the enslaved mother and her daughter had, it seemed, was Turchin, who ordered his second-in-command, First Lieut. Chauncey Miller, to investigate. This meant another trip to Federal lines for the young girl, another, probably agonizing, recounting of the assault, and another identification of her rapist. Bowers was then sent under arrest to the provost marshal in Huntsville, while Miller hoped to gather some "white witnesses." After that, the inquiry stalled when the brigade was ordered to move. Soon after, Bowers returned to his regiment.[74] The enslaved mother and her daughter would not get justice, although the presence of the Federal army had encouraged them to assert their right to live lives free of sexual violence. While the arrival of Federals had caused the family irreparable harm, the presence of the Federal army caused this woman and her daughter to insist on an end to the sexual abuse of Black women and girls.

The Army of the Ohio's commander, Brig. Gen. Don Carlos Buell, was ultimately responsible for Bowers's lack of prosecution. Instead of investigating Bowers's offense, Buell concerned himself with complaints by Athens's Confederate elite. And so, in July, Buell had Turchin court-martialed for depredations committed by his men. Athens's rebel townspeople testified about the Federals' behavior. Several reports concerned the sexual abuse of enslaved women, the most extensive of which being the rape of the young enslaved girl.[75] Individual soldiers did not face charges for sexually assaulting Black women and children.

A few weeks after Turchin's trial concluded, Buell continued to deal with Federal soldiers raping enslaved women—perhaps because Bowers and other men of the Eighth Brigade had done exactly that and faced no consequences. In a strongly worded letter to a subordinate, Buell complained about "disgraceful outrages" committed by Federal soldiers. "Negro women are debauched," Buell informed the officer, chastising the man that such abuses "disgrac[e] the army" and are "destructive of the public interests."[76]

Following the disastrous loss at Perryville, Buell faced a trial of his own. In addition to inquiries about his military decisions, the commission questioned Buell's interpretation and implementation of conciliation. One exchange was particularly damning. The commission questioned Gen. J. B. Steedman, a witness for the government: "What would have been the effect of a kind, conciliatory policy toward the negroes . . . by your army?" Steedman replied, "They might have been made more useful to the Union army than they have been." The commission continued their line of questioning, asking Steedman, "What has been the policy of Major General Buell in this respect?" Steedman replied, "His policy has been generally to exclude them from the camp and in favor of returning them to their owners." Like many commanders, Buell had focused his civilian policy on the restoration of the Union, which he believed could be accomplished by conciliatory treatment toward white Southern civilians. He afforded enslaved people no redress of grievances (and, if Steedman is to be believed, he refused to honor the Confiscation Acts).[77] While these policies might have been acceptable in 1861, by 1862 the tide had turned. As the Buell Commission's line of questioning indicates, Federals had to wonder if they had conciliated the wrong civilians, and if their kindness had merely been interpreted as weakness.

WHILE PRESIDENT LINCOLN, his generals-in-chief, and several key commanding generals initially favored a policy of conciliation concentrated on white male Southerners, white and Black Southern women made clear that they would play a role in the conflict. White Unionist women expected that in return for their material support, the Federal army would protect their persons and property. Displays of Federal might only encouraged elite Confederate women into boisterous displays of secessionist sentiment. Rebel women interpreted the very presence of the U.S. Army as a threat to them and their homes, and they sought to oppose the Federals at every turn. African American women in particular did not behave as expected. Black women insisted that the war was about slavery, and they sought to bring this to fruition by migrating to Federal lines. Even if they remained on plantations, enslaved women made demands of the U.S. Army, insisting that it make redress for grievances and treat them as people rather than "contraband." While Lincoln, Scott, McClellan, and others had intended to only wage war on the battlefield, Southern women quickly drew them to the home front.

Southern women's demands of the army caused key figures in the U.S. Army—from Commander-in-Chief Lincoln to Major General Halleck—to wonder whether the conciliation policy required adjustment. Many regimental commanders and enlisted men were inclined to agree with them, particularly as initial encounters turned into social interactions. Throughout the next year of the war, as the U.S. Army occupied more territory and Federals and civilians lived in close proximity to one another, soldiers' and women's initial impressions of each other became more detailed as they assessed each other's appearance, observed their character, and interacted with each other socially and even romantically. These interactions eventually led many officers and enlisted men to realize the astonishing breadth of rebel women's rebellion. Elite Confederates' treasonous behavior stood in for the behavior of all women, encouraging a vocal contingent within the U.S. Army to do away with conciliation once and for all.

CHAPTER TWO

Social Relationships and the Turn Toward Hard War

By mid-1862, U.S. soldiers had gone from invaders to occupiers. In this capacity they became well acquainted with Southern women. Elite rebels stood out because these women seized on the presence of the army to make clear their Confederate allegiance. Initially, officers and enlisted men were certain that rebellious ladies were a vocal minority. To prove their point, they sought out and praised Confederate women who adhered to the standards of true womanhood.[1] Sarah Childress Polk, widow of former President James K. Polk, was one of these women. Polk's sympathies lay with the Confederacy, yet she welcomed both Federals and rebels into her home. Thus the Tenth Indiana Volunteer Infantry of Buell's Department of the Ohio paid her a visit soon after arriving in Tennessee. Regimental historian James Birney Shaw wrote approvingly that once the soldiers arrived, "Mrs. Polk came out on the verandah and greeted us kindly, the boys responding with cheers." Polk allowed soldiers to tour her late husband's plantation and entertained many officers. Although the former first lady publicly stated that her "womanly sympathies [were] with the South," Union soldiers applauded Polk's equitable treatment of both armies. The men of the Tenth Indiana, much like their commanding general, hoped that all elite Confederate women would emulate Polk's behavior, creating an environment of mutual respect.[2]

As the Civil War dragged into its second year, the conflict brought regimental commanders and enlisted men and civilian women into close contact, causing them to assess each other's appearances, observe each other's character, and interact on social occasions.[3] Examining these social relationships reveals the ways in which men and women altered antebellum standards of behavior, as war provided space to redefine and renegotiate the country's ideals about race and gender. White soldiers and white women, particularly those from the upper classes, found that peacetime strictures of gentlemanly and ladylike conduct, such as protection of "worthy women" for men and "kindness toward all" for women, did not fit wartime situations. Enslaved women found space to challenge the country's racial and gender hierarchies through their assertion that true humanity lay in treating all people with dignity and respect. As the war upended accepted standards, all parties—white and Black, Northern and Southern, rebel and Unionist—changed their behavior, if not their ideals, in order to meet wartime realities.

Regimental commanders and officers from privileged backgrounds found adhering to standards of gentility during war quite difficult. Antebellum gender roles expected these men to prioritize refined manners, care for dependents, and protection of worthy women.[4] During war, men's obligation to "weaker" members of society meant leaving home to protect the nation through armed service. But there was an inherent tension between their roles as protectors and warriors. Many of the South's "worthy women," women of supposed good character and good morals, were rebels. At first, officers sought out these women because they wanted to associate with people from similar class and racial backgrounds, and they assumed that rebel women's good character would eventually win out over their treasonous notions. These men sought to apply conciliation to social settings, reasoning that gentlemanly behavior could persuade elite Confederates out of rebellion.[5]

That Federal officers spent time with rebel women irked Unionist white women, who could not fathom why they would spend inordinate amounts of time with the country's enemies. As those who had experienced the treachery of Confederate friends and neighbors firsthand, white Unionists hoped that the arrival of the U.S. Army would bring them not only protection but also companionship. War made these women quite vulnerable due to their political sympathies, necessitating that they depend on men they did not know while their own kinfolk hid from Confederates or enlisted in the army. Federals who spurned loyal women to spend time with rebels demonstrated foolishness and naivete. These men had been deceived by Confederate women's performance of kindness and gentility, and the ease with which they had been duped caused white Unionist women to question their judgment and character.[6]

The South's most loyal women were enslaved Black women, whom many officers and enlisted men regarded as neither worthy nor women. Their enslaved status and their Blackness supposedly signified deficiencies in their character, making them beneath the notice of gentlemen.[7] But Black women used the conflict to articulate their own standard of behavior. The highest honor these women could bestow on white Federals was not the label of "gentleman" but that of a friend to their race.[8] Enslaved women only spoke highly of Federals who treated African Americans with dignity and respect. Through social interactions with Union soldiers, enslaved women demonstrated both their loyalty and their desire to be treated equitably.

Elite Confederates had difficulty reconciling their political sympathies with the standards of true womanhood. In order to be treated as ladies by the Union army, they needed to behave like true women. But their ladylike status depended on maintaining slavery, and that necessitated supporting the Confederacy. And so rebel women took the idea of "Confederate womanhood," which they had formulated during the secession crisis, and extended it to wartime.[9] Often embraced by young rebels, this new standard glorified elite women's resistance, creating space for female patriotism and national devotion. Rebel women used this new standard to insist that the Federal army treat them like ladies even when they behaved in rude, impolite, and even treacherous ways.[10] "Confederate womanhood" meant that rebels did not have to treat Federals politely even if they behaved like gentlemen. Since these men were the enemy, elite rebels felt emboldened not only to treat them with disdain but to engage in espionage and treason.

Soldiers' and women's social interactions reveal that Southern women's behavior created a crisis for regimental commanders and enlisted men. White Unionists demanded that soldiers spurn rebel women, who seemed to be worthy women in need of protection. Enslaved Black women insisted that Union troops treat them with respect. Worst of all, the South's worthiest women, elite rebels, maintained friendly relationships with Federals in order to hide their brazen acts of treason. The result was that, by the end of 1862, the attitudes of many regimental commanders and enlisted men hardened toward all Southern women.[11] Not all women were rebels—that much was true. But the actions of elite rebel women caused soldiers and officers on the ground to advocate an end to the policy of conciliation. Because of the duplicity of wealthy Confederates, all women would be made to feel war's hardships.

Assessing Appearances and Observing Character

Wartime social relationships can be best viewed through the stages mandated by gentility. While not all Federals and Southern civilians adhered to these standards, gentility provided nineteenth-century Americans with helpful guidance for navigating a world of strangers, and these guidelines became particularly useful during war. Gentility's first stage was for strangers to assess appearances and observe character. Because women in particular were not to acknowledge strange men, men and women "read" strangers' appearance and character through physical characteristics. Since a person's exterior form revealed their inner character, strangers paid special attention to how a person looked and behaved in order to decide whether they wanted to know them better. And so Federals and civilians "read" the clues contained in appearance in order to better understand the newcomers they confronted. But these assessments could never be accurate because gentility's raison d'être was to preserve the country's racialized gender order. Thus, Federals remarked on the dignified demeanor of slaveholding elites even as Rebel women endlessly faulted even the behavior of officers from privileged backgrounds. In addition, gentility's racist undertones were on full display in the contemptuous ways some white Federals treated Black Unionist women. Early in the war, race and socioeconomic status, rather than political sympathies, determined which Federals spent time with which Southern civilians.[12]

Polished and well-dressed Federals inspired the praise of African American women. Formerly enslaved woman Patsy Hyde of Nashville, Tennessee, patriotically concluded that Federals were "de prettiest men" she had ever seen, and she admired how dressed up soldiers looked in their uniforms. Even years after the war, formerly enslaved women remembered the shininess of soldiers' buttons or described the beautiful sight of hundreds of bluecoats marching along the road. After women had spent decades enslaved and endured months of war, swarms of blue uniforms occupying Middle Tennessee came as a relief. The United States was gaining ground, and liberty seemed that much closer.[13]

Even so, enslaved women living in loyal areas worried whether individual Federals would live up to their shiny appearance. These women were aware that, this early in the war, commanders expected Union soldiers to uphold the fugitive slave clause. Perhaps for this reason, Hannah Davidson, enslaved in Kentucky, was "scared and ran away crying" when Federal cavalry arrived with "their swords hung at their sides." Eventually, Union soldiers' kindness overcame her fear. Davidson recalled one man telling her, "We won't hurt you, child," and said, "It made me feel wonderful." Other young enslaved women feared Yankees because their enslavers taught them to expect the worst from bluecoats. Jennie Small, a formerly enslaved woman from Pocahontas County, West Virginia, had been taught by her enslavers to be afraid of the Yankees. Her mind was changed when one officer took her on his knee and told her that "they were our friends and not our enemies; they were here to help us. After that I loved them instead of fearing them."[14] Black women insisted that the Federals who had earned their affection were those who showed them kindness and respect.

Invading Federals inspired alarm because as soldiers and white men they could easily inflict violence. Enslaved women wondered whether the U.S. Army would respect their political sympathies, which might differ from those of their enslavers. Such was the case for Millie Simpkins, living in Dickson County, Tennessee, near the Cumberland River. As Simpkins watched Ulysses S. Grant's command steam toward Nashville, she felt afraid. She lived in the household of her Confederate enslaver, and for that reason she "wuz skeered dey [Federals] would shoot."[15] Simpkins did not want to be caught in the crossfires of violence if Federals refused to recognize that enslaved people's loyalty might differ from that of slaveholders.

Enslaved children vividly recalled that much depended on the individual temperament of Federals. Rather than offering them protection, some white soldiers used dehumanizing and violent language toward them. Lucy Brooks of Montgomery County, Maryland, was playing one day with friends but grew concerned when Federals approached. In order to avoid them, she "ducked through a hole in the fence and ran out in the field. One of the soldiers seed me and he hollers 'look at that rat run.'" Particularly in areas still a part of the Union, where the Federal army's orders upheld the institution of slavery, some Northern white soldiers made it clear that they did not regard Black girls as they did white children. While white children were "innocents" in need of protection, some Federals viewed enslaved children as vermin. Enslaved girls learned early to be wary of such men.[16]

Much like the soldier who yelled at Brooks, some white Federals—particularly those from more racially homogenous regions—gawked at and insulted Black women and children. As part of the occupying force in northern Alabama, Illinoisan William A. Smith openly stared at an enslaved woman who "was white with nearly smooth hair." Similarly, after the Federal invasion and occupation of Beaufort, South Carolina, Col. Thomas Wentworth Higginson of the Thirty-Third USCT, declared that "most of the black women are utterly repulsive in aspect & attire." Occupying soldiers gaped at Black women, asserting that they were not the soldiers' equals since genteel standards forbid social equals to openly stare at each other. In this way, white U.S. soldiers made clear that social conventions did not require them to treat Black women with respect.[17]

Even once confiscation policies brought enslaved people within Federal lines, white Union soldiers often made clear their racist assumptions that Black men and women were not equal human beings. Illinoisan Douglas Ritchie Bushnell, stationed in Helena, Arkansas, under Henry Halleck's Department of the Mississippi, recounted what he termed a "curious" sight one summer evening as he made his way back to his tent. Bushnell watched a "poor n[egro] and his wife laying on the ground out in the open moonlight, they were both fast asleep, the man lay on his back and his poor wife lay up by the side of him, with both arms around his neck." What Bushnell found remarkable was not the presence of African Americans (he had written his wife earlier that the "whole army and town is swarming with *darkies*"), nor that the couple were asleep on the ground. Instead, Bushnell was struck because the Black man and his wife "looked as loving and as affectionate as white folks." Bushnell's shock over loving relationships between Black men and women was not uncommon: Many white soldiers, chaplains, and commanders questioned if African Americans were capable of love and lifelong partnerships. In essence, they questioned their humanity.[18]

Federal soldiers seemed unable to interpret Southern African Americans' behavior. The men of Buell's District of the Ohio, under command of a general who refused to enforce the Confiscation Acts, had been told to expect slave revolts.[19] Instead they found enslaved Black people more celebratory than insurrectionary. In Versailles, Kentucky, African Americans gathered from miles around to greet the Seventy-Second Indiana Infantry regiment. Commander Benjamin McGee and his men found the "shout[ing], danc[ing], leap[ing], yell[ing], and pray[ing]" to be "quite amusing . . . and touching." The men of Buell's command found such displays humorous rather than gratifying, assuming that enslaved men and women misunderstood the nature of the conflict. Under Buell's army, Federals were fighting a war to preserve the Union. Why enslaved people would celebrate Union soldiers' arrival under these circumstances did not make sense.[20]

Federal soldiers did not question poor white farming women's status as human beings but instead emphasized the ways in which these women did not live up to the standards of true womanhood. In Florence, Alabama, Union officer Jenkin Jones considered local factory girls a mixed group, "some of them good looking, others passable." That the young women had to work meant that they were not ladies. And if they were not ladies, then they could not be beautiful, because being beautiful required good character and good morals, something only elite women possessed. Beauty depended not only on race but on class, and thus white working women inspired contempt.

In addition to lacking beauty, officers found poor white farming women lacking in cleanliness and education. Officer Madison Bowler of Minnesota was shocked to find that even Kentuckians who practiced a skilled trade were ignorant and poor. Bowler could not believe that a shoemaker's house contained "the shop, hencoop, and pig-pen . . . in the same room with the family." In addition, none of the family could read or write. Chaplain George S. Bradley of the Twenty-Second Wisconsin described the ignorance of Southern women as "sad" and "lamentable," remarking that their grime and tobacco habits disgusted him so much that he "prayed that my destiny might never be linked with any of them." These Midwesterners implicitly critiqued the peculiar institution for the poverty, ignorance, and uncleanliness of poor farming women. Uneducated, dirty, and snuff-chewing white women demonstrated that chattel slavery perverted all of Southern society and prevented white women from reaching standards of civilization.[21]

Federals from farming backgrounds had more practical reasons for critiquing loyal white women. Charles Musser, son of a small farmer from Iowa, contemplated marrying "some loyal Arkansasians' fair daughter" while stationed in Little Rock. "There are plenty that wants to marry," he declared, and he "almost lost [his] heart among the beautyfull Daughters of the 'Sunny South.'" For Musser, the only hiccup was that although "clever and amiable," these young women could not compare to those of his acquaintance back home. Arkansas women lacked the buxomness, rosy cheeks, intelligence, and "edjucat[ion]" of Western women. Political sympathies could not overcome the fact that loyal Southern white women did not meet frontier standards of domesticity. Musser needed a companion who was hardy, smart, and educated. Although Arkansas's white Unionist women were beautiful, Southerners emphasized manners over learning and never adequately funded public education.[22]

While Federals focused on poor white women, elite and middle-class white Unionist women felt proud of men in the U.S. Army. These women had eagerly awaited the arrival of Union soldiers because they felt that common political sympathies linked them to Northern soldiers. Julia Chase of Winchester, Virginia, noted that once the soldiers of General Banks's command took possession of the town, "it was so good to see some one outside of Dixie." Frances Peter of Lexington, Kentucky, referred to Federal soldiers within Buell's District of the Ohio as "our men." Unionist women even emphasized that Federal soldiers embodied the ideal citizen soldier, a man who was both a warrior and a gentleman. Peter noted a striking contrast between Federal prisoners of war and their Confederate captors: "[I] couldn't help comparing *them*, so clean & gentlemanly looking & looking so well fed [with] the half starved, half clothed, dirty [Confederates]." The good health and cleanliness of Union soldiers demonstrated to Unionist women that these men lived up to standards of genteel manhood.[23]

Federal soldiers, however, had little to say about white Unionist women. Instead, elite rebel women made an impression on them, because they seemed just about the only white women who came close to domestic ideals. Newspaper correspondent Zenas T. Haines and his fellow soldiers under Gen. Ambrose E. Burnside's Department of North Carolina visited the plantation of a North Carolina farmer and commented that the female members of the family, although only "tolerably good looking," did have "a quiet, venerable aspect." The Fifth Pennsylvania Cavalry, passing by the Front Royal home of Virginian Lucy Rebecca Buck, admired her sister Nellie's manners and elegant apparel, calling out "Little Secesh in a white dress!" as they passed by.[24] Through their dress, etiquette, and leisure, Federal forces knew elite rebels to truly be ladies.

While Union soldiers quickly identified which Southern women looked like ladies, they noticed that not all of them acted like ladies. While occupying Jackson, Tennessee, under Grant's District of West Tennessee, Charles Lutz sounded shocked by how the women behaved, noting that "they are so mad at the union soldiers that they will scarcely look at one of us." Not only that, "they say that they will not walk under our flag." Lutz believed the Union army should "make them come to terms" or else put them outside of Federal lines.[25] Soldiers seemed shocked by elite women's behavior because real ladies would never call attention to themselves in public and in front of strange men. To the army, ladies who openly defied Federal authority seemed to be daring the military to treat them as hostile.

Begrudgingly, Confederate women admitted that some Federal soldiers did *look* attractive. Civilians in Winchester nicknamed Federals "Lincoln's Fancy

FIG 2.1. Alfred Waud, "Your Men Bin Stealing My Hogs"—Poor white women had a more difficult time preventing Union soldiers from taking their possessions. Part of the reason may have been that many Union soldiers viewed them much as did war correspondent Alfred Waud: shoeless, slovenly, and haggard. (Library of Congress)

Men" on account of their brass buttons, "polished guns," and "shining" boots. Sarah Morgan noted that Union soldiers in New Orleans were "fine, noble looking men . . . showing refinement and gentlemanly bearing." Elite Confederate women had to at least be truthful when it came to Federal soldiers' appearance, but they also maintained that fine clothing did not necessarily reflect character.[26]

Rebel women insisted that well-dressed Union soldiers failed to meet the standard of genteel manhood. Lucy Rebecca Buck made the distinction that the Federals of Brig. Gen. Nathan Kimball's First Brigade of the Department of the Shenandoah were "Men, but anything else than *gentle* men" and described them as "ruffianly fellows" because of their destructive behavior on her family's plantation. In Nashville, Elizabeth Pendleton Hardin faulted the men of Buell's Army of the Ohio for their rudeness. Not only was Hardin almost run over by Yankee cavalry one day, but the officer who reproved them yelled expletives. "[I] sneer[ed] at his cursing in the presence of ladies," Hardin recounted. Young rebel women used their status as true women to point out the flaws in Federal soldiers' behavior. These men, who resorted to violence and used foul language in the company of ladies, showed themselves to be unfit for polite society.[27]

And yet elite rebel women admitted that they themselves violated the standards of true womanhood by wearing Confederate symbols or behaving contemptuously toward Federals. In New Orleans, Clara Solomon criticized one of her friends for being "very patriotic" and still wearing "a [Confederate] flag," insisting that she and other women "should not lay ourselves open to insult." Sarah Morgan concurred, declaring that "Southern women" had "disgraced themselves by their rude, ill mannered behavior" toward the men of Butler's Department of the Gulf. Solomon worried about the consequences if women did not shape up quickly. When she found out that her female instructors intended to close their school in order to observe a Confederate fast day, disregarding the Union commander's orders, she pleaded, "*We* are the captured in a captive city and as servile to them as the slave to his master." As elite enslavers, wealthy Confederate women were accustomed to behaving how they pleased and commanding others to treat them with respect.[28] They now faced nearly unprecedented circumstances: They could either behave as true women toward enemy soldiers and gain the protection due to ladies, or openly defy Federal authority and face the consequences.

Social Outings and Social Relationships

After observing each other and deciding who met the standards of gentility, soldiers and women began to interact socially. These social occasions could be casual, such as sharing a meal or stopping in to call, or more formal, as when soldiers and women hosted a dance or picnic. Here again, political sympathies were not the determining factor. There were few occasions in which white Federals and Black women interacted at social events, since the 1850s witnessed white Americans increasingly committed to racial segregation.[29] And while white Unionist women sought out Federals, many soldiers still did not consider rebel women to be their enemy, instead insisting that women could be persuaded out of their Confederate sentiments with good treatment. But by mid-1862, many soldiers began to realize the depths of rebel women's disloyalty. Rebels' adherence to "Confederate womanhood" sanctioned rude and contemptuous treatment toward the U.S. military. Federals took notice of rebel women's treason once they stopped behaving like ladies but still insisted on being treated like them.

Relatively few interracial social outings occurred in the war's early years. Most Black Southerners were enslaved and thus had little to no leisure time. Even those who had seized their freedom by 1862 faced the difficult struggle of maintaining and expanding freedom. The experiences of Susie King Taylor illustrate this point. Taylor escaped slavery, along with family members, in spring of 1862. Perilous months followed, where hundreds of formerly enslaved men, women, and children attempted to evade attacks by Confederate militia. Once she and her compatriots were more secure, Taylor had more occasions to interact with white Federals in David Hunter's Department of the South. These officers sought to direct her labor. Commodore John R. Goldsborough told Taylor that he "was pleased to hear of my being so capable . . . and wished me to take charge of a school for the children." Teaching forty children by day and many adults at night kept Taylor quite busy.[30] But having been born into slavery, Taylor was well acquainted with a life of work. Her labor continued into freedom, although now she was at least working to benefit her community. Even so, her labor left little time for leisure and no time for social interactions with white Federals.

Taylor did form strong opinions about the white Federals with whom she interacted. Some she simply did not comment on. A very select few she praised. Capt. C. T. Trowbridge of the Thirty-Third USCT was one of these men. The two met in August 1862, when Trowbridge came to St. Simon's Island to fill the First and Second South Carolina regiments. But Trowbridge was not simply interested in military matters: He visited Taylor's school and showed an interest in Taylor's work. Thus began a long friendship between the two, with Taylor commenting, "When I knew him better I found him to be a thorough gentleman and a staunch friend to my race." To Taylor, being a gentleman and a friend to African Americans went hand in hand. Trowbridge was concerned with more than winning the war on the battlefield; he was also interested in the Black community's self-improvement. For these reasons, he earned Taylor's respect and praise.[31]

For its part, the military actively discouraged social interaction between white soldiers and Black women. Those who did so, particularly if they were officers, could find themselves in front of a court-martial. Two officers in McClellan's Army of the Potomac found themselves in such a predicament. First Lt. Francis W. Usher of the Thirty-Fourth New York faced charges for drunkenly visiting "the houses of lewd black women, mingl[ing] with them, [and] play[ing] cards with them" in Sandy Hook, Maryland. Officers charged First Lt. James L. Goddard of the Seventy-Sixth New York with roaming "the streets of Fredericksburg, Virginia in company with a Negro woman at night." In Henry Halleck's District of the Mississippi, Maj. James M. Ruggles of the Third Illinois Cavalry faced a court-martial for visiting "a negro wench after taps." Also in the District of the Mississippi, a court-martial charged Second Lt. Richard Lewis of the Second Indiana Artillery with "conduct prejudicial to good order and military discipline" for "playing cards with two negro wenches."[32] Overall, the army charged thirty-nine men with various offenses related to Black women, and most of those charged were officers. These trials seem to indicate that both the current and future general-in-chief frowned upon white officers interacting with Black women. And language used in the trials to refer to African American women—"lewd" and "wenches"—indicates that some officers, similar to the nation's white population, considered Black women to be of low morals.[33] Even during a civil war, commanding generals such as McClellan and Halleck concerned themselves with enforcing the country's racialized gender order.

White Union soldiers and white Southern women had many more occasions to interact. As members of similar social institutions, they often attended church together and interacted at Sunday worship. Oftentimes the presence of Yankees in church caused a stir. Kate Foster of Natchez contemptuously observed that "there were a great many Yankees at church and the officers thought they were dressed killingly but their uniforms cannot compare the least with ours." Indeed, Union soldiers' behavior during worship services became yet another area for rebel women to find fault. Kate Carney seemed appalled when one Sunday morning "just after service began, the Yanks got up and left." Such behavior reinforced Southern women's beliefs that Federals were not gentlemen because they behaved little better than infidels.[34]

White Union soldiers hoped that their presence in local houses of worship would demonstrate their good character and break the ice socially. Alfred Pirtle joined his cousin Laura one Sunday morning at the Church of the Nativity in Huntsville, Alabama. Pirtle reported to his parents that there were "few gentlemen present except Federals," and that his presence "excited the secesh ladies a good deal." Thomas Speed recounted a notable visit to George Washington's place of worship, Christ Church, in Alexandria, Virginia, during which he attracted notice for quite a different reason: lack of familiarity with the Episcopalian service. A young Confederate woman "had to find all the places for me in the prayer book," although when it came time to sing he triumphed "at the fact that I knew how to find [the hymns]." Pirtle believed that his and other officers' church attendance "convinced [some Confederates] that there are a good many gentlemen, even among the 'Yankees.'"[35] By attending church services, soldiers hoped to demonstrate their personal piety and remind rebels of shared religious beliefs.

Once soldiers and women got to know each other better, officers felt free to call on white Southern women. According to Alfred Pirtle, this was so that the men did not "los[e] a good deal of [their] small share of refinement," a refinement they associated with "the pleasure of ladies society." Some soldiers seemed to prefer women who remained loyal to the Union. Lewis Bayard Smith had the good fortune to spend an evening with a family "living in very handsome style" near his camp. And even though the family resided in the secessionist haven of Baltimore, Smith found "the ladies of the family" to be "very pleasant," mostly because they were all "strongly Union in feeling." More often than not, soldiers sought a refuge when they visited Unionist civilians, looking for "things [to be made] quite homelike for us after the routine of the day's work," as Julian Wisner Hinkley put it. White Unionist women tended to agree. Katherine Couse and her family only extended invitations for meals to officers, those who Couse referred to as "refined hansome looking men," noting that she and her sisters had become "so attached to them." Officers, then, sought out loyal white women's company so that they were not deprived of feminine moral and religious influence during war.[36]

Once wealthy white Southern women and white Union soldiers became better acquainted, they began to organize dinners, dances, and picnics. If possible, loyal women and men excluded rebels entirely from these gatherings. In Lexington, Kentucky, elite enslaving Unionist women spent weeks planning a Thanksgiving Day dinner for injured Federal soldiers in Ambrose Burnside's Army of the Ohio. The "delighted" soldiers "hoped the Lexington ladies would live forever" and "paid the ladies all kinds of compliments." Josie Underwood of Louisville marveled at "how war and gaiety go together" when the men of William K. Strong's District of Cairo occupied the town. "The soldiers [give] 'hops' at headquarters—visit the girls," she noted, and "they are often up here to call—take tea and I ride quite often with several of them." Near Nashville, wealthy enslaver Cynthia Brown described her Melrose plantation as being the "social headquarters for U.S. officers."[37] Social occasions gave Unionist women a chance to display their political sympathies as well as providing a social outlet during a chaotic and divisive war.

While some soldiers preferred to spend time with Unionists, they did not limit themselves to associating with loyal women. For many, particularly those in the Army of the Potomac, the only requirement was that the women be of good character, and this frequently led soldiers to the homes of wealthy slave-owning Confederates. Under Hooker's command, a Pennsylvania soldier exulted at being posted near the house of "one of the F.F.V. [First Families of Virginia]." Some soldiers even admitted a certain attraction to plantation society. New Yorker William Mickle felt "quite taken up" with the "style of living" of wealthy Virginians, admiring how they "cherish[ed] [the] *house* as the most sacred spot on earth & concentrat[ed] all affection in their families." Mickle was so infatuated with upper-class Southern ways that he contemplated accepting an invitation to dine with some prominent families even though he despised slavery. With large houses, fine possessions, and many enslaved people, upper-class Southerners had clearly attained the comfort and ease that genteel culture required.[38] Even for soldiers who hated slavery, elite Southerners' adherence to genteel values made social contact both desirable and pleasant.

In fact, Federals seem not to have viewed Confederate women as their enemies, and some expected rebel women to treat them well. In a letter back home while stationed with Bayard's Brigade of Pope's Army of the Virginia,

Freland Holman of Maine found it unsurprising that he had been "treated kindly and respectfully by all the Secession Ladies." The kind treatment was, perhaps, owing to Pope's harsher war tactics. In Huntsville, Alabama, Alfred Pirtle of Buell's Army of the Ohio sounded guardedly optimistic about the prospect of a social truce. Admittedly the civilians treated Union soldiers "as enemies," and there was "none, or very little of, good feeling between the citizens . . . and our troops." However, Pirtle hoped that "time and an interchange of views" would soften the Huntsville ladies. In Halleck's Department of the Mississippi, Illinoisan Douglass Ritchie Bushnell and a friend called on a notorious "secesh" lady at her plantation near Batesville, Arkansas, and received a warm welcome given that the woman's husband was, conveniently, a Union man.[39] Federal soldiers believed that, due to elite rebel women's embrace of true womanhood, the women would behave kindly even to their enemies, meaning that the two groups could spend pleasant social occasions together.

U.S. soldiers labeled women who displayed rebel sympathies as lower class. Frequently outside of the home, and showing little shame by interacting with strange men, these women clearly did not embrace true womanhood and could not be expected to behave well. While marching through Pulaski, Tennessee, Federals in Buell's District of the Ohio seemed unsurprised when young factory women called out to them, "Run you cowards" and "[The rebel army] will catch you before you get to Nashville." The soldiers did not expect better behavior from working-class women and felt emboldened to respond with threats of violence. Brig. Gen. John M. Palmer alerted the women that if they did not quiet down, the soldiers would burn the building. Off the coast of North Carolina, Federals began their occupation of New Bern with white Southern women who "look[ed] secesh daggers" at the soldiers. Newspaper correspondent Zenas Haines regarded such women as "doleful and disgusting," labeling them all "white trash."[40] Since rebellious behavior contravened standards of true womanhood, Federal soldiers believed it was only poor white Southern women who would engage in treasonous behavior.

Time soon changed soldiers' outlook, especially for those men serving under conciliationist commanders in areas where Confederate sympathy dominated. Pirtle's relationship with Huntsville's Confederate ladies still had not thawed after several weeks. Exasperated by their obstinacy, Pirtle admitted to his sister that he had a "right spicy conversation" with several secessionist women, uncaring if his bitter rejoinders hurt their feelings. Illinois soldier

Richard H. Watson, serving in the Trans-Mississippi under the command of John Pope, exacted revenge by calling on rebel ladies without an invitation to do so, an egregious breach of genteel behavior. Watson was provoked by the "aristocratic" and rabidly secessionist white women of Lebanon, Missouri, who did not "hesitate to own it although the Town is full of Soldiers." As retaliation for their treasonous behavior, Watson frequently called on these women, asserting his power as a Federal soldier to go into "any *Mansion* that I took a notion to and with out being requested to do so, take a seat. And with all the sangfroid request to hear a few pieces on the *Piano*." While these soldiers knew that they had defied gentlemanly standards when they got angry or called without an invitation, they responded to women's unladylike behavior by asserting their dominance as soldiers in an occupying army.[41]

Elite rebels' rude behavior caused some white Union soldiers to avoid their company entirely. After several more weeks enduring Confederate women's spite, Pirtle declared to his mother that "we are starting a society that will be as exclusive as the secesh. . . . The 'Feds' think they can get along without the secesh quite as well as they can with the 'Feds.'"[42] While unpleasant social encounters did not convince soldiers to reclassify rebel women as enemies, they did motivate Federals to find other women with whom to spend their time.

Elite Confederate women unequivocally labeled Federal soldiers as their enemies, but many older women recognized the wisdom in behaving courteously. Lucy Rebecca Buck's mother reproved her daughter for allowing the Federals of the Department of the Shenandoah to upset her, instructing her that it was "wicked to allow [her] passions to get such an ascendancy over [her] better feelings."[43] More mature rebels knew that they needed to behave like ladies toward enemies who were their social equals. Misbehaving would only invite ill treatment.

Some elite rebels, most of them young, insisted that wartime allowed them to deviate from true womanhood and invented new standards of behavior. This was true throughout the Confederacy, in areas occupied by commanders with conciliationist leanings and those who took a firmer hand toward the civilian population. In Murfreesboro, Alice and Mattie Ready left their house to avoid spending time with Union general Ormsby M. Mitchel. In New Orleans, women "turned [their] backs" on the men of Butler's Department of the Gulf while walking on the street. Lucy Rebecca Buck and her rebel friends went so far as to wear "thick brown veils" to church once the men of Banks's Department of the Shenandoah occupied the town, vowing "not to let a Yankee see our faces." In Glencoe, Virginia, forty-eight-year-old Elizabeth Curtis Wallace remained busy when soldiers of the man she referred to as "the Beast" Butler came for a "social chat," forcing her husband to entertain them by himself. These women blamed Union soldiers for having the impudence to look at them or call on them, insisting they would rather "die [than] receiv[e] Yankees." Through these behaviors, these women developed the idea of Confederate womanhood, which allowed elite women to treat Federals in a way that demonstrated their loyalty to their Confederate families and the Confederate nation.[44]

Confederate women justified rude remarks and angry words as wartime exigencies. Betty Herndon Maury proudly observed that her four-year-old refused a soldier of Irvin McDowell's command when he offered her candy, instructing him, "Yankee candy would choke me." When an enlisted man in Mitchel's command "spoke in disrespectful terms" about Confederate soldiers, Kate Carney laid aside her sewing and "blazed out at him." Lucy Rebecca Buck and her sister took it on themselves to "quarrel" with two young Virginian officers in Banks's Department of the Shenandoah. "[We] tr[ied] to shame them in their treason," Buck declared, drawing on ideas of women as the gatekeepers of Confederate nationalism.[45] Through Confederate womanhood, elite women maintained that they could transgress peacetime standards of true womanhood and still keep their status as ladies.

Although young women maintained their hostility to Federals throughout the war, every once in a while one or two kind and well-mannered Federal officers made an impression. Kate Carney and her sister came to like the well-behaved officers who guarded their home and resolved to join them for a meal. "Bettie & I haven't eaten with them yet," Carney disclosed, "but thought as they were so kind to us, we would." Nannie Haskins of Clarksville, Tennessee, felt that Col. Rodney Mason of the Seventy-First Ohio was a person whom "the citizens thought as much of . . . as one could of any enemy."[46] Northern Federals who behaved in a gentlemanly manner did not change young women's categorization of them as enemies, but their genteel manners did inspire these elite young ladies to make exceptions to their new standard of Confederate womanhood.

While individual Federals might pass muster, young Rebel women stood firm in giving most U.S. soldiers the cold shoulder. In Louisville, Confederate Lizzie Wright refused to dance with Federal officers at a ball. Nannie

Haskins's patriotism prevented her from attending a "grand picnic" held by the Federal commander of the town. Avoidance became much more complicated as time went on. While attending a barn dance with friends, Haskins was horrified when two Union soldiers showed up; worse, her friends refused to leave early.[47] The extreme stance of young Confederate women—that Federals were not fit to dance with, let alone associate with—underscored the strength of their patriotism. Their behavior also displayed the way in which they used the war to define new standards of behavior for themselves.

Social relationships became fraught during a time of war, and yet in many ways they still replicated the nation's divisions along lines of class and race. Even when divided by political sympathies, white soldiers preferred to spend time with women from similar backgrounds. Black women's loyalty made little impression on white Federals, and the army spent an inordinate amount of energy trying to keep white officers away from Black women. The most significant change came from elite young Rebels, who reinvented true womanhood to fit their new identities as Confederate women. These young ladies labeled Federals as enemies and treated nearly all of them precisely along these lines, making the case that they would not simply be persuaded out of their rebellion by kind words or courteous gestures.

Conclusion: Women's Treachery and the Turn to Hard War

The Civil War raised uncomfortable questions about gender roles, particularly when ideas about appropriate behavior clashed with wartime realities. One of the central tenets of true womanhood and the "self-made man" was the need to conduct oneself with sincerity. Prominent reformer William Alcott insisted that sincerity held up the entire social fabric: "The whole framework of society is upheld and kept in order by truth, and nothing but truth. Let deception become universally prevalent, and communities as such could scarcely exist, much less flourish and be happy."[48] But white women found deception to be necessary during war. This behavior caused the U.S. Army to question their status as ladies and to raise the possibility that it should hold them responsible for their treasonous behavior.

Federals did not have a problem excusing women's dishonesty if it benefited the cause. Indeed, many white Unionist women found deception to be a reality of living in an enemy country. In Fayette County, Tennessee, Elizabeth F. Tucker and her husband, who was "known . . . to the army as a true

Union man," took care of a Federal surgeon. Tucker stated in her testimony before the Southern Claims Commission that she had "concealed [the surgeon] and his politics" for a month, even when Confederate soldiers came to search the house. The surgeon was able to escape imprisonment because Tucker had "secreted him between the feather bed and the mattress in one of the rooms." A few months later, Tucker's husband died, but she nursed two officers back to health and kept them from Confederate forces by commanding two of her enslaved people to secret the men in the barn. When Confederates knocked on her door, she could allow them to search because "there were no soldiers there." Tucker and other Unionist women held that deception was perfectly fine during war because the Federal army required women's assistance to be successful.[49]

The army considered white Unionist women with Unionist husbands to be above suspicion, but because married women owed obedience to their husbands, some Federals became suspicious of loyal women with husbands who were rebels. Even though Unionist Ellen Tompkins's husband served in the Confederate army, she welcomed several regiments of the Federal Quartermaster's Department to her western Virginia farm in summer of 1861. Tompkins put all of the land and buildings on the farm "[to use] in various ways for the benefit of the troops" and cared for sick and wounded soldiers herself. Although Tompkins's behavior displayed her loyalty, men in the ranks did not trust her. Insisting that Tompkins could not be truly loyal since her husband was a Rebel, rumors swirled in camp that she used the cover of darkness to signal troop movements to Confederates stationed nearby. Other soldiers surmised that Tompkins sent her enslaved men and women to pass information while running errands. These concerns led Gen. William S. Rosecrans to remove Tompkins and her family from their farm, sending them outside of Union lines. Even so, after the war he supported her request for compensation, declaring that she "kept unstained faith as not communicating with our adversaries."[50] The Tompkins affair demonstrates the impact of coverture on married women's loyalty, since a patriarchal society expected women to be submissive to the political loyalties of male relatives. A married woman most certainly could not have separate political sympathies from her husband; her actions, no matter her words, would always be suspect.

Rebel ladies in occupied areas seized on assumptions about true women to outwardly comply with the Federal military while undermining their enemies at every turn. In Port Royal, Virginia, Helen Struan Bernard hid

Confederate officers in her home while surrounded by Burnside's Army of the Potomac. In Tennessee, Alice Ready's parents behaved kindly to the men of Ormsby M. Mitchel's command, but the family made plans on several occasions for Alice to pass information about Federal forces to Confederate general John Hunt Morgan. The Readys felt certain that Alice would avoid suspicion because she was a respectable upper-class woman. The most daring among these women were fellow Murfreesboro residents Kate Carney and her mother. The Carney women sheltered an escaped Confederate prisoner while Federal soldiers questioned them in their parlor about the man's whereabouts. By allowing the man to bathe, shave, and change clothes in their home, the escapee walked past his former captors without being recognized. Carney admitted that she didn't "like to act deceitfully," but she shrugged this off by observing that "occasions require it, in war time." Confederates took advantage of Federals' assumption that elite white women's innate goodness prevented them from deceiving others. Women's politeness secured the trust of Federal authorities so that they could secretly aid the Rebel army.[51]

After months of this behavior, regimental commanders and enlisted men finally began to realize that it was elite Confederate women who betrayed them. Upon closely monitoring elite Rebel women's behavior, officers in the Trans-Mississippi found an appallingly brazen pattern of deception. In St. Louis, Provost Marshal F. A. Dick wrote to his superiors in Washington, D.C., informing them that "the wives and daughters of officers in the rebel service" smuggled medicine, Confederate paraphernalia, and letters. The wealthy women, who wielded "great influence," also "[encouraged] their husbands and sons to continue the war; they convey information to them and by every possible contrivance they forward clothing and other support to the rebels." Elsewhere in the Show-Me State, Maj. Edward B. Eno described the women as so "intensely secesh" that he worried a Confederate victory would encourage them to take up arms and fight. Eno advised his commander, Maj. Gen. Ulysses S. Grant, to take firmer measures when dealing with rebel ladies. Through treasonous behavior, these elite women no longer deserved protection or preferential treatment.[52]

Elite women made fools of Rosecrans's Army of the Cumberland. In Gallatin, Tennessee, Maj. Gen. George Thomas was so fed up with the conduct of Confederate women that he ordered that they not be allowed to pass through his lines. Thomas considered women "more insinuating and far more dangerous than men." General Rosecrans's Fourteenth Army Corps bitterly remembered the duplicity of Nashville's Confederate women. While pretending to be agreeable, women smuggled goods and information right under soldiers' noses, boasting to their friends how they had outwitted the Yankees. Comparing the deceptive Nashville residents to prostitutes, the soldiers described the women's "secret enterprises," which "waited for execution only until darkness."[53] Because they used their gender and class status as a shield for treasonous actions, the army reasoned that these women should no longer be afforded the protection that belonged to true women. Their behavior made them the worst sort of women, clear in the ways in which Federals conceived of the threat in sexual terms. Elite rebels showed themselves to be painted women, deceitful creatures who "poisoned polite society with deception and betrayal." These women's deceitful actions removed them from the protections of true womanhood, putting them on the same level as "women of fashion" and sex workers, women to whom gentlemen owed neither respect nor protection.[54] Not only were treasonous Rebel women not ladies, they were—just like prostitutes—a danger to the military and to society. Their deception caused the U.S. military to distrust all Southern women, convinced that women were enemies that the army needed to neutralize rather than protect.

In New Orleans, Louisiana, Gen. Benjamin F. Butler instituted the most infamous policy holding elite women responsible for their actions. Recognizing that because of the strictures of true womanhood, no lady would acknowledge a strange man on the street, let alone talk to him, Butler ordered that Louisiana women "calling themselves ladies" who "by word, gesture, or movement insult[ed] or show[ed] contempt" for Union soldiers "shall be regarded and held liable to be treated as a woman of the town plying her avocation," that is, as a prostitute. It is clear in Butler's enforcement of the order, however, that he dealt with these women not as sex workers but as women who declared themselves as independent and not requiring men's protection. Eugenia Phillips, the wife of a Confederate officer, stood on the balcony of her house laughing and mocking the funeral procession of a Federal officer. In his order regarding her imprisonment, Butler insisted that Phillips deserved to be treated like an "uncommon, bad, and dangerous woman, stirring up strife and inciting to riot." Phillips, then, had "unsexed" herself, requiring not that the army protect her, but that the army defend themselves from her. At Ship Island, Mississippi, where Phillips was imprisoned, Pvt. Lafayette Bailey remarked that her sentence was just because "she laughed when our men was going to bury a soulger." Butler and his men insisted that to receive the protection ladies desired, they would have to act like ladies, respecting military authority and conducting themselves in a quiet, respectable manner. If women did not behave this way, Butler threatened to treat them as traitors fully subject to the rules of war.[55]

BY LATE 1862, Southern women and Federal soldiers had become well acquainted with each other. As the army came to occupy more territory, regimental commanders and enlisted men had more opportunities to interact with Southern women. These social interactions reveal that white Federals spurned relationships with loyal African American women and scorned impoverished white women they termed "poor white trash." They sought out genteel ladies, mainly elite Southern women who were also Confederates. Officers in particular expected that elite rebels would still conform to the standards of true womanhood, which mandated kindness and sincerity toward all. But for Confederate women, particularly young women, family and country now came first, and these women dispensed with kindness and sincerity toward enemies. Officers suffered elite ladies' rudeness in the parlor, believing it was only womanly bluster. As soldiers on the ground and their commanders came to realize the depth of wealthy Confederates' sentiments and the extent of their deception, a new approach to civilians crystallized. Women no longer required protection. They were enemies who would be made to feel the might of the U.S. military.

During the summer, fall, and winter of 1862, Federal commanders embraced and officers and soldiers implemented new policies that brought war into women's homes. Foraging, confiscation, and emancipation subjected women to war's hardships. But the policies did not affect them all equally. Wealthy enslavers forged direct relationships with the military in the hopes of influencing policy, characterizing confiscation and emancipation as "making war on women and children." African American women faced difficult choices of remaining on plantations or migrating to Federal lines. Whatever their choice, they insisted that they be treated as loyal civilians in need of aid. All told, these policies reveal that Southern women still had fight in them as they tried to influence and negotiate harsh policies toward civilians.

CHAPTER THREE

Domestic Struggles over Confiscation, Foraging, and Emancipation

THE SECOND AND THIRD YEARS of the Civil War brought new policies and, with them, new conflicts between soldiers and civilian women. No story better illustrates this contentious period than an altercation between a formerly enslaved woman and a white Federal soldier in Pine Bluff, Arkansas. Recalling his mother's wartime experience, Sam Word described how she came upon a Union soldier in her cabin stealing handmade quilts. She chastised the soldier: "Why, you nasty, stinking rascal, you say you come down here to fight for the n——s, and now you're stealing from 'em." The soldier defended his larceny by saying, "You're a goddamned liar. I'm fighting for $14 a month and the Union."[1] There is much to glean from this exchange. Foraging policies brought Federal troops into women's homes, and some soldiers did not stop at requisitioning supplies but also helped themselves to women's personal items. Part of what motivated the quilt-stealing soldier was unhappiness with the turn the war had taken: From a war to preserve the Union, it became a war to end slavery. Confederates might have brought on the war, but the soldier did not target them, instead reserving his ire for an elderly Black woman. He was not fighting to end slavery, and while he could not alter the army's war aims, he could take out his displeasure by stealing the belongings of a formerly enslaved woman. Word's mother interpreted the conflict in light of emancipation. All Federals were now tasked with fighting for African Americans, and for her this did not just mean an end to slavery. It also meant respect for Black women's loyalty, and recognizing loyalty meant respecting their homes and possessions.

Between 1862 and 1863, the Federal army embraced the harsher war policies of confiscation, foraging, and emancipation, spelling the end of conciliation.

While they were three separate policies, they emerged within days of each other and often worked in tandem. Congress approved a strengthened Confiscation Act on July 17, 1862. The next day, Gen. John Pope, commander of the newly formed Army of Virginia, ordered his men to "subsist upon the country." Three days after that, President Lincoln met with his cabinet to discuss an emancipation policy, and a preliminary version appeared two months later. That same day, he issued an executive order condoning Pope's foraging policy, extending it throughout Virginia and much of the Western theater.[2] These policies had profound consequences for Southern women, their political loyalties, and their homes.

Under the new guidelines, the U.S. Army exerted its presence in concrete and material ways. In the Eastern theater, Federals foraged liberally from loyal and disloyal women, expecting all civilians to support the war effort. The army was more circumspect in applying confiscation and emancipation. They targeted rebels, leading enslaving women to argue that confiscation and emancipation made war on white women and children by depriving delicate Southern ladies of enslaved people's domestic labor. Confederate women understood that Federals intended this policy to punish them for their rebellion, and they sought to move enslaved people out of the way of the army. These actions motivated even more enslaved people to self-emancipate to prevent family separation, and Black women within military lines advocated that they be treated as loyal civilians in need of aid.

In the West, Federals tried to distinguish between loyal and disloyal civilians while foraging, seeking to visit war's hardships on wealthy Confederates. But they also delayed implementing confiscation because many Western officers and enlisted men despised African Americans. Enslaved women's struggles for freedom faced a hostile Federal army resistant to waging war on slavery. When Federals did resort to confiscation, they pressed Black women into service. This misuse of what was supposed to be a voluntary policy angered Black women because it separated them from their families and their homes, undermining the primary reason for their loyalty. Overall, Southern women viewed harsher war policies with suspicion because the policies challenged their ability to control their homes. Union soldiers who asked for or demanded meals, requisitioned property, or stole belongings angered women because the actions made feeding, clothing, and caring for themselves and their dependents during war even more challenging.

This chapter considers all three of these policies in tandem because this is how the army implemented them and civilian women experienced them. In the East, Federals implemented confiscation and foraging at the same time. As a result, rebel enslavers attributed most Federal actions to confiscation and few to foraging. Civilian women in the West had a bit of lag time between foraging and confiscation, but enslavers confusingly referred to both policies as either "stealing" or "thieving." African American women did not label these policies but fit them into their larger freedom struggles. Black women in the Western theater focused on the abuses of forced confiscation and forced enlistment, arguing that such treatment undermined the cause of freedom. Ultimately, what mattered to civilians was not which policy they experienced but the effect of the army's actions on themselves, their homes, and their wartime loyalty.

The army did not design these policies to target women. Even so, women bore the brunt. Rebel and Unionist enslavers vociferously decried confiscation and emancipation as subverting the bedrock of Southern civilization: free white homes. Federals who attacked slavery waged war on white Southern women and children by forcing them to do backbreaking physical labor. African American women faulted Federals for ignoring their political sympathies and physical circumstances when it forced them to labor or took away their husbands, fathers, and sons to serve in the army. Poor white farming women held that when the army requisitioned supplies from them, it placed them in positions of uncertainty and even dependency. What resulted from the harsher war policies of 1862 through 1863 was a struggle between Southern women and the Federal army over Southern domestic spaces. At stake was the very nature of the Southern home.

Early Days of Foraging and Confiscation, Spring 1862

At the heart of conciliation was the idea that Federal soldiers would not meddle in domestic spaces. That meant not bothering Southern civilians in their homes and not taking their property. But by early 1862, the U.S. Congress and the U.S. Army were aware that they faced the problem of a large, vocal, and hostile class of Confederate enslavers. The First Confiscation Act, although adopted in 1861, was not widely used until commanders faced extensive opposition from rebel civilians. Federals did not apply the policy everywhere. While soldiers did ask Southern civilians for food, particularly in the border states, the recalcitrance of rebel civilians motivated the army to apply the First Confiscation Act in places like Winchester, Virginia, and New Orleans, Louisiana.

Soldiers saw a world of difference between taking property and asking for food. In Kentucky, Col. Madison Bowler, part of Buell's Army of the Ohio, saw nothing wrong with walking right up to a white Unionist woman's door, in spite of Buell's express orders that "peaceable citizens are not to be molested in their persons or property." Nevertheless, Bowler came away with "three canteens [of milk] . . . a dozen (all they had) of eggs, and . . . half a bushel of very nice biscuit."[3] In Bowler's mind, he had not coerced the woman but had asked nicely for provisions, and the loyal woman, perhaps grateful for the presence of Federals, complied with his request. The state's white Unionist women had very different expectations. Frances Peter of Lexington believed that Federals' arrival meant a reprieve from Confederate soldiers constantly asking "'Is there any chance of our getting something to eat out here.'"[4] But Josie Underwood reported with dismay that the first regiments to arrive in Bowling Green, composed of men from Ohio, Indiana, and Illinois, were "a lot of hungry coarse Dutchmen" who "treat[ed] Union women with a great deal of rudeness." Underwood herself did not have to labor to feed the Federals because her family's enslaved people shouldered the backbreaking work, giving the soldiers "breakfast . . . and fed them till 12 o'clock."[5] In the border state of Kentucky lay the seeds of conflict between Federal soldiers and Southern civilians. Soldiers had gendered expectations of Southern civilians, believing they could ask white women to feed them. White civilian women expected Federals to stay out of their domestic spaces because soldiers posed a threat to their domestic management. With enslaved people busy feeding soldiers, they could not labor to care for their enslavers. Thus, white women expected soldiers to stay in camp and eat their rations.

As Buell's Army spread into Middle Tennessee, soldiers continued their practice of asking civilians for meals. They did so, once again, contrary to orders, with Buell instructing his soldiers soon after entering the city that they were "forbidden to enter the residences or grounds of citizens on any plea without authority." Even so, Nashville's Confederate women faced a plague of Federal soldiers expecting home-cooked food. Lizzie Hardin believed that the stationing of Federal guards at each house was only to give "the appearance of protection." Rather than protecting the city's residents, the stationing of guards "resulted in nothing but the feeding of these guards by the

Southerners."[6] Soldiers believed that they could engage in a gendered exchange with Confederate civilians by giving them protection in exchange for meals. Elite rebels were even less likely than enslaving white Unionists to see this as a bargain. Federal soldiers should not ask them for a thing, not even breakfast. These privileged women expected that their domestic spaces would be entirely spared not only war's hardships but also its irritations.

Once Western Federals in Middle Tennessee realized that many of the town's residents held rebel sympathies, they did not stop at asking for meals. They soon overran elite women's property. Elizabeth McGavock Harding of Belle Meade plantation observed that although the Union soldiers who swarmed over her property were "generally very polite," they seemed "totally unconscious that their presence could by any possibility be deemed an intrusion. . . . [They] seem wanting in sensibility." Wealthy Confederates like Harding did not view Federal encampment on their land as protection but regarded it as a violation of proper manners. That the soldiers did not realize their faux pas demonstrated that they were uncivilized. Even if Federal soldiers did not take anything from them, elite rebels found their very presence to be an imposition.[7]

African American men and women abandoned by enslavers did not receive the protection of guards, and so their possessions were not spared. In Doncaster, Maryland, Federal soldiers in McClellan's Army of the Potomac "robbed" an unnamed Black woman, elderly man, and four children "of all their provisions . . . and they were left in a starving condition." There was no gendered exchange for this family, even though in his August report to President Lincoln, McClellan indicated the necessity of "pursuing a rigidly protective policy as to private property." Southern law and custom did not include Black women in the category of "women," and so even Federal soldiers did not extend to them the rights and privileges they automatically conferred on white women. Enlisted men did not supply the family with a guard or ask to be fed a meal but stole from them, plunging them into poverty and hunger. While white women—even recalcitrant rebels—automatically received protection from Federal soldiers, Black families did not.[8]

The U.S. army behaved quite differently toward white Unionists. When Irvin McDowell became commander of the newly created Department of the Rappahannock in April 1862, New York–born Margaret Tilloston Kemble Nourse of Fauquier County suddenly encountered almost daily visits from Federal soldiers. Nourse applied for and received a written safeguard from Union command, which she could show to squads of soldiers in order to prevent property requisitions. When five Illinois soldiers showed up on her property after her grain, Nourse "showed them the safeguard." One responded, "'They darsn't touch it'" because of the protection papers. While enlisted men initially attempted to seize upon army reorganization to forage from civilians, McDowell's command quickly instituted policies to prevent indiscriminate plunder. From then on, soldiers requested rather than requisitioned supplies, requests that Nourse and her husband honored. The safeguard restored the ability of the Nourse family to regulate the taking of their possessions, allowing them to more effectively balance providing for their family and for the Union cause.[9]

Even Confederates had access to safeguards to prevent property requisitions. As April turned to May, Helen Struan Bernard of Fredericksburg recorded that "the enemy are in full possession of the country all around us." Although she and her family were staunch rebels and quite wealthy, Bernard did not face requisitions from McDowell's Department of the Rappahannock. Enlisted men followed their commanders' injunction to only take supplies when authorized by a division or brigade commander. Bernard marveled at the order the town experienced. In addition to a picket on the road, Federals also placed "a guard in the yard to protect us from the marauding parties of their own soldiers" without her even having to ask for one.[10] Even as Federals began to implement limited requisitions of property in the Rappahannock, they sought to do so in a controlled manner. Recognizing that soldiers might target wealthy rebels, the Army of the Rappahannock was cautious, placing a guard on the Bernard plantation to protect Confederates' property rights.

In areas newly occupied by the Federal army, or in which rebel women did not kick up a fuss, the army tread lightly. But the Federals of Banks's Department of the Shenandoah, elated from their occupation of the former Confederate stronghold of Winchester, began to forage. Laura Lee noted that in spring of 1862, Federals were "beginning to carry off numbers of servants . . . [and] foraging parties go all around the country and carry off everything moveable." U.S. soldiers, with the permission of their officers, do seem to have targeted Winchester civilians. Commander Banks noted such actions with disapproval in his orders on March 13, lecturing his men that "officers in some cases, from mistaken views, either tolerate or encourage depredations on property," and he cautioned his men that "pillage is the most certain method of

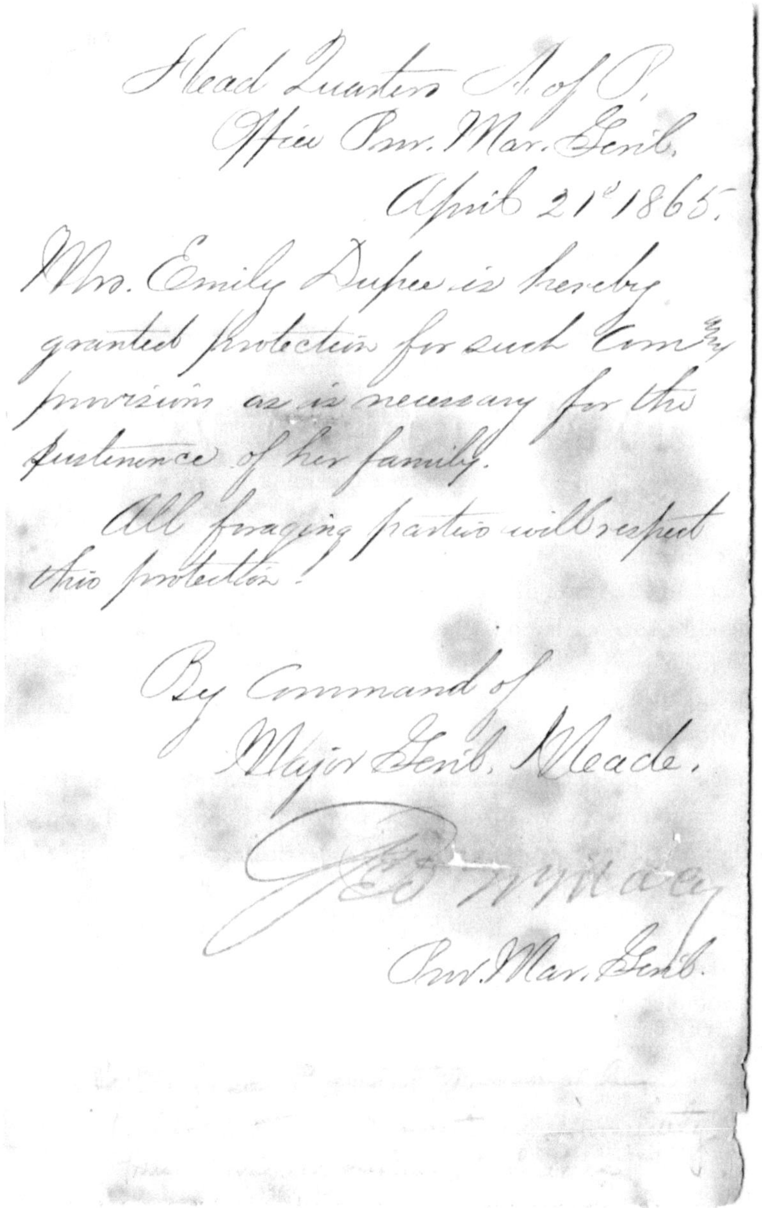

Head Quarters A. of P.
Office Pro. Mar. Genl.
April 21st 1865.

Mrs. Emily Dupee is hereby granted protection for such amt of provision as is necessary for the sustenance of her family.

All foraging parties will respect this protection.

By Command of
Major Genl. Meade.

Geo. [illegible] Macy
Pro. Mar. Genl.

FIG 3.1. Referred to as "safeguards" by civilian women, papers exempting women from foraging were sometimes doled out by Federal commanders. This order by Major General Meade, issued by Provost Marshall of the Army of the Potomac George Macy, protected Mrs. Emily Howe Dupuy of the Linden plantation in Prince Edward County from foraging after the war. (Virginia Museum of History and Culture, Mss1.D9295.b91) disorganizing and destroying an army." For her part, Lee attributed the foraging to rebel women's sentiments, noting that the soldiers "are very much disappointed in their reception here. They say they were never treated with such scorn, as by the Winchester ladies." Revenge does seem to have been the reason for U.S. soldiers' depredations on the property of disloyal civilians in Winchester, and once begun, commanders like Banks had difficulty reigning in such behavior.[11]

Lee believed that the consequence for the town's unrepentant Confederate sympathies was for Union soldiers to implement confiscation, even though neither the current commander, Banks, nor the subsequent commander, Franz Sigel, authorized such practices. "Great numbers" of enslaved people began leaving the city in spring of 1862, including her enslaved man Evan. She noted with despair that "it is only young men and boys who [the Yankees] entice off." By May, "nine-tenths of the servants" had gone, and in November, Lee and her sister decided it was better to "distur[b] . . . our household" by sending their enslaved women away. Lee was remiss in faulting the "Yankees" for "enticing" enslaved people to leave slavery. The reason was actually more simple: Jackson's Confederate cavalry was impressing enslaved men into the rebel service. A May report from Front Royal noted intelligence from a Confederate prisoner of war that "the enemy were impressing militia, mostly timid Union men, slaves of all and any ownership." Faced with forced service in the Confederate army or taking a chance with Federal soldiers, Evan and others chose Federals.[12]

If Lee believed that Federals had done their worst during their first occupation of Winchester, she revised her opinion when they reoccupied the town that summer. By that point, even the civilian provost marshal made clear that he was "not placed here to protect rebel women and children," a viewpoint Lee characterized as "odious and audacious." Lee accused Federals of "behaving outrageously" in June, faulting them for "breaking into homes."[13] The soldiers of Banks's and Sigel's command did, in fact, forage more widely in Winchester that summer. Rather than a targeted attack on Confederate women and children, the practice was due to a constellation of factors, including resistance from Confederate forces, unrepentant rebel women, and destroyed infrastructure. The frosty reception from Winchester civilians and victory over Thomas Jackson's Confederate cavalry certainly contributed to foraging that summer. But so did Confederate militias' burning bridges in the Shenandoah, as well as torrential rains that washed out other infrastructure. If the Federals who occupied Winchester took supplies from Southern civilians, they had good reason to. Low on rations, they had to subsist among the local population.

Just south of Winchester in Front Royal, eighteen-year-old Lucy Rebecca Buck believed that her elite, enslaving family fared no better. At first the soldiers of Banks's command called on the family requesting meals, but by April soldiers requisitioned the family's hay. Soon, "great uncouth Yankees" paced the plantation, "as though they really considered Bel Air a prison and we their lawful captives." The prison metaphor was apt: Federals expected good behavior of civilians, or they threatened punishment. Buck's father relayed a message from a Federal lieutenant, who warned that Front Royal had a reputation as a "*fast* place" and that "if the people did not behave themselves very nicely it would be *slower* before sundown."[14] While young women such as Buck chafed against Yankee restrictions on their Confederate sympathies, they also well understood, by late spring of 1862, that the army would make their lives infinitely more difficult if they refused to behave.

What saved the Buck family from inordinate destruction was both a blessing and a curse: Gen. Nathan Kimball camped his brigade on the family's plantation and made his headquarters in the house's west wing. Housing a Federal commanding officer among these staunch Confederates was hardly ideal. Even so, Buck acknowledged that Kimball "did all he could" to "prevent unnecessary destruction." That did not keep soldiers from dismantling nearly all of the plantation's fencing, even around the wheat fields, and then setting loose the pigs and cows and helping themselves to milk.[15] As Kimball's command hunted down Thomas Jackson's Confederate cavalry, they were required to live off of civilians. During this campaign, avoiding "unnecessary destruction" meant soldiers did not cut down the wheat and did not enter the house or yard.

More distressing to Buck than property destruction was the appearance of formerly enslaved men as laborers within the Federal army. Buck connected the two, declaring that after the Federals had confiscated physical property, "the climax of our indignation" was the passing of a cavalry company "and among them we recognized a mulatto in uniform." The U.S. Army was not yet enlisting Black men in the ranks, and so the man most likely wore the clothing allowance issued to him by the Federal army. Such distinctions were lost on Buck, who focused instead on the damage done to the man's enslaver. She declared that this young man "a short time since had fled from the best of masters and joined these miserable hypocrites [Federal soldiers]." Even so, Buck declared, "I should not blame him near as much as I do his instigators." Buck connected the presence of Federal soldiers with a supposed decline in fealty on the part of enslaved people. For Buck, the specter of African American freedom was more chilling than the requisitioning of hay or the destruction of pasture fences.[16]

Although African American men working with Federals terrified Buck, she consoled herself with the knowledge that U.S. soldiers were hardly abolitionists. From enlisted men to commanders, the men of the U.S. Army made it quite clear that they were no friends to African Americans. General Kimball instructed Buck's father that "if any man wanted to raise a fight all he had to do was to go down to camp and tax one of his men with being an emancipator." Buck struggled to reconcile these attitudes with the fact that the army "permit[ted] contrabands to go with them and harbor all who flee their masters." She was uncertain why the army was not encouraging enslaved people to come within Federal lines. "I have endeavored to detect them in some way trying to influence our slaves," she recorded that May, but "thus far the effort has been in vain." So while the army kept "servants" and also had "black attendants," whom Buck suspected of being abolitionists, their numbers were few. With her own enslaved people seeming "cheerful[l]," Buck ceased worrying about Federals' designs on slavery.[17] Buck associated the presence of the U.S. Army with the immediate decline of slavery, particularly since slavery was the bedrock of the Confederate war effort. She could not understand why Federals did not press their advantage.

A variety of factors influenced the Federal army's welcoming of enslaved people into their lines and enslaved people's decision to leave slavery. For instance, once McDowell's soldiers occupied Fredericksburg in April 1862, Betty Herndon Maury found that "the negroes are going off in great numbers and are beginning to become very independent and impudent." The army's status as occupiers rather than invaders and the proximity to refugee camps influenced bonded people's decision to leave. So did McDowell's policy of putting the local enslaved population to work "at depots and on railroads." Maury's household was far from unaffected. While she only had few enslaved people residing with her at her family home, she gained intelligence that all three of them were "going soon." It was not so much their leaving that troubled Maury. "I am afraid of the lawless Yankee soldiers," she recorded in her diary, "but that is nothing to my fear of the negroes if they should rise against us."[18] Similar to Buck, Maury worried about an alliance between Federal soldiers and vengeful formerly enslaved people.

The formerly enslaved did not intend to revolt, but that was small comfort to Maury. She was incredulous when bonded people left "their owners by the hundred," most likely to live within McDowell's lines, while others began "demanding wages." Enslavers tried to maintain some semblance of the racial hierarchy by refusing "to hire out their own or other peoples [*sic*] slaves." The result was that "there are numbers of unemployed negroes in town." Unlike many of her ilk, Maury did not fault Federals for the slow decline of slavery. That was perhaps because Fredericksburg's formerly enslaved had made it clear that they created freedom for themselves. What irked Maury about Federals was that they did not side with the city's white residents. "Many little difficulties have occurred since the Yankees have been here, between white people and negroes," she stated. "In every case the soldiers have interfered in favor of the negroes."[19] Alliances between Federal soldiers and formerly enslaved people worried Maury. Suddenly, she and other rebel planters distinctly felt the lack of any mechanism that would help them enforce the bounds of slavery and freedom.

Enslaved people and their free Black allies underscored that their decisions to leave or stay prioritized their families and their freedom. If the Federal army welcomed their kin and provided a path out of slavery, then they took that route. In the lower Potomac region, George E. Stephens remarked on the number of freedmen entering McClellan's Army of the Potomac. "It is a sight to see these men and women who, though born and bred in slavery, boldly grapple with death itself for the sake of freedom." Bonded people's antislavery ideology motivated them to take such a risk: They saw a path toward freedom and they took it. They did not leave slavery because they were "badly fed or poorly clad," they confided in Stephens. In fact, there was "an abundance of provisions in secession." To white soldiers these men and women told an entirely different story, "shrewdly knowing that in the majority of cases the white man's idea of the wrongness of slavery, lies in the bad treatment of the slaves." Black men and women understood that white Federals did not believe they had "an unalienable right to liberty." So they lied about poor treatment and the lack of provisions to obtain sympathy from the army.[20]

Hundreds of miles away in New Orleans, enslavers faced similar difficulties once the men of Butler's Department of the Gulf arrived. Confederate Clara Solomon was particularly troubled by the behavior of one of her family's enslaved women, Fanny. Fanny frequently absented herself, taking up company with another enslaved woman, Lucy. Solomon faulted Lucy as a bad influence, characterizing her as "weak-minded." The family believed it was only a matter of time before Lucy convinced Fanny to follow in the footsteps of other formerly enslaved people and seize her freedom. What Solomon could not fathom was how a "house-servant" like Fanny might desert them. She marveled at the "many instances in which . . . those who have been raised by people, have deserted them, though they have received the kindest treatment at their hands; but they imagine no sacrifice too great with which to purchase freedom." Like many enslavers, Solomon believed those who labored in the home to be well treated, and thus she characterized freedom as a "betray[al]." Solomon proposed dealing with freedom-seeking enslaved people by meting out "severe punishment" and then "discard[ing] them forever."[21] The mask of paternalism slipped entirely when enslaved people refused to perform absolute loyalty and obedience. In response, enslavers turned coercive and violent.

They also blamed the men of Butler's command. Solomon was indignant that New Orleans's enslaved people "sought the protection of the Yankees" and that Federals allowed this behavior. "They say they do not intend to interfere with slavery," she bemoaned, "then why do they encourage them to come to them?" To add insult to injury, the army would only "allow a master to take his slave, *if he be willing to go*. But is not that harboring them?" Her solution was that the U.S. Army "should drive them away."[22] Whether enslavers lived in Front Royal, Fredericksburg, or New Orleans, their main concern was with confiscation. That the Federal army refused to forcibly return their enslaved people to them was ludicrous. No matter that congressional legislation and military policy ruled against such an action. The Federal presence was interfering with slavery, and enslavers wanted the enemy army to return their important war resources to them.

Southern civilians experienced a range of policies that brought war into their homes during the spring of 1862. Women in border states and recently occupied Union areas found that safeguards did not mean that Federal soldiers would leave them alone. Instead, they found themselves deprived of domestic labor when enslaved people cooked for enlisted men. While soldiers framed requests for meals in terms of a gendered exchange, Unionists and Rebels alike hoped that Federals would stay out of their domestic affairs. In contrast, women in the path of the Army of the Rappahannock felt fortunate to receive safeguards, a practice that prevented unnecessary destruction. Rebels in the Shenandoah Valley experienced the harshest treatment, as Federals applied confiscation to Confederate sympathizers. The presence of the formerly enslaved among Federal lines drew the ire of enslavers, and their ire did not lessen when they found that the army did not entice men and women from their owners. These patterns—complaining about Federal requisitions and enslaved people within the lines—would only increase during the summer months, as Federals adopted a much more stringent policy of confiscation.

Second Confiscation and Foraging in the 1862 Eastern Theater

New policies in summer of 1862 brought war even further into the homes of Southern civilians. In July, Congress approved the Second Confiscation Act, which paved the way for any person enslaved by a rebel to find freedom. Soon after, Western commander Gen. John Pope moved east, ordering his Army of Virginia to live off the land. These policies had profound effects on Southern civilians. Confederate enslavers quickly equated a strengthened confiscation policy with Federals warring on women and children, as enslaved people's absence deprived them of domestic labor. While enslavers preoccupied themselves with confiscation, Virginia's Unionists discovered that the new policy of foraging did not spare loyal folks from Federal requisitions. And a disturbing pattern emerged in the wake of Federal defeats: some white Union soldiers used these new policies to destroy the lives and livelihoods of Black civilians. As the war became more about ending slavery than preserving the Union, some white soldiers decided that they would maintain supposed Black inferiority through violence.

Rumors swirled among enslavers that the summer would bring harsher policies. Lucy Rebecca Buck of Front Royal overheard adults "discussing a bill before the Federal Congress for the confiscation of all Secession property in the hands of their troops." Soldiers in Samuel W. Crawford's division of the Department of the Shenandoah, and subsequently the Department of the Rappahannock under Maj. Gen. James Shields, had already started appropriating the Buck family's possessions for army use, but Buck herself was concerned with the effect that a new confiscation policy would have on the family's enslaved people. She linked a new, more extensive policy to the destruction of white Southern families. Buck declared that the new confiscation bill's "awful consequences" would include "the ruin and exile of hundreds of families and our own large family of little children."[23] Over the ensuing months, Confederate and Unionist enslavers would make the same arguments: Federal confiscation was tantamount to warring against women and children. So bound up was the Southern family with slavery that freedom for Black families—for Black women and children in particular—spelled the destruction of white families.

The Buck family faced more immediate threats, as the continued presence of the U.S. Army encouraged enslaved people to make known their loyal sentiments. One man, Rob Roy, stood out because the family had placed "so much confidence" in his fealty. Roy now made no secret that he "espous[ed] the cause of the Yankee." Buck felt nothing but anger, stating that she "never was half so mad in my life." She blamed U.S. soldiers for Roy's supposed change of heart. Like many enslavers, Buck believed that enslaved people would have no thought of freedom or Unionism without outside interference, but they gave Federals far too much credit. Major General Shields himself acknowledged that enslaved people came to him willingly sharing intelligence, writing to a fellow officer, "A negro man came in and just now reports the enemy coming 8,000 strong through the mountains." The unnamed enslaved man, much like Rob Roy, required no outside interference. Desiring the demise of the Confederacy, they shared intelligence with Federals and shared their Union loyalties with their enslavers. Buck took the wrong lessons from Roy's espousal of the U.S. cause. To her, supposedly loyal enslaved people who openly praised the Union signaled the precise dangers of an occupying enemy army.[24]

As spring turned to summer, the Federal presence continued, and foraging increased. In early July, the Buck family had a new brigade of Federals encamped on their property, these belonging to Nathaniel P. Banks, now in John Pope's Army of Virginia. The Buck Family soon felt Pope's orders to his soldiers to live off the land. In addition to the usual burning of fencing and consuming of wheat, the family faced "raids on the garden and cherry trees, dairy and kitchen" and almost endless requests for meals. The next day, the Federal quartermaster announced to Buck's father the "military necessity" of "cutting and appropriating the remainder of the wheat standing in the field." Federals had begun to use the language of foraging in the valley. Buck disparaged the entire incident as "quite a crude proceeding." While in the spring, Federals under General Kimball attempted to limit the damage to the Buck family's property, by the summer the men of Pope's command insisted on the need to subsist off of the land.[25]

Non-slaveholding Unionists in Gen. John Pope's path grew increasingly concerned about foraging. Soon after Pope ordered his soldiers to live off the land, his army visited Unionist Ann C. Brandt, the guardian of her deceased Confederate son's young children. Soldiers made quick work of nearly $5,000 of her grandchildren's inheritance. Their behavior surprised Brandt, who proudly displayed the national colors, "thinking the soldiers would protect [her] because of [her] sentiments." But Pope's orders were clear: His men were to "subsist upon the country in which their operations are carried on," and vouchers would be issued, "payable at the conclusion of the war, upon sufficient testimony . . . that such owners have been loyal citizens of the United States." Eventually Brandt received guards and passes from Federal officers, but not before enlisted men confiscated her mules, broke open her granary, and treated her quite rudely. One German cavalryman told her "Go away old woman" when she tried to keep some of her horses.[26] Loyal white women assumed that even the men of Pope's command would direct their foraging at rebels. While officers proved willing to spare Unionists and prevent unnecessary destruction, enlisted men carried out Pope's orders to the full extent.

Federals foraged liberally from white Unionists in the lead-up to the Battle of Cedar Mountain. Susan P. W. Hall of Culpeper County found that not even poverty spared her from foraging. Hall and her husband "took no interest in politics" but even so "wanted the union to stand as it was." Their loyalty did not deter Federals from killing and dressing their hogs "in plain sight of the house." When Hall's husband tried to achieve redress by lodging a complaint within Federal lines, officers told him "they were obliged to have the property for the Army, but that he would be paid for it." Elsewhere in the county, Sarah Thomas operated a 277-acre farm while caring for her sickly husband. In addition to nursing him, she also "fed the soldiers" and took "care of the sick." Her attention to U.S. soldiers did not exempt her from foraging, as Federals "took all [the corn] we had left."[27] With orders to live off the land, the men of Pope's command often did not take women's political sympathies or class status into account. The only protection that the army offered Unionist women was the promise of postwar payment.

The army, decentralized as it was, did not treat Unionist women and Confederates the same in Fredericksburg. Instead, the men of Brig. Gen. Rufus King's command, near the end of the Peninsula Campaign and while enduring frequent attacks by Confederate cavalry, subjected the notorious rebels of Fredericksburg to foraging and property destruction. Elizabeth Maxwell Alsop reported that "the Yankees have destroyed most if not all of Uncle Tom Chandler's furniture." She believed it was a targeted attack because her uncle had "entertained the Confederates last week." In addition, both her paternal and maternal grandmothers faced requisitions by Federal foraging parties. One group took mules and horses from her mother's mother, and the other took hams and bacon in addition to mules from her father's mother. The men of King's command exceeded Pope's orders to forage when they engaged in property destruction but targeted their attack on civilians who were clearly disloyal.[28] In doing so, enlisted men put the French and Alsop families on notice that support for the Confederate army now came with material consequences.

What was most disconcerting to Alsop was not the foraging but the way one of her grandmother Alsop's enslaved women responded. Similar to Rob Roy, enslaved woman Georgiana openly embraced Unionist sentiments. After U.S. soldiers had confiscated the property, "Georgiana clapped her hands and said 'She was glad the Yankees had taken the mules & wished they would, take ole Miss off too.'"[29] The presence of the Federal army emboldened Georgiana to give voice to her hope for reverse confiscation, one that would liberate enslaved people from enslavers. For why should Georgiana have to leave the only home she had ever known and abandon the plantation she had worked for decades to sustain? At least in the Eastern theater, Federal soldiers confined themselves to taking the property of enslavers rather than the property of the enslaved, causing some bonded people to hope that the army would also carry off their oppressors.

By the end of July, Virginia's enslavers finally received news of the Second Confiscation Act. This new law was so notorious that women called it by name. Unionist enslaver Margaret Tilloston Kemble Nourse sorrowfully recorded in her diary that "the confiscation bill has passed." She pleaded with the Almighty that the war might end soon, and she railed against a Federal army that would "war now against women and children for it will personally affect them most." Nourse's concerns, like Buck's, stood with white women and children. Any attack on slavery was interpreted as the actions of a "ruthless" government intending to "crush all these poor people without a thought of regret." Nourse lamented the end of the slave codes' reification of racial and gender difference. Confiscation (and the Militia Act) gave Black women status as wives and mothers, recognizing their gender rather than subsuming it into the category of bonded laborer. Enslavers like Nourse found the new law to be troubling precisely because white women's status as ladies depended on Black women's labor.[30]

Enslaving women sought to reshape their households in response to the legislation. In Fredericksburg, Betty Herndon Maury recorded, "The Yankees have . . . passed a new confiscation bill seizing the property of all who refuse to take the oath." Maury's central concern was with a particular kind of property: enslaved people. Discussing her uncle's plans to move somewhere safe from Federal incursions, Maury commented, "We have to be very cautious and careful speaking of these things, for if the negroes have any suspicion that they were to be carried away they would run off." Protecting enslaved property took on new urgency with an updated law, one that sheltered any enslaved person, whether their enslaver was Confederate or Unionist. The law was such that Helen Struan Bernard had entirely given up on punishing recalcitrant enslaved people. "I take comfort in the thought that this is no time for discipline," she consoled herself in her diary, "for if the least feeling of discontent is produced, off goes the servant to the Yankees & we have no means of redress."[31] Maury and Bernard recognized a new reality in which their enslaved people could find shelter within Federal lines, so they had to tread carefully. No longer worried about slave revolts, they worried over slave abandonment.

Meanwhile, Pope's army regrouped in northern Virginia, spreading foraging policies further. Straggling soldiers informed Margaret Nourse that "Lee and Pope are fighting," and the next day some enlisted men "robb[ed] the corn field." Although she once again obtained a guard, she did not enjoy the same protection that she had earlier in the summer. The very next day, an officer ordered the Nourses to supply him with chickens, and seven cavalry soldiers "demanded corn for their horses." While most of the soldiers abided by Pope's orders, others did not: On August 6, Pope prohibited his men from "enter[ing] any house without a written permit from his brigade commander." Nevertheless, ten Federals requested dinner from the Nourses. By the end of the week, Nourse had to bribe soldiers with hams and chickens so that they would leave her sheep alone, to no avail: Federals shot "two hogs from mere mischief," "killed a sheep and left it," and "killed both old turkies."[32] While safeguards prevented soldiers from destroying personal property, they no longer prevented foraging, which sometimes devolved into unnecessary destruction.

Foraging could, particularly after a Federal defeat, lead to property destruction. The Read family of Baileys Crossroads found themselves in Federals' path after the defeat at Second Bull Run. The Thirty-Fifth New York Infantry and Fourth Michigan Cavalry encamped on the property, "us[ing] and appropriat[ing] to themselves the hay that was in two barns" and killing "two fat hogs." But soldiers did not stop there, as matriarch Charlotte S. Read stated in her postwar claim: "What of the property the troops could not carry away and use and appropriate to themselves they destroyed," including twelve chairs, one washstand, nearly all of the family's clothes, plates, cups, silverware, jugs, and kettles, and the family's national flag. Read estimated the damage at $1,253. The officers and enlisted men in these two regiments engaged in unnecessary destruction of Read's property, contravening their commanding general's orders about entering private property. These Northeastern and Midwestern troops took out their defeat on a Unionist family. Retreat provided the opportunity and foraging provided cover to engage in pillaging.[33]

For those still enslaved in Virginia, the army's advance toward Fredericksburg brought the possibility of freedom. Stationed at Union Mills, Virginia, with Sickles's Division of the Army of the Potomac, George Stephens told the *Anglo-African*, "As is ever the case when our troops fall back from the enemy's country, large numbers of contrabands . . . follow in our wake." A new urgency propelled people. As enslavers worried about the Second Confiscation Act, they made plans to send away their bonded people. George and Kitty Washington and their six children, enslaved near Warrenton, Virginia, were one such case. Their enslaver, Joe Weaver, had already seized two of the couple's children and sent them to Richmond, and he planned to do the same with Kitty and the rest of the children. So Kitty "took as many of their things as she and her husband could conveniently carry, and turned her steps northward." When the Rebel cavalry came near catching them, the Washington family "struck [for] the woods," remaining there in the drenching rain for hours. Their urgency was acute. Once the Washingtons reached camp, they informed Stephens that "all negroes caught attempting to escape are ordered to be shot."[34] To the Washingtons, slavery was clearly collapsing when those who held them in bondage could only resort to fleeing or violence to stabilize the institution. The risks within Federal lines outweighed the certainty of family separation or death.

The close of 1862 brought one last major campaign in Virginia, the ill-fated Battle of Fredericksburg. With a cold, wet, and hungry army came visitors to the farms of Virginia's women. Pleasanton's Cavalry Division of the Army of the Potomac visited Mary Latham, a widow and mother of four from Rappahannock County, Virginia, where they slaughtered all eight of her sheep. Latham, a Unionist, entreated soldiers to leave her one or two as she had four children to feed. But a winter campaign did not allow for sympathy. Federals told Latham that "their supplies had not come up and they were obliged to have them for food."[35] Newly widowed Martha Bailey of Culpeper County watched as Federals took her mule, horse, buggy, and harness (but thankfully left her food supplies alone). Asked after the war why she did not go after her possessions, Bailey explained that "it was the same week my husband died, and I was not in a condition with five young children to look after it and gave it up."[36] Without male relatives around to insist on protection for domestic spaces, Fredericksburg's widowed, loyal women faced a hungry and demoralized army unconcerned with family size or political sympathies.

After the Federal defeat, George Stephens and his regiment remained in camp. In the wake of the battle, "comparatively few people . . . have taken refuge among us" as "the slaves were all run off" by their enslavers. Other men and women "did not succeed in making their escape when we retreated, the movement was so suddenly and quickly performed." That meant that those who did make their way to Federal lines were not bonded people but free people. Seizing freedom was as much an issue of luck and timing as anything else. Those who had waited for a Federal victory or a slow retreat to self-emancipate would need to find another opportunity.

In the wake of defeat by Confederates, some white Federals took out their anger on African Americans. Stephens faulted a regiment of Zouaves for their "rowdyism and brutality to colored men," noting that "more than one poor slave has met his death at the hand of this mob." Rather than seeing African Americans as their allies, some Federals took out their aggression on them. On the day Stephens and his regiment retreated from camp near Fredericksburg, the Zouaves grew angry with African American teamsters and began attacking them with iron bars. Even the teamsters' boss had difficulty subduing the soldiers. When the boss broke up the fight, the Zouaves merely ran off to their tents to grab their firearms to "murder in cold blood a few unarmed negroes," as Stephens put it. The Black men only escaped by hiding themselves away.[37] When these white Federals failed to subdue Confederates on the battlefield, they took out their frustrations on the men who labored along with them to ensure the success of the Union.

The advent of harsher war policies in Virginia raised the stakes for Southern civilians of all stripes. Poor loyal white women found that foraging did not spare even those who favored the Union. Meanwhile, Unionist and Confederate enslavers decried the Second Confiscation Act, arguing that it waged war on women and children. Those same enslavers warred on Black families, who increasingly made their way to Federal lines to avoid family separation. Even within those lines, they did not find a welcome reception and were still subjected to racist violence. In the Eastern theater, confiscation emerged before foraging and proved much more widespread and controversial during the last half of 1862.

Foraging and Second Confiscation in the 1862 Western Theater

In the Western theater, Federals implemented harsher war policies in reverse. At first they foraged throughout the countryside, supplying their armies with the fruit of the land. While in the East the armies foraged from both rebels and Unionists, Western armies tried to protect the white and loyal. And as rebel resistance to Federal occupation continued even after implementing foraging, some officers and enlisted men encouraged confiscation. While their actions defied the orders of conciliationist commanders like Don Carlos Buell, they also did not explicitly benefit enslaved people.[38] Western armies often forced Black men and women off plantations to labor for Federals, a practice that enslaved people condemned. While in the East, armies tried to encourage Unionism among the enslaved, Western armies coerced enslaved people, treating them more like laborers than like human beings.

Initially, Federal officers tread lightly in Middle Tennessee. Col. Madison Bowler, who felt no qualms asking loyal Kentucky women for food, behaved differently in Nashville. In this region of intense secessionist sentiment, Bowler and his men took care to make distinctions between loyal and disloyal civilians. As he described in a letter to his wife, "The 'secesh' give us a wide berth, and when we want anything all we have to do is take it. Union men's property is sacredly respected by us, though they must hold out the sure sign of a little red, white, and blue waving over the premises."[39] While in

Kentucky Bowler and his men had operated from the assumption that civilians were Unionists and would be happy to share their bounty with their friends in uniform, Middle Tennessee was notorious for being rife with secessionist sentiment. Requisitioning supplies from rebels was one way for Bowler and his men to make these folks feel war's hardships.

Wealthy rebel women tried to avoid foraging by using their connections and resources to demand the Federal army's protection. Elizabeth McGavock Harding, one of the wealthiest residents of Nashville, secured several audiences with military governor Andrew Johnson to obtain a guard for her 250-acre plantation. Even though Harding was a Confederate and her husband was imprisoned in Fort Mackinaw, Johnson promised to write orders that her house not be molested because of her "unprotected position." The orders, however, never materialized. Weeks later Harding lamented that "law and order are at an end" as "marauders [U.S. soldiers] . . . shoo[t] turkeys and sheep." While in the Eastern theater officers automatically placed guards at the homes of wealthy rebels, Harding could not get Johnson to bend to her will. And so Federal soldiers foraged liberally from her large plantation, subjecting Harding to war's hardships.[40]

Other elite Confederates had more success when they took advantage of the diffuseness of the Federal command. Just south of Nashville, the Carney family felt entitled to Federal protection even though they were in no way defenseless—the Carney patriarch was only briefly imprisoned in summer of 1862. Nevertheless, Kate Carney's mother went to great lengths to secure a guard. She first visited the provost marshal, who had no men to spare, and then called on Gen. William Nelson. Once Nelson found out the family were rebels, he ordered the elder Carney woman to "go home, & stay there . . . if they didn't wish to be eaten out of house and home." But later that day, a Federal officer inquired into the family's complaints and sent over a lieutenant as a guard. The Carney family's travails demonstrate that, while some Western theater commanders refused to conciliate rebels, their orders depended on subordinates for implementation. Confederates could usually find a sympathetic officer who would acquiesce. Wealthy rebels used the vastness of the Federal war machine to receive protection of their property.[41]

Rebel women knew that foraging and pillaging depended on the disposition of individual officers. In Madison Parish, Louisiana, Kate Stone reported that while some plantations had been "burned by the Yankee bands," others had "not [been] molested." Stone attributed the difference to the "temper of the officer in charge." Those officers who were more "good-natured" might refrain from burning rebel property, yet "most" were "malicious." Stone knew of which she spoke: Her house remained intact because an officer dissuaded enlisted men from raiding and burning. The officer believed the plantation posed no threat because there were "only ladies and children" in the home.[42] Even as conciliation began to fade in the Western theater, some officers resisted visiting war's hardships on wealthy ladies.

Foraging became widespread once enlisted men realized just how little Unionist sentiment prevailed. That spring in Murfreesboro, Tennessee, Kate Carney referred to Federals who foraged, most likely cavalry under command of Gen. Ormsby M. Mitchel, as "stealing from the garden." Carney refused to recognize these actions as an official policy, instead characterizing the requisitioning of supplies from the country's enemies as the work of unprincipled soldiers. In McMinnville, Lucy Virginia French recognized that foraging was official policy but highlighted its invasive character. In her town, "large foraging parties ravage[d] . . . [and] broke into every store . . . took out everything they wanted, went into everybody's garden poultry house, dairy etc. and helped themselves." The behavior continued for a week, at which point French characterized the U.S. soldiers as "graceless tramps of Yankees" who "are stealing and prowling about the place." Rebel women in the Western theater did not connect Federal policies to their treason, instead characterizing U.S. soldiers as predators who invaded ladies' homes.[43]

Murfreesboro's enslavers characterized both foraging and confiscation as stealing. The Federal commander in charge of the region, Ormsby M. Mitchel, followed War Department orders to confiscate enslaved people belonging to rebels, a stance that put him on a collision course with his conciliationist commander Don Carlos Buell. These discrepancies caused young rebel women, Alice Ready being one of them, to characterize Mitchel's actions as thievery. She recorded in her diary that "Old Mitchell [*sic*] and his division have left, started to day about 2 oclock, I suppose they thought they had stolen enough negroes."[44] Once again, elite rebels refused to consider confiscation as official policy or as punishment for their treason. Instead, they accused Federals of "negro stealing," equating the U.S. Army's policy with illegal behavior that violated their property rights.[45]

Characterizing confiscation as thieving allowed female enslavers to engage in the pleasant fiction that their enslaved people would not voluntarily desert them. Elizabeth McGavock Harding noted that while many of her bondspeople seemed discontented, the grumblings were "nothing of any consequence" and certainly no indication that they desired freedom. Harding remarked to her husband that while "many servants have run away from their homes," she assured him, "not one of ours has disgraced himself and you by such conduct." Kate Carney seemed only amused, not troubled, when one of her family's enslaved women, Prissy, no longer took pains to hide her joy over Confederate losses and dismay over Union reverses.[46] In contrast to their Eastern counterparts, Western enslavers initially remained untroubled when enslaved people complained or expressed loyal sentiments. They wrongly assumed that enslaved people who did not immediately leave for Federal lines did so because they felt attached to enslavers, and not because of commanders' conflicting policies about sheltering enslaved people within U.S. Army lines.[47]

Enslavers in the Western theater rejoiced when the U.S. Army treated enslaved people poorly. Southeast of Murfreesboro in the loosely held town of McMinnville, wealthy planter Lucy Virginia French referred to Federals as sending "a stolen negro" to her house to obtain their dinner, once again characterizing confiscation as thievery. French exulted in the fact that soldiers treated African Americans as servants, for "it has shown the negroes very plainly that the war has not been made on purpose to free them." In addition, word had spread quickly within the enslaved community by "those who have tried Yankee masters and life in the army" that it was not "the state of perfect beatitude which it has been represented to be."[48] French, of course, drew the wrong conclusions. She took some Federals' poor treatment of enslaved people as evidence that plantation owners treated their bonded people well. French believed that the Yankees had demonstrated that enslaved people fared better in slavery than in freedom.

French spoke too soon. Not a month later, one of her enslaved men, Cooper, was found "missing, gone off with the Yankees." Cooper had joined up with an Ohio regiment, and not even the intervention of French's husband could stop him.[49] The presence of the Federal army created space for enslaved people, like Prissy and Cooper, to take action against slavery. As a woman, Prissy might have faced constraints in leaving for Federal lines due to family obligations, but this did not stop her from vocally supporting the Union. As a young man, Cooper had more opportunities and thus left McMinnville entirely, removing himself from the jurisdiction of his enslavers. Both had declared war on the plantation household, whether or not their enslavers interpreted their actions as such.

Federal policies of confiscation toward enslaved people were supposed to be voluntary: Enslaved people could seek protection within Federal lines if they chose to do so. This was largely how the army behaved in the Eastern theater.[50] In the West, African Americans realized to their dismay that some Federal soldiers thought nothing of carrying enslaved people off to camp if they required labor. Julia Casey of West Tennessee bitterly remembered that Yankee soldiers took two of her sisters during the war. Minnie Fulkes found these episodes painful to talk about even decades later. "Dem times too over sad 'cause Yankees took lots of slaves away an' dey made homes, an' whole heap of families lost sight of each other. I know of a case whar after hit wuz ten years a brother an' sister lived side by side an' didn't know dey wuz blood kin." Enslaved people in the Western theater deplored coercive policies of confiscation. Rather than welcoming them into Federal lines and allowing them to decide what freedom looked like for them, some soldiers forced enslaved men and women to labor, treating them as if they were still enslaved.[51]

The problem of Western Federals forcing enslaved people to labor for them became so widespread that in summer of 1862, William Tecumseh Sherman, commanding the Army of the Tennessee, issued orders clarifying army policy. Sherman declared that "the well-settled policy of the whole army now is to have nothing to do with the negro." Citing Henry Halleck, Sherman declared that Federals must "exclude [enslaved people] from camp." But he also acknowledged that "the laws of Congress command that we do not surrender back to the master a fugitive slave." In this instance, Sherman insisted that it was not the army's business to become involved, but one that should be decided by civil authorities. Even so, commanding officers could "appropriate . . . labor through the quartermaster." The rampant contradictions within Sherman's orders indicate that Federal policy toward enslaved people was anything but well settled. One need only look slightly east to Buell and Mitchel to see conflicting interpretations of army policy. Rather than coherent policy, Sherman's orders were an attempt to rationalize the exclusion of African Americans from his lines, concerned that large numbers of African Americans would slow his army down. He envisioned "our trains encumbered by them" and insisted, "nor can we afford to feed them."[52] Sherman did not view African Americans as a loyal population that would be an asset to his army, and his views trickled down to some of his men.

Western soldiers often did not treat enslaved people with equal respect. Federals intruded into their domestic spaces and, rather than requesting meals as soldiers did with white women, issued commands. In Missouri, Harriet Casey recalled how Federal soldiers would "come at night and rout de slave women out of bed and make 'em cook de soldiers a square meal." Josie Martin of Helena, Arkansas, remembered similar treatment. Her most salient memory of Federal soldiers was when they "found old colored people, went out, took their hog and made them barbecue it. . . . They wasn't so good to Negroes. They was good to their own feelings. They [ate] up all that old couple had to eat in their house . . . and worked the old man and woman nearly to death." Black civilians took issue with Western Federals who refused to treat the African American population as their allies. Rather than respecting their domestic spaces, Union soldiers expected African Americans to be at their beck and call. This lack of basic decency intimated that many Western soldiers held proslavery sentiments.[53]

Western Federals made clear that they had not come south to bring freedom when they requisitioned supplies from plantations now inhabited by enslaved people. Around Cartersville, Tennessee, Adeline Taylor resided on the plantation that her enslavers had fled, making a home in freedom with other self-emancipated people. The arrival of Union soldiers was a curse more than a blessing, and she reminded her children of this fact until the day she died. Federals "et up and wasted the rations, then humor up the black folks like they was in their favor when they was settin' out wasting their living." These soldiers merely pretended to be antislavery while squandering the hard-earned fruits of African American labor. In Huntsville, Alabama, enslaved women welcomed Jenkin Jones and his men onto their plantation until the soldiers helped themselves to their chickens and corn. After that, the women protested Union soldiers' plundering of the supposedly "abandoned" plantation because it depleted their resources and undermined their free and independent household.[54] Black women labeled these experiences with Federals as deliberate destruction motivated by racism. Taking food from enslaved people living on plantations abandoned by rebels did nothing to further the war effort and everything to reinforce racial hierarchies.

To add insult to injury, Western theater armies refused to allow Black women and children into their lines. In Helena, Arkansas, Henry S. Eggleston of Curtis's Army of the Southwest decided that it would be "impossible to forage for the immense numbers that were flocking to our camp daily." So he ordered that no more women or children be admitted within his lines. While the law stated that "all slaves . . . taking refuge within the lines of the army . . .

FIG 3.2. Edwin Forbes, "Spotsylvania C[ourt] H[ouse], Va."—Even though white Federals disdained Black women for not exhibiting "proper" behavior, they intruded on women's private spaces. War correspondent Forbes depicts an intimate scene as Black women and children sit around a fire while another woman cooks a meal. (Library of Congress)

shall be forever free of their servitude," enslaved women in Tennessee, Alabama, and Arkansas faced obstacles in securing freedom. The only place in which their freedom would be secure was in U.S. lines, but some Federal commanders refused to give them refuge. Individual enlisted men and officers forced enslaved women to labor within their own homes or carried them off to Union lines when they required assistance. But when women made their own way to army lines, commanders treated them as drains on military resources.[55] The double standard alienated enslaved women in the Western theater from the U.S. Army and forced them to labor for their enslavers supporting the country's enemies rather than contributing to the Union war effort.

Some Western Federal soldiers made clear their proslavery sentiments as they occupied new areas of the Confederacy. After the invasion of Memphis in summer of 1862, Grant's Army of the District of West Tennessee spread into Mississippi. Just outside of Holly Springs, young Cordelia Lewis Scales endured many of the indignities undergone by Tennessee's plantation elite.

Federal soldiers "staid in our yard all the time" and would "order the milk to be churned any time & they took corn fodder, ruined the garden & took evry thing in the poltry line."[56] As occupiers, Federals encamped on the Lewis plantation and foraged as much as they could from the wealthy rebels. While Lewis was indignant at their orders, the family's bonded people, not their pampered daughter, did the actual labor of providing for Union soldiers.

Yet foraging, as maddening as Lewis found it, was not the main topic of conversation. Enslavers and soldiers were on edge as news of the Preliminary Emancipation Proclamation spread. Scales entered into a heated conversation with a group of cavalry and infantry officers, accusing them of being cowards and running away in battle before levying the ultimate insult: They were "negro thieves." The soldiers denied the charge, asserting that they were "western men." The "western men" grew irate when Scales retorted that she "judged people by the company they kepted that they fought with them & staid with them that 'birds of a feather would flock together.'"[57] If it was not already clear from the actions of Western officers and soldiers, they had no sympathy for enslaved people and did not support emancipation. They took pains to make this clear to Scales by both their words and their behavior.

Similar scenes occurred in Kentucky. Here the U.S. Army struggled to whip the Confederate army on the battlefield, neutralize the threat from rebel ladies, and preserve the institution of slavery. In sum, the army placated white Unionists while punishing Confederates. In Lexington, Frances Peter praised Gen. Quincy Adams Gillmore, commander of the Second Brigade of the Army of the Ohio, because he "does not allow his soldiers to gad about like the secesh or interfere in any way with private property." In fact, Gillmore issued orders to that precise effect, encouraging guards and pickets to "refuse admission within the lines to that class of people known as 'contrabands.'"[58] Not only that, Gillmore and his staff made clear distinctions in their treatment of secessionist and Unionist civilians. In November, Gillmore's subordinate, Gordon Granger, ordered notorious secessionist Mary Gibson (wife of lawyer turned Confederate officer Hart Gibson) to supply the rebel hospital with wood fuel "until she received orders to quit." Peter commented approvingly, saying that Granger "seems to know how to deal with the secesh."[59]

And deal with them the Federals did. When Margaret Preston, wife of Confederate major general William Preston, asked Gillmore to send a guard to protect her property, Gillmore said that he would only do so to prevent "pilfering," but that if his men wanted to forage for supplies he would send them to her, giving her "a receipt for what they took, to be payable after the war, or at such time as she should declare herself loyal to the Union, or should bring her husband back and make him a union man." Preston declared this to be a "perfect farce" and then tried to convince General Granger to comply with her request. Granger was not only unmoved but gave the secessionist "a complete setting down." Granger and Gillmore's harshness toward Confederate women was partly due to continued threats from rebel guerrillas, particularly John Hunt Morgan's command.[60] Federals' refusal to intrude on the domestic spaces of white Unionist civilians, and their harsh treatment toward the families of notorious Confederate officers, cheered young Unionist women like Peter, as occupation brought them material benefits.

Peter came to find that while commanders had clear policies of protecting Unionists and punishing secessionists, some enlisted men could easily upset the balance. For months, Lexington's loyal population existed peacefully with the Ohioans and Indianans in the ranks because the men were proslavery. Then came an influx of Michigan soldiers, a group Peter described as "not near as nice" because "there are so many mean fellows among them and more Abolitionists than in all the Ohio & Indiana regiments put together. In fact I have never seen an Ohio Abolitionist yet."[61] Enlisted men's support of or antipathy toward slavery depended on the state from which they hailed, and those who were antislavery could cause headaches for Unionist enslavers.

The Michigan soldiers wasted little time in applying confiscation to Lexington, upsetting Gillmore and Granger's status quo. Peter recorded that an enslaved man "stayed at the camp a day or two (though it is against orders I think to let negroes in)." When the man's enslaver came to collect him, the Michigan officer refused to give him up, telling her, "Well now I think that n[egro] has served you long enough." The unnamed female enslaver applied to the commanding general, who handed him over. This did nothing to deter the antislavery soldiers. Several days later, the Michigan men were at it again, and this time their commanders made an example out of them. Peter recorded that "several officers were arrested today for running off negroes from their owners." Whether they actually "ran them off," though, remains in question, for Peter also noted, "There are a good many negroes in jail here who have followed the soldiers here from T[ennessee] and A[labama]." The discrepancy between the practices of enlisted men and the policies of commanders became such a problem that H. G. Wright, commander of the Department of the Ohio, wrote to General-in-Chief Henry Halleck about the issue. Wright complained to Halleck that Granger was "much harassed by complaints of Union men in Kentucky of the abduction of their slaves by officers and men of his army; that many of the camps are crowded with worthless negroes, to the great demoralization of the troops, and he asks that some definite policy be laid down for his guidance." Halleck responded, rather unhelpfully, the next day, instructing Wright to refer to "the law of Congress of last session, the President's proclamation, and the printed orders of the War Department."[62] Lack of clarity in Federal policy left Wright and Granger in a bind: They could welcome enslaved people into their lines and anger white Unionists, or exclude them completely and alienate a loyal population (and entire groups of enlisted men). White Unionists such as Peter deluded themselves into thinking that enslaved people left slavery because Federal soldiers encouraged them. In reality, the presence of sympathetic Michigan soldiers ready to apply confiscation to the border state was all the encouragement that enslaved people needed.

In the Western theater, Federals embraced foraging but distinguished between rebels and Unionists. Although some women secured guards from sympathetic officers, enlisted men embraced taking what they wanted from civilians with clear rebel sympathies. Confiscation came much later to the West, as some proslavery commanders and enlisted men refused to put it into practice. When Federals did employ confiscation, they ignored its voluntary nature and forced enslaved people to labor for them or excluded from their lines enslaved people who willingly sought out Federals. Soldiers self-identified as proslavery Western men and upheld the institution in Confederate and border states. But the arrival of antislavery regiments spelled trouble, particularly in Kentucky, when enlisted men defied commanders' orders to deprive rebel and Unionist enslavers of enslaved labor. Disagreement in the Western theater over whether and how to implement confiscation foreshadowed the coming struggle over emancipation.

Emancipation and Foraging in 1863

The Emancipation Proclamation might not have freed very many enslaved people at the moment it was announced, but it brought immense changes to the slaveholding South. Wherever a Federal presence existed, people held in bondage pushed even more forcefully for freedom, first affecting slave owners in Confederate states and eventually in border regions as well. But the new policy did not mean that the Federal army welcomed African Americans into the lines, as it still preferred men to women and children. Combined with the continued practice of foraging, Southern civilians faced a desperate struggle over food, labor, resources, and freedom.

Virginia's enslaving women noticed emancipation's effects almost immediately. By the end of January, Unionist Julia Chase of Winchester recorded in her diary, "The blacks are leaving in great numbers, and probably in the course of a few weeks there will be but very few left." The presence of Federals and the length of time Winchester had been occupied made leaving bondage much easier for these people. The Emancipation Proclamation promised freedom but only if enslaved people left the homes of their enslavers. Rather than a struggle over freedom, Chase viewed these changes primarily as a loss of domestic labor. She complained that with so many people gone, "we shall be [at] a great loss to get anything done."[63] Without enslaved people, work within the household would go much more slowly and be much more difficult. Chase's comments reveal that the maintenance and continuation of the plantation household utterly depended on the labor of enslaved people.

Western Virginia's enslaved women viewed the Emancipation Proclamation through the lens of antislavery ideology. The United States's commitment to ending slavery was finally bringing the country closer to its founding ideals of freedom and equality. An African American woman in Harpers Ferry, whose name was unrecorded by Wilder Dwight, gave Dwight a civics lesson in the wake of emancipation: "De Union is broderly love. Dat's what de Union is. Dese yere secesshnists ain't got no sich principle. In de Union day do good to one another, but dese yere secesshnists dey don't do no good to you. Dey wont' help yer out when yer's in trouble. Lord bress yer! Dy can't help derselves out, let alone other folks. I's for de Union and love, dat's what I's for." This woman expressed her political principles as favoring the "Union and love," the bedrock of antislavery ideology and one that recognized the equality of all. Rebels, committed to the expansion of slavery, only cared about preserving their wealth and influence. They did not care about advancing the interests of the community. In contrast, both the Declaration of Independence and the Constitution embraced the ideals of brotherly love and natural rights. The nation had not yet lived up to those ideals, but emancipation brought it closer. This was the lesson the woman sought to impart to Dwight, an abolitionist who, like many white Americans, could not see beyond ending slavery to ending racism. Black civilians articulated a grand vision of the

FIG 3.3. David B. Woodbury, "A Negro Family coming into the Union Lines"—In this photograph, Woodbury captures an image of African Americans entering Federal lines around the time of the Emancipation Proclamation. Black men, women, and children sit around and inside a wagon driven by a mule. (Library of Congress)

conflict and the nation, one in which the country would finally live up to its highest ideals.[64]

As emancipation slowly spread throughout Virginia, non-slaveholding rebels experienced continued foraging. In Stafford County, twenty-year-old Virginia Hammett, daughter of a small farmer, began keeping a journal in 1863 to keep track of the "painful horrors" of war. By this time, Hammett had seen her "home and that of all my neighbors made desolate, . . . robbed *almost* to starvation." But Hooker's Army of the Potomac kept coming. In early February, a brigade camped on the farm, and Hammett recorded that they had

FIG 3.4. Alfred Waud, "Contrabands coming into camp in consequence of the proclamation"—War correspondent Waud used Woodbury's photograph of African Americans entering Federal lines to create this sketch on January 1, 1863. The difference between the two images is striking—Waud has exchanged ill-fitting clothing for nicer outfits, and the figures are smiling. (Library of Congress)

"completed the destruction, have left the house and farm both a wreck." War took its toll but did not dampen her support for the Confederate cause. Even in the face of occupation and requisitions, she had "several quarrels" with a "Mass. Yankee of the first water." "I hope I may be forgiven for hating him with all my heart," she reflected. "May I never see his ugly face again."[65]

No matter what the U.S. Army did, Hammett found fault with it. When Major General Hooker issued orders allowing county residents to purchase food from the commissary, Hammett was incensed that it came with stipulations. "Destitute families" had to "take the oath of allegiance to the United States." Hammett characterized loyalty oaths as "another instance of Lincoln's despotism." She despised hungry soldiers showing up at her doorstep asking for something to eat. Hammett questioned, "How can they expect us to be able or willing to give or sell them anything, when they have wrested from the citizens everything they could lay their hands upon."[66] Hammett was disinclined to do anything that the Federal army asked of her, whether that was taking the oath to purchase food or feeding hungry soldiers on picket duty. Her interactions with Union soldiers only made her more contemptuous of the United States.

Policies of emancipation and Black military service did nothing to endear Federals to her. Hammett disparaged Lincoln's "call upon the Militia," which she characterized as a desperate attempt to round up "every sort of person" to rally to his cause of "freeing the negroes." She insinuated that emancipation was so unpopular that the United States had to expand its recruiting to "Indians [and] negroes." While Hammett disparaged these policies in the abstract, she was more circumspect about the practical effects. When planting season came around, Hammett observed that she and her neighbors did not have the "essentials" needed for the task, from fences to horses to "servants." And she questioned the practicality of agricultural production during a time of war. "We should not like the idea of planting for the Yankees to reap," she observed. The symmetry between these concerns is telling. Hammett disparaged a war to free people held in bondage because it deprived her and her neighbors of the unpaid, bound labor they relied on to make their living.[67] These scenes repeated themselves all over Virginia. In Front Royal, the Buck family's enslaved people left as a group under the cover of darkness, taking nothing but their clothes and the family's three horses. Buck was indignant "at their ingratitude in taking the horses when they knew they were our main dependence of support." With no enslaved people and no horses, field work would be difficult to accomplish. Like Hammett, Buck's primary issue with emancipation was that enslaved people could now deprive Southern whites of their labor.[68]

Female owners of large plantations witnessed the breakdown of agricultural production *and* household labor. In Gloucester County, Harriotte Hopkins Lee Taliaferro kept her Confederate officer husband abreast of the changes. Taliaferro was unhappy that "the servants are still leaving in great numbers." While Hammett and Buck had worried about planting and harvesting, Taliaferro belonged to one of Virginia's first families, so her primary concern was maintaining her ladylike, leisurely lifestyle. Taliaferro hoped that "those about the house remain" so that "we may have sufficient to perform the necessary household duties." Her reasons were straightforward: "I do not feel at all inclined to undertake scrubbing, washing[,] cooking and such like employment."[69] While non-slaveholders and smaller plantation owners worried about food production, Taliaferro acknowledged that the maintenance of Southern civilization, and all its niceties, depended on the labor of enslaved people.

Even as they recognized the coercion at the heart of the plantation household, planter women clung to paternalist ideology, which infused their complaints about emancipation. Taliaferro took it personally when enslaved people who worked in the house left for freedom. "I do not think anything of field hands going. . . . They do not know any better and imagine they are going to improve their condition," she complained. "But those who have been raised in *the* house, treated & more like children than servants, in whom every confidence has been placed and to whom every kindness has been shown. Such behavior makes my blood boil and I think no fate is too bad for them."[70] The departure of enslaved people, especially those whom enslavers felt had been coddled and indulged, belied enslavers' insistence that the plantation was held together by familial bonds. So too did their response. Taliaferro wished the worst for the people she formerly held in bondage, revealing that she believed them entitled to nothing more than lives of hard work and perpetual bondage.

With the summer campaigns came further struggles over resources and labor. In Warrenton Junction, George E. Harvey, who worked in the Quartermaster's Department, supervised a squad of African Americans laboring for the War Department. Their job, according to Harvey, was to take "Grain[,] Hay & every thing else a person can think of" from civilians.[71] Harvey and the Black laborers may have encountered resistance while foraging. But Black Unionists understood that complying with foraging and caring for the army was a way to demonstrate their loyalty. After the Battle of Chancellorsville, Hooker's Army of the Potomac used Catherine Alford's home in Spotsylvania County as a hospital. In her postwar claim, Alford stressed her family's charity toward the wounded, juxtaposing her loyalty with the disloyalty of her neighbors. She declared that she and her husband "were the only family around . . . that would do anything for [the soldiers]."[72] Here Alford strategically downplayed how much of her property Federals had requisitioned. Instead, she emphasized her generosity and kindness as proof of her loyalty. Her compliance with Federal requests highlighted her status as a loyal property owner who had willingly provided for the army.

While Virginia's women struggled over foraging and emancipation, civilians in Tennessee and Mississippi faced armies experimenting with much harsher policies, from removing rebel civilians to living off the land. After subduing Confederates in Middle Tennessee, Maj. Gen. Joseph Reynolds proposed confiscating wealthy rebels' possessions and distributing it to destitute loyal neighbors. In order to make Unionists feel truly secure, he hoped to "send the rebels out of the country, and make safe room for the return of loyal men. . . . [so that they would] feel that the country is once [again] in their possession."[73] Western soldiers increasingly looked to harsh measures to deal with resistance from civilians, even if they were women.

While Western men had no patience for rebel women aiding Confederates, they respected women for standing up to soldiers who took their possessions. Around Readyville, Tennessee, U.S. soldiers out foraging tried to take a horse from a young woman. Unwilling to let the horse go, the woman beat the soldier "unmercifully over the head" with a hickory goad. Federals characterized the actions as "brave" and gave her a round of applause. In Holly Springs, Mississippi, Cordelia Lewis Scales recorded how foraging now turned into property destruction. "Thirty & fourty . . . Yankees would rush in . . . take every thing to eat they could lay their hands on, & break, destroy, & steal every thing they wanted to." Scales remained defiant. When soldiers insisted on searching the family home for arms, she refused to allow them to look inside her trunk. The soldiers merely laughed, saying, "She's a trump." While Federal commanders might prescribe harsh treatment for recalcitrant civilians, enlisted men found young white women's resistance to be admirable or humorous. Shielded by their age, race, and gender, these young women could successfully protect some of their possessions even from hardened Western soldiers.[74]

While enlisted men in Mississippi and Tennessee often took what they wanted, they preferred it when women gratefully complied with Federal requests. In Columbia, Tennessee, Chaplain George Bradley lauded the behavior of a woman who made soldiers "welcome to everything she had." Bradley believed this showed her to be "truly loyal" and "noble hearted."[75] Other soldiers continued to frame these interactions in terms of a gendered exchange. Illinoisan Oliver Boucher, stationed near Vicksburg, "stoped in to a good looking house" and "toled the lady that I was sent to guard her house & person against any assaults whatever." He then hinted that he had not eaten dinner. To his delight, she replied that "if [protection] was my business I could get the best she had."[76] Foraging allowed Federals to direct women's household labor and soldiers then equated compulsory giving with patriotism and womanly virtue.

The advance of Grant's Army of the Tennessee and the fall of Vicksburg led to a new reality in Mississippi. Federal occupation brought the unwelcome policies of foraging and emancipation to the doors of Mississippi's plantation elite. In Natchez, Catherine Olivia Foster watched as over one hundred U.S. cavalry passed by her door, and she was relieved that they "did not come in." Foster's only hope was that "they will remember that they have mothers, wives, & sisters at home and treat us as they would wish them to be by our men." Two days later, they did visit, advancing by the garden and "pulling & eating apples along the way." Intercepted by one of Foster's enslaved women, the men only took watermelons. But they kept returning, demanding milk and meals.[77] Federal officers promised Foster protection but did not station a guard, and enlisted men would only be put off so long by an enslaved woman's harangue.

Natchez residents soon realized that they had common ground with Federal soldiers from the West: Both had low opinions of African Americans. Although Grant received orders from General-in-Chief Halleck to welcome Mississippi enslaved people into the lines and employ them as "laborers, teamsters, cooks, &c.," enlisted men resisted such orders. Soon after the army's arrival, Foster recounted that "the negroes are flocking to the enemy in town and the Yanks are cussing them and saying they wished they had never seen a negro. They are an ungrateful set and we are all tired of them." Still, Foster held out hope that her bonded people would "all prove faithful to the end." That was not the case. About a week later, Foster considered all of Natchez's Black residents to be "a lot of ingrates" and consoled herself with the fact that "God punishes us for ingratitude as much as for any other sin." Confronted with such "faithlessness," Foster wanted them to all leave for Union lines. "The sooner we are rid of them the quicker we will whip our enemy," demonstrating that Foster recognized the ways in which her enslaved people actively hindered the rebel cause. Unable to rely on the people she held in bondage to labor for her, Foster considered them a nuisance. But so did the men in Grant's army. The result was a standoff, with African Americans caught in between: Federals tried to convince planters to take Black women and children back to plantations, while planters tried to rid themselves of an "ungrateful" labor force.[78]

Even as Federal armies in the West continued to treat African American women and children as a nuisance, they coerced Black male civilians into enlisting in the Federal army. As some had done with confiscation, Federals ignored the voluntary portion of the 1862 Militia Act and rounded up Black men to put into the ranks. Enslaved woman Candis Goodwin declared that Union soldiers went around to the homes of enslaved people under cover of darkness and ordered Black men that it was their "civil right" to enlist. Jane Wallis protested to Union authorities that Federals took her invalid husband against his will, leaving her and her three children to fend for themselves. Avalena McConico of Mississippi noted that her uncle Franke Genes was "gathered . . . up out of the woods and put . . . in the battle lines" by U.S. soldiers. Henderson Kurkendall, a formerly enslaved man who served in the Union army, articulated Black men's complex attitudes toward military service. Kurkendall told his daughter, Maggie Snow, that "the Yankees made all the slaves fight they could run across. Some kept hid in the woods." Kurkendall framed Black men's reluctance as the fact that the men "wanted freedom but they didn't want to go to war."[79] As these men and women made clear, choosing to serve in the U.S. Army was one thing. Being forced to serve separated them from their families and placed loved ones in a vulnerable position in the midst of a hostile white population. While commanders focused on how they could best make African American men useful to the Federal army, Black women insisted that only they and their families could make that decision. When Federals decided for them, it undermined the very nature of the freedom they sought.

Similar scenes occurred in Kentucky, where commander of the District of West Kentucky Horatio G. Wright, enlisted men, and enslavers engaged in an all-out war over the institution. Some Federal soldiers hoped that enslaved people would rise up in revolt against their enslavers. This was the experience of Mattie Mooreman of Hartford, who lived on her enslaver's plantation. One day Union soldiers arrived, went straight to the slave quarters, and commanded the bondspeople to "rise up. Told 'em to come on in the big house and take what they wanted. Told 'em to . . . take Master's silver spoons and Miss' silk dress. 'If they don't like it, we'll shot their brains out,' they said."[80] Mooreman's interaction with Federals demonstrates that enslaved women sought lasting freedom brought about through peaceful means, while some white enlisted men wanted to incite violent insurrection as a way of exacting retribution on the enemy. Enslaved women well knew that neither army commanders nor local enslavers would abide revolt, and so they chose the path of limited resistance to preserve their families and their communities.

What neither Federals nor enslavers wanted was for African Americans to be able to make their own choices and move about freely. In Lexington, Frances Peter was dismayed when "some of the negroes" assembled in "the negro quarters at Headquarters" and "had a ball" in which they "danced on the porch, stamped, shouted, got drunk and kicked up a great row until a very late hour," which she characterized as "insolent" and a "great piece of impertinence." Peter laid the blame for the event on there being "a great many bad negroes in this neighborhood" and lamented that "our boy is one of them." Peter also faulted Federals for being lax in their duties, for they had left headquarters unattended and had not set up a watch.[81] Once again, Peter faulted the U.S. Army's interference with bonded people acting as autonomous human beings. Peter believed that a central duty of the Federal Army was to closely monitor the enslaved population, preventing them from engaging in behaviors disallowed in slave codes, including holding public gatherings, drinking alcohol, and staying out past curfew. In Kentucky, African American men and women began asserting their right to behave how they chose, to move about freely and associate with whom they wished, raising the specter of social equality to white enslavers like Peter.

Peter approved when, under command of Maj. Gen. Ambrose Burnside, the Army of the Ohio engaged in harsher policies toward African Americans that compelled them to work. That summer, the army required labor, and thus it required African Americans. But commanders could not agree on whether to spare Unionists' bonded people. While Gen. Speed Fry ordered "the negroes of rebels [and] rebel sympathizers" to "work on the railroads," his counterpart General Boyle instructed soldiers to "take all negroes between 16 and 45 without making any difference between Union and rebel." In Peter's mind, it was still Federals' duty to protect white Unionists' bonded people and place the brunt of forced labor on rebels' enslaved people. Like many Unionist enslavers, Peter approved when the army forced African American men to work because she believed that bonded people did not have the right to choose how to spend their time. Those freedoms were reserved only for elite white Southerners like Peter and her family, and so she approved of policies that hurt rebel enslavers and kept Black men and their families in what she believed was their station in life.[82]

By December, Peter no longer concerned herself with whether Burnside's army coerced labor from the enslaved people of Unionists or rebels. Some of her fears may have been allayed because Major General Grant had removed Boyle to the field over concerns that he was overly political. Now Peter rejoiced anytime Federals appropriated the labor of Black men without their consent. In one instance, she exulted when "the darkies met with a great mishap." "Just as their churches were being dismissed," she recorded, "a number of soldiers . . . captur[ed] all the men they could lay hands on . . . whom they sent off to Camp Nelson to work on the wagon road." In Peter's eyes, African American men had risen far above their station when they moved about freely, attended their own churches, and dressed finely in "go to meetin' clothes."[83] White Unionist enslavers such as Peter believed that African American men forced to labor for the Federal army learned an important lesson about freedom: Freedom would not entail the freedom to remain in their communities, with their families, and attending their own churches. Freedom would simply mean receiving wages for forced, menial labor.

THE HARSHER WAR policies of confiscation, foraging, and emancipation ignited conflicts with Southern civilians. Intended to make Southerners feel war's hardships, the Federal army applied them unequally and in confusing ways. In the Eastern theater, the army foraged from rebels and white Unionists, making little distinction based on political sympathies. When it came to confiscation, the army applied these policies to Confederates, encouraging Unionism among enslaved people and welcoming them to Federal lines. In the Western theater, soldiers distinguished between Confederates and Unionists while foraging, seeking to spare loyal people from requisitions. Confiscation came late to these areas, as Federal "western men" often held proslavery views. When commanders like Fry, Boyle, Wright, and Burnside did resort to confiscation, they forced African Americans to labor or refused to admit women and children into the lines. Federal commanders, based on orders from General-in-Chief Halleck, made decisions for enslaved people rather than letting enslaved people make their own decisions. By 1863, emancipation spread slowly as foraging increased. In the East, Federals created space for enslaved people to make their way to Union lines. In the West, enslaved people faced forcible conscription and hostile army policies. And while emancipation did not apply to Kentucky, wartime realities encouraged enlisted men and eventually commanding officers to resort to confiscation and forced labor. The fluctuating enforcement of foraging, confiscation, and emancipation increased hostilities on the ground, undercut Unionism, and limited the scope of emancipation.

In the wake of emancipation, proslavery forces would devise unofficial wartime policies of their own in 1864, policies intended to undermine emancipation and equality. Using sexual assault and claims of sexual assault as their weapons, some white Federals and white Southern women characterized African Americans as sexually deviant and dangerous, people unfit for freedom.

CHAPTER FOUR

Wartime Sexual Assault and the Progress of Emancipation

NEAR THE END OF NOVEMBER 1862, Jane Whittimore busied herself with the washing in the kitchen of her enslaver's Nashville home. She was interrupted by a white Federal soldier who tried to force her to have sex with him. A day or two later, she made her way south of the city to Camp Mill Creek where she identified Pvt. Charles Pratt of the Twenty-Fourth Wisconsin, who was court-martialed on charges of attempted rape and robbery. Whittimore took the stand to testify against him, alleging that he "came in the house where I was washing, tried to make me give up to him, he tried to turn my clothes up."[1] Whittimore's testimony is only one page in a much larger trial, but it is powerful in its singularity: She was one of the first enslaved women to testify against a white Federal soldier during a court-martial. Whittimore went to significant lengths to complain about Pratt's behavior toward her. Perhaps she felt she had a particularly strong case because Tennessee law did not specify that only white women and girls could be raped. She traveled to Federal lines to report the crime and identify Pratt, and then she took the stand as a witness, a practice that broke with the Tennessee law barring Black people from testifying against white defendants.[2] Whittimore's actions insisted that she had been treated improperly and that the Federal army was responsible for ameliorating the wrong.

This chapter considers Black women's use of the court-martial system against white defendants and white women's use of the court-martial system against Black defendants as these victims and defendants attempted to secure for themselves the full benefits of emancipation. While white-on-white sexual assault did happen, cases of white-on-Black and Black-on-white assault reveal the use of the court-martial system in powerful ways. Before the war, Black women could not demand justice with a hope of receiving it. During the war, the door cracked open, and they were determined to make sure it opened wide. Black women marched into offices, courtrooms, tents, and homes to demand justice for themselves and the generations of Black women to come. Just six months into the conflict, enslaved and free women and girls filed complaints of rape or attempted rape against white soldiers.[3] These women insisted that even if Southern law did not recognize the rape of an enslaved woman as a crime, the Federal military must make redress. Because of the pressure placed on it by Black women, commanders and political figures realized the glaring omissions in the articles of war, which made no provision for charging soldiers with crimes committed against civilians.[4] These omissions meant that some commanders declined to charge individual soldiers with rape while others tried soldiers under the Ninety-Ninth Article of War or by holding a military commission.[5] While progress was slow and halting, and white Federals continually objected to Black testimony and tried to discredit the Black women who testified against them, African American women continued to demand that the army punish the soldiers who harmed them.[6] Their complaints eventually resulted in the military trying and convicting white soldiers for the rape or attempted rape of Black women and girls. These trials are indicative of one of the many ways that enslaved and free women sought to secure for themselves the benefits of emancipation.

With emancipation came Black military service, and one of the many obstacles that Black Federals faced was accusations of sexual assault by white

TABLE 4.1 Soldiers court-martialed for rape and attempted rape (April 1861–June 1, 1865)

Year	Rape	Guilty	Attempted rape	Guilty
1861	0	0	1	1
1862	15	9	13	6
1863	30	24	23	12
1864	44	30	23	7
To June 1, 1865	28	18	27	12

SOURCES: Data from Records of the Office of the Judge Advocate General (U.S. Army), National Archives; Thomas P. Lowry, Courts-Martial Spreadsheet.

NOTE: I excluded defendants who were civilians or noncombatant military laborers as well as trials after June 1865.

Southern women. Although these cases are few and far between, they reveal a sharp break with antebellum prosecutions of free and enslaved Black men for the rape or attempted rape of white women and girls.[7] Prior to the Civil War, Black men accused of raping white Southern women found a community inclined to trust the legal process yet divided over white women's character. Poor white women who accused a Black man of rape faced intensive investigations into their family ties and sexual history. Much less scholarly attention focuses on Black soldiers court-martialed for the rape of white Southern women.[8] But these trials indicate a break with the past: Poor white women, emboldened by opposition to emancipation, lodged flimsy charges against Black Federals. These women interpreted the very presence of Black soldiers in their home as a violation, and white officers proved sympathetic to their claims. Unlike powerful white Southerners, Union officers had no investment in and few ties to Black soldiers. Particularly to Northeastern and Midwestern men, the widespread association of Black men with the rape of white women made poor white women's claims seem credible.[9] Black Federals who stood in front of courts-martial for the sexual assault of white Southern women faced a hostile white population incensed by their military service and an indifferent court inclined to see African American men as rapists.

Focusing on the experiences of Black women and men in sexual assault courts-martial during the Civil War reveals important insights. Black women and girls went to extraordinary lengths to report their rapists, insisting that the Federal army recognize their loyalty by punishing soldiers who assaulted them. On the other hand, white Southern women and their families sought to weaponize the court-martial process against individual Black Federals by wildly exaggerating or even wholly fabricating charges of rape in order to link wartime emancipation with attacks on the purity of white Southern womanhood. Narrowing the focus to Black victims and Black defendants advances decades of scholarship and reveals troubling continuity and marked change. Building on the strength of previous work, this chapter argues that reading court-martial records in light of emancipation reveals that Black women seized the opportunity presented by the presence of the U.S. Army, bringing their claims straight to Federal command just months into the war and insisting the army punish soldiers. Their efforts pushed the military toward stricter control of white soldiers and indicate Black women's expectations that their loyalty entitled them to respect of their persons. On the other hand, white Southern women who charged Black Federals with sexual assault made no mention of loyalty or disloyalty. Their testimony indicates that they regarded the mere presence of Black soldiers in their homes as sexual assault. The army's response to women's claims is instructive. While Federals put obstacles in the way of Black women's accusations, white commanders sometimes proved too credible toward white Southern women. Black women accused white Federals but faced hostile courts even as white women from poor and middling backgrounds gained a credibility they had never before received. Wartime trials for sexual assault reveal Black women insisting on new rights as they accused white men of sexual assault, sometimes obtaining a conviction. On the other hand, emancipation and military service cost Black men some of the protections of slavery, as widespread stereotypes of them as violent rapists influenced courts-martial when poor white women accused them of rape.

Data and Definitions

Context is needed in order to fully understand individual court-martial cases: the process of military justice, wartime perceptions about rapists and victims of rape, and data illustrating where perception differed from reality. This chapter will first examine the court-martial process, then consider perceptions, and finally consider the data about who assaulted (or attempted to assault) whom, and what we can learn from those numbers.

Perhaps the most important aspect of the Civil War court-martial was that there was no uniform code of military justice. While the Articles of War and army regulations spelled out important aspects of general courts-martial, they left much to the discretion of the chief officer of the court. Even so, cases shared some similarities. A court-martial for sexual assault began when an offense was either discovered by or brought to the attention of the U.S. Army. From there, an officer wrote out specific charges and specifications against the accused and placed the defendant under confinement (in the case of enlisted men) or confined to quarters (in the case of officers). Those charges and specifications, along with a list of those arrested, went to the officer commanding an army or colonel commanding a department, who had the power to call a general court-martial. The court-martial itself consisted of commissioned officers, anywhere from five to thirteen, with the highest-ranking officer serving as president of the court. The president encompassed the roles of prosecutor for the United States and counsel for the defendant. In this capacity he administered oaths to the members of the court, the defendant, and witnesses; objected to leading questions; and protected the defendant against self-incrimination.[10]

The defendant had rights, although limited, throughout the process. He was to be informed of the charges and specifications levied against him before the beginning of the trial, and custom dictated that he also be shown a list of witnesses. He could ask a fellow soldier or officer to serve as his counsel, although this counsel was restricted to giving advice and offering legal objections in writing. The defendant could also object to a member of the court if he felt they might be prejudiced against him. Once the charges and specifications were read, the defendant entered a plea of guilty or not guilty, and most defendants in a sexual assault court-martial pleaded not guilty. From there the court considered witnesses. The military could only compel testimony from members of the armed services, and civilian witnesses often had to travel in order to be present. Army regulations did allow the military to compensate witnesses up to three dollars per day for their trouble. Rules of evidence were similar to those in civil courts. Witnesses had to have firsthand knowledge of either the accused or the circumstances, and hearsay was inadmissible. Defendants had the right to cross-examine the prosecution's witnesses as well as summon witnesses on their behalf. After testimony concluded, the defendant could make a statement in his defense.[11]

The court then cleared for judges to deliberate. Members voted on each charge and specification, with a two-thirds vote needed to convict. Then the court decided on sentencing. In cases of enlisted men convicted of sexual assault, guidance from the War Department enjoined courts-martial that sentencing should be no more severe than the penalties for the same offense in civil courts. For officers convicted of a military offense—generally Article of War 99—punishments could include death, cashiering, dismissal, suspension from rank and pay, confinement, and reprimand. A two-thirds vote was needed to sentence a defendant to death. After sentencing, the officer ordering the court-martial reviewed the proceedings and could either confirm or disapprove them. If the officer disapproved, he could reconvene the court, pardon the defendant, or mitigate all or part of any punishment except the death penalty. From there, the proceedings went to the War Department, and in some instances underwent review by the judge advocate or the president.[12]

If neither the judge advocate nor the president suspended the sentence or pardoned the defendant, the defendant's sentence was carried out by the appropriate military authority. Throughout the process, military officers exercised extraordinary authority, defendants had limited rights, and civilian witnesses were at a severe disadvantage. All of these factors affected the ability of Black women to obtain justice and Black U.S. soldiers to receive a fair trial.

The army's system of military justice did not allay the fears of Southern civilians. Southern women in particular worried about the presence of the Federal army, as it brought large numbers of unknown men roaming the countryside. Invading armies caused fear among civilian women, leading to rumors spreading like wildfire. Some rumors functioned like the grapevine telegraph, warning enslaved women about the harm that white Federal soldiers might inflict. Other rumors, spread by elite Confederates, warned that Black Federals would visit unspeakable horrors on virtuous Southern ladies.[13] Rumors tell us about the fears that Southern women harbored about the presence of the U.S. military. Sometimes their fears mirrored reality. At other times, rumors spread unfounded accusations meant to reinforce the Confederacy's commitment to slavery. The common perception throughout the Confederacy was that Black soldiers posed a significant danger to elite white rebel women, particularly the danger of sexual assault.

Data from wartime courts-martial tell quite a different story. As table 4.2 illustrates, white Federal soldiers were far more likely to rape Black women than white women, with forty-nine soldiers tried for raping white women and

TABLE 4.2 Soldiers charged with rape in court-martial trials

Race of soldier	Race of victim	Cases	Guilty verdicts	Conviction rate (%)
White	White	49	36	73
White	Black	70	57	81
Black	Black	1	1	100
Black	White	20	12	60

SOURCES: Records of the Office of the Judge Advocate General (U.S. Army), National Archives; Thomas P. Lowry, Courts-Martial Spreadsheet.

NOTE: Civilians and noncombatant military laborers are excluded. Some trials only identified that "a woman" accused a soldier of rape, and I interpreted this to mean a white woman.

seventy tried for raping Black women. From these numbers it is clear that white soldiers raped Black women at much higher rates than white women, particularly when we consider that African American women made up a much smaller portion of the Southern population.[14] Only twenty Black soldiers went to trial for raping a white woman, and fifteen of those trials occurred on or after June 1, 1865. The significance of the fact that the vast majority of trials of Black Federals charged with sexual assault of a white woman occurred after the cessation of hostilities cannot be overstated. In all fifteen cases, charges of rape against Black Federals originated in areas with a significant presence of occupying African American soldiers. In some instances, as that of Pvt. Peter Small of the Seventy-Fourth USCT, merely being near a white woman was enough to result in a trial. Small was not convicted because the only witness to the supposed assault was the white woman he was accused of assaulting, and she testified that nothing happened between them.[15] Five privates of the 104th USCT found themselves in front of a court-martial for plundering a home in McPhersonville, South Carolina, and raping three white women. The court convicted and executed two men and convicted and dishonorably discharged two others and sentenced them to hard labor for the remainder of their term of enlistment. Only one was acquitted. One other enlisted man received the death penalty for raping a white girl, and that was Pvt. Evan Williams of the Forty-Eighth USCT. Stationed in Thibodeaux, Louisiana, and accused of raping Georgiana Josephine Bryan, the eleven-year-old daughter of a wealthy sugar broker and planter, Williams insisted that the encounter was consensual. He was shot.[16] Data gleaned from courts-martial paint a very different picture from that of wartime rumor. During the conflict, white soldiers were accused of raping Black women more frequently than white women, while Black Federals were rarely accused of raping white women. It was only the end of the war—and the presence of occupying Black Federals—that brought about a rampant increase in white women accusing Black soldiers of rape.

Disparities also exist in courts-martial for attempted rape. As the table on the next page demonstrates, white soldiers stood trial for attempted rape of a white woman forty-nine times and Black women thirty-seven times. The slightly higher number of white victims of attempted rape indicates white Southerners' family and community ties. White women had male relatives or neighbors close at hand to intervene when Federal soldiers

TABLE 4.3 Soldiers charged with attempted rape in court-martial trials

Race of soldier	Race of victim	Cases	Guilty verdicts	Conviction rate (%)
White	White	49	29	59
White	Black	37	11	30
Black	Black	1	1	100
Black	White	11	5	45

SOURCES: Records of the Office of the Judge Advocate General (U.S. Army), National Archives; Thomas P. Lowry, Courts-Martial Spreadsheet.

NOTE: Civilians and noncombatant military laborers are excluded. Some trials only identified that "a woman" accused a soldier of attempted rape, and I interpreted this to mean a white woman.

threatened. The data also shows only ten Black soldiers standing before a court-martial accused of attempted rape of a white woman. This demonstrates that rebel fears of Black Federals preying on elite Confederate women had no basis in reality. Courts-martial indicate that white Southern women had much more to fear from white Federal soldiers. Rumors about African American soldiers reveal rebel anxieties about the destruction of slavery, the fear that without the "civilizing" influence of bondage, free Black men would revert to their supposedly aggressive and hypersexual tendencies.

Although this data is helpful, court-martial trials alone cannot give a complete picture of sexual assault during the Civil War. Rape, then as now, was an underreported crime. Primary sources indicate that even when women reported sexual assault, officers did not always investigate the crime or bring charges against the accused. And some soldiers, most of them African American, did not make it to trial but were executed on the spot.[17] For these reasons, this chapter uses court-martial records cautiously and supplements them with evidence from other sources, such as the WPA Slave Narratives and Black soldiers' letters. This more fulsome picture demonstrates the tension between military regulations designed to protect civilians from soldier depredations and women's accusations against men considered to be good soldiers. The trials themselves sometimes had little to do with justice and more to do with whose loyalty mattered and whose bodies and homes the army felt it needed to protect.

The Sexual Assault of Black Women Before and After Emancipation

Black women and girls' accusations of sexual assault resulted in the courts-martial of white soldiers just six months into the conflict. Near the close of 1861 in Newport News, Virginia, a private and a sergeant left the lines, went to the home of the aged Harriet Lane, and subjected her to such violent assaults that she died before the army could convene a court-martial. In Irvin McDowell's Department of the Rappahannock, sexual assault of civilians was so rampant by May 1862 that McDowell issued General Order No. 12 to his army, reminding his men that "the punishment for rape will be death" and instructing them that "any violence offered a female, white or colored, with the evident intent or purpose to commit a rape, will be considered as one, and punished accordingly." Stern orders, the threat of capital punishment, and the insistence that the attempted rape of a Black woman was a punishable crime did not deter Pvt. Lewis B. Trost from raping Polly Walker, a Black woman, at Sperryville that July.

As the army spread south, so did Federal soldiers' sexual assaults of Black women. As discussed in chapter 1, Federal soldiers' sack of Athens, Alabama, was accompanied by the rape and attempted rape of many enslaved women and girls, one of whom reported her assault to Col. John B. Turchin. The assaults became so widespread that Brig. Gen. Don Carlos Buell, himself no friend of African Americans, admonished a subordinate officer that "such conduct is disgracing the army and is destructive of the public interests."[18] The assaults continued throughout occupied areas. During the summer of 1862, a white officer raped washerwoman Mary Ellen de Riley on a boat in New Orleans. On the Sea Islands, sexual assault of Black women was rampant. The army had only occupied the region for a month when Pvt. James Meoliff tried to force a woman referred to only as Tina to have sex with him. That summer, a colonel ran after a Black woman, threw her on the ground, and attempted to rape her. Esther Hill Hawks, a Northern relief worker and doctor, was appalled by Federal soldiers' behavior, insisting that "no colored woman or girl was safe from the brutal lusts of the soldiers," alleging that the commanding officer of the Fifty-Fifth Pennsylvania, Col. Richard White, kept local women captive in his quarters as sex slaves.[19] The situation became so dire that Congress called Maj. Gen. Ormsby M. Mitchel to respond to an inquiry into reports of the widespread rape of Black women by white soldiers.[20] The prevalence of assault, combined with Black women and girls reporting the mistreatment, created pressure at the very highest levels of the military and the U.S. government.

As the data and cases discussed above indicate, commanders were entirely unprepared for the number of Black women and girls sexually assaulted by the men of their command. Not only were white soldiers more likely to rape African American women, but punishing offenders was difficult under the existing regulations. The Thirty-Third Article of War, which dealt with crimes committed against civilians, specified that officers and soldiers be turned over to a civil magistrate if they "used violence, or committed any offence against the persons or property of any citizen of the United States, such as is punishable by the known laws of the land." However, Southern laws recognized the rape of an enslaved woman not as a crime against her person but as a crime against her enslaver. And the Federal military, at least early in the war, considered enslaved women and girls not citizens but property. Articles of War and Southern law notwithstanding, Black victims reported the men who assaulted them and expected the army to make redress. These women knew they had been wronged, no matter what antebellum laws and military definitions had to say. And so they brought their complaints to anyone who would listen: commanders, provost marshals, and Northern relief workers. Even when results were inconsistent—McDowell insisted the behavior was a crime while Buell insisted officers better control their men—African American women and girls kept up the pressure, to the extent that the women on the Sea Islands forced a congressional inquiry into their complaints. One need look no further than Francis Lieber's distillation of the articles of war to see their imprint. The code explicitly prohibited soldiers from committing crimes against civilians and explicitly mentioned rape as one of these crimes. In addition, the Lieber Code included Black women as sexual assault victims and placed no limitations on African American testimony against white soldiers. Along with Section 30 of the Enrollment Act, which allowed the army to charge soldiers with murder, assault, robbery, and rape, the Lieber Code gave Black women and girls important rights in the court-martial process. Due to their advocacy, they now had a better chance of securing justice for themselves.[21]

Black women and girls brought even more accusations against white Federals in the last two years of the war. Courts-martial were concentrated in two locations, Tennessee and Virginia, both with large numbers of African

Americans and sizable occupying Federal forces. The similarities end there. Trials in Tennessee largely involved white soldiers who attacked Black women in refugee camps, often as ways of displaying their displeasure with new war aims focused on ending slavery. In this region, Black women had to fight to ensure that officers in courts-martial followed the Lieber Code, as white officers often refused to interview Black victims and objected to Black testimony. While Black women and girls reported the soldiers who assaulted them, the army fought over the rights of formerly enslaved women.

Instances of sexual assault display the contested nature of emancipation in Tennessee and the ways in which the Black community worked together to protect themselves. On Emancipation Day in Murfreesboro, Tennessee, Pvt. Henry Murphy of the Thirty-Fifth Indiana refused to discontinue his assault of an enslaved woman until removed from the woman's quarters by the commanding general. Although emancipation itself would not be official policy until later that summer, Murphy's violent rape of the unnamed enslaved woman sought to reinforce her subordination. A few months later, Pvt. William Swift of the Seventy-Second Indiana quit his post and raped a Black woman, whose neighbor traveled to Federal lines to complain about the assault. Near Memphis, Sgt. Thomas Graham snuck into a refugee camp, entered the tent of a young Black girl, and attempted to rape her. His attempt was foiled when another Black refugee alerted the guard that there was a "white man in the negro tent." The African American community banded together to watch over and report individual white soldiers who took out their displeasure with emancipation on the bodies of Black women and girls.[22] Reporting a crime was only the beginning, however, as Black women and girls would have to fight to be able to testify against their assaulters.

Even though Tennessee law allowed for the possibility of the rape of Black women and the Lieber Code allowed them to testify against white defendants, Black victims struggled to testify about the wrong done to them when officers of the court put obstacles in their way. East of Memphis in the summer of 1863, two privates entered the tent of Harriet Ragan and another Black woman who were "under the care and employ of the quarter master." This language seems to indicate that the women's presence within the lines was contested and that the soldiers who snuck into their tent aimed to drive them from the lines. The quartermaster's clerk heard the disturbance and recalled Ragan saying to one of the men, "I won't. I shan't." The clerk ordered the soldiers' sergeant, Joseph Lafferty of the Twelfth Illinois, to arrest the two men.

Lafferty refused to do so, saying that "he did not like to arrest them as they were clever fellows." Lafferty's defiance also indicates his opposition to the women's presence in camp, clearly stating that he sided with his soldiers over enslaved women that the quartermaster was trying to protect. Eventually the men were court-martialed, facing a court in which the captain of their regiment served as judge advocate and a lieutenant of their regiment served as a member. The court administered an oath to Ragan but as soon as she began her testimony, a member of the court challenged her competency, stating that she did not know the nature of an oath. This procedure was entirely irregular. Benét's treatise on courts-martial instructed courts that "any objection to [a witness's] competency ought to be stated before he takes the oath." It also made convicting the two soldiers impossible. The court sustained the objection to Ragan's testimony, so the only witness called before the court to testify about what happened in the tent was barred from testifying. Ragan's experience demonstrates that even with Section 30 and the Lieber Code, individual courts placed obstacles in the way of Black women receiving justice. Ragan faced a hostile environment before a court stacked with members of the same regiment as the men she had accused. Even though she now lived in Federal lines and was legally free, officers opposed to emancipation bent the rules of courts-martial in order to give favorable treatment to their own soldiers. Some within the U.S. Army continued to treat her as though she were enslaved and asserted that she could not be trusted to tell the truth. Nevertheless, Ragan spoke out about the wrong done to her, reported her attackers, and tried to testify against them, all important steps in securing expansive boundaries to emancipation.[23]

Attacks on Tennessee's self-emancipated women continued into 1864, but by this point women took the stand to testify against their attackers. That summer, Mary Hindspeth left her work in Nashville's refugee camp when she was accosted by seven white soldiers. Two of them raped her while five others looked on until soldiers from the 101st USCT came to her rescue. The white soldiers threw rocks at the USCT soldiers to give them enough cover to get away, resulting in only one of the rapists being apprehended. Hindspeth reported the attack and was the first witness to testify at the trial. With emancipation now in effect, she was legally a free woman and had standing as an army employee. Not only that, she had relationships with USCT soldiers who could come to her aid and testify at her trial. While the rapist was ultimately not convicted, Hindspeth's status as a free woman and a laundress for the army established her loyalty and her right to claim protection. The army had to consider what it owed laborers like Hindspeth and the Black Federal soldiers who apprehended her rapist and testified against him at trial. By 1864, sexual assault in Tennessee was no longer the word of an enslaved woman against a white Federal soldier. With emancipation well under way, trials became a web of loyalties and obligations. Some white soldiers defied military regulations and assaulted Black women in order to affirm their racial subordination. Black women insisted that their loyalty and their status as army employees entitled them to protection. And African American soldiers protested women's blatant mistreatment within Federal lines.[24]

Sexual assault trials looked very different in Virginia. In the Old Dominion, commanders recognized the abuses that resulted when refugee camps stood near soldier encampments and took steps to separate the spaces. This did not prevent white soldiers from sexually assaulting Black women and girls; it just meant that rape occurred in Black homes. This was particularly true in the case of free Black woman Fenton Frazer and her niece Irene Ann Satturwhite. Fenton, her mother, Susan, her husband, John, their daughter, and their niece resided in Stafford County. After months of being "very much interfered with by the soldiers," Fenton's husband secured a guard from Federal lines. Even so, eleven white soldiers visited the family home late one evening in April 1863, stating that they had come "to fuck these women and we are going to do it too."[25] Several soldiers removed John from the house and beat him violently, three dragged Fenton into a ditch and took turns raping her, while the others held thirteen-year-old Irene Ann down while one soldier assaulted her.[26] The soldiers intended to send a message: The Frazers might be free, but they could not protect themselves if white Federals decided to subject them to violence. At the trial, John, Fenton, Irene Ann, and Susan testified that the soldiers believed that the level of violence they meted out would discourage the family from reporting the incident. The Frazers made clear that as a free Black family loyal to the Union, the Federal army owed them better treatment. When one defendant tried to challenge Susan's testimony "because she is a colored person and slave" and "does not understand the nature of an oath," the judge advocate refused to sustain the objection.[27] The Frazers' refusal to be cowed by threats meant their pursuit of justice was not in vain. They knew their rights, knew their way around the legal system, and believed that the military was obligated to take their side when its soldiers subjected the women of the family to brutal assaults. As a result, the ringleader of the attack was stripped of his rank as a noncommissioned officer, dishonorably discharged, and sentenced to hard labor for five years. One of the privates involved was convicted of assaulting the family and fined ten dollars.

Virginian Black women and girls faced fewer obstacles in reporting attacks and testifying against their attackers, but they still faced assumptions about their supposed sexual promiscuity and loose moral character. White Federals' tendency to give fellow soldiers the benefit of the doubt was on display in two spring of 1864 attacks. Southeast of Norfolk, seven members of the Twentieth New York Cavalry dragged freedwoman Grace Barnes into the woods and took turns raping her. The next day, Barnes journeyed to camp to report the assault. When she could not locate an officer, Barnes had the camp surgeon conduct an examination. At trial, Federals did not request testimony from Barnes's housemates or the camp surgeon, turning the trial into a he-said she-said situation between Barnes and one of the defendants, who insisted that Barnes "went into the woods ahead of [the soldiers]" and "prostitut[ed] herself willingly."[28] Seventy miles northwest in City Point, young Jennie Green followed the Eleventh Pennsylvania Cavalry into Federal lines, where she and an older, married woman went to officers' quarters to cook them dinner. When she arrived, First Lt. Andrew J. Smith pulled her into another room, locked the door, and raped her. The older woman reported Green's assault to the superintendent of contrabands, who caught Smith in the act.[29] Given testimony from Green, the older woman, and the superintendent of contrabands, the court found Smith guilty but pleaded for leniency on the basis of his "previous good character." President Lincoln ordered lawyer William Johnston to review the case, and Johnston found that "the most that can be made of the proof is that a young woman was caught abruptly in an act of shame, and pretended to be ravished."[30] While Barnes and Green could give testimony and marshal white and Black witnesses to buttress their cases, their status as self-emancipated and their need to work for a living made them vulnerable. Separated from family and near or within Federal lines, Black women and girls confronted squads of white soldiers who believed age-old tropes that they were sexually promiscuous. These attitudes made them vulnerable to assault and then vulnerable once again in the court-martial process.

In spite of attitudes about their supposed promiscuity, young Black girls continued to go to great lengths to file complaints against Federal soldiers who mistreated them. While a patient at the smallpox hospital in Point Lookout,

Maryland, in September 1864, sixteen-year-old Mary Campbell requested that the assistant surgeon visit her sick tent. When he arrived, she told him that one of his men "had been committing violence on her" and then identified Pvt. John F. Hall of the Fifth New Hampshire. Campbell herself did not testify at the trial, which took place seven months after the attack, as by that point she had recovered and moved upstate. Even so, the evidence against Hall was damning: Another patient, a Confederate prisoner of war, testified that Hall had bothered Campbell in her tent late at night and that she had loudly complained. Campbell went to great lengths to report the rape, a fact established at the trial by Pvt. James Moore of the Thirty-Sixth USCT. Moore worked at the hospital and testified on her behalf, recalling that he had seen Hall standing in Campbell's tent the morning after the incident and that he "heard him tell her not to say anything to the Doctor, or any of the rest about it." Campbell paid Hall no mind.[31] Campbell benefited from the testimony of the USCT soldier Moore, who used his standing as a Federal soldier to protest Hall's coercion of and threats toward Campbell. Although we do not have Campbell's direct testimony in the trial, it is clear that this young Unionist girl expected better treatment while she was within Federal army lines. She insisted on her right to be free from unwanted advances, ignored the threats of a Federal soldier, reported his assault, and pushed the military to do something about white Federals who preyed on young Black girls.

White men's threats of retaliation did not work on Black women who could see freedom within their grasp. Near the small town of Pocahontas, Virginia, just across the border from West Virginia, lived Laura Ennis, an African American woman who frequently traveled to Federal lines to visit her daughter, who most likely worked for the army. One day in January 1865, Ennis and her friend James Carey were traveling in a cart toward the lines when two Federal soldiers stopped them, pushed her from the cart, and dragged her into the woods, where one of them raped her. The rapist, Pvt. Charles Clark of the Twentieth New York Cavalry, then threatened Ennis. "He told me if I reported him in the Camp that he would shoot me, hang me to a tree and would skin me," Ennis testified during the trial. Clark's threats did not dissuade Ennis. She reported Clark even though the army remained encamped in the region in which she lived and her daughter worked within Federal lines.[32]

New patterns in sexual assault accusations emerged during Sherman's March to the Sea and through the Carolinas. As the war drew to a close, white soldiers continued to subject Black women and their families to attacks on their homes and persons, indicating that their animus to the destruction of slavery continued to be taken out on the bodies of African American women. Even so, closely knit communities in these regions used the grapevine telegraph to protect enslaved Black women and girls from assault by white Federals.

Only a few courts-martial exist of white soldiers who raped or attempted to rape Black women during Sherman's campaigns. The WPA narratives indicate that although few soldiers faced court-martial, sexual assault may have been more widespread. Black women and girls passed information along the grapevine telegraph warning each other to take precautions. Anna Parkes was just a girl at the time of Sherman's March, but she remembered that in Athens, Georgia, there was "a heap of talk 'bout de scandalous way dem yankee sojers been treatin' Negro 'omans and gals." Bessie Myers's mother, Jennie Bell, enslaved in North Carolina, would "run and hide every time the Yankee men come. She said she felt safer in the dark." At times, entire plantations came together to protect young Black women. Rachel Sullivan of Edgefield, Georgia, remembered that when Union soldiers came to the plantation, the Black men put all of the women in one house with a guard in front. Sullivan stated that the men did not "want to put no temptation in [th]e way o[f] [th]em soldiers."[33] Direct evidence from formerly enslaved women and girls indicates that courts-martial cannot give a full picture of the dangers white Federals posed during Sherman's March. These women testified that they, their relatives, and their communities believed that Sherman's men posed a danger to Black women and girls.

Black mothers in particular worried over white soldiers' penchant for sexual abuse and took steps to protect their daughters. In South Carolina, Tena White's mother locked her in the house to guard against attacks by "brutish" Federal soldiers. Mamie Riley's mother, perhaps because her daughter did not listen to her instructions, went to great lengths to keep soldiers away. When Federals began to break into enslaved people's cabins, Riley's mother grabbed "a quilt off de bed an' cover herself all over wid it . . . and she yell out when she hear 'em comin': 'Dere's de fever in heah!"[34] The grapevine telegraph functioned as it was intended during Sherman's March, warning the vulnerable about the possibility of white Federals sexually assaulting Black women and girls.

Court-martial trials corroborate the evidence from the WPA narratives that some of Sherman's men behaved like brutes toward the Black women they encountered. In the Catawba River region of South Carolina in February 1865, a squad of white Federals came upon a cabin outside of Federal lines. They decided to cook dinner and spend the night there. At some point in the night, five of the soldiers subjected "a woman of African descent" to a brutal assault. The woman did not testify at the trial, which was not held until May in Washington, D.C. None of the soldiers who testified knew her name or how she came to be in the house—some said she lived there, but others were not sure. The soldiers who watched but did not participate characterized the incident as "rough. . . . Killgore took her down, and committed a rape on her, while four of them held her." The men then tortured her, saying they wanted to "see what for a 'thing' she had," and took a lighted torch, pulled up her clothes, and threw the torch between her legs, where it burned the inside of her thighs. "They left her lying on the floor crying," the witness testified.[35] Killgore and Kunkle's rape of the unnamed South Carolina woman demonstrates the ways in which some white soldiers used rape as an instrument of racial subordination. While raiding, as we will see in the next chapter, could be used as a tool of emancipation, these soldiers used the leeway that raiding provided to go outside of army lines, forage for dinner, take over a cabin, and brutally sexually assault an enslaved woman.

The next time one of Sherman's soldiers raped an African American woman, she testified against her rapist, using the protections afforded to her in the Lieber Code to insist that the army make amends for the harm done to her. On an April evening in Raleigh, North Carolina, Sgt. Enoch George of the Fifth Veterans Ohio went to Nisa Grimes's home. Grimes was in a sickly state but agreed that George could spend the night in the house with her and her family. Once inside, however, George ordered Grimes's husband and children out of the house, locked the door, and sexually assaulted her. Grimes's husband attempted to intervene but could not get the locked door open; he then ran toward the Federal camp and reported the assault to a commanding officer. By the time of the trial, the court referred to Grimes as "a colored female resident" of Raleigh, indicating her status as a free woman. Her testimony was unwavering: "He came to my house and forced me. . . . I told him to go away from me, and tried to get away, but he would not let me go. . . . I did not want to have anything to do with him."[36] Grimes's forceful testimony, and her husband's reporting of the assault, gave George no leg on which to stand during the trial. He attempted to frame the encounter as consensual, stating in his defense that "the woman Nisa Grimes agreed to let him sleep with her all night." Grimes and her husband successfully navigated the military justice system, insisting on their rights to their bodily autonomy and security of their home. As a result of Grimes's unwavering testimony, the court was unmoved by George's flimsy defense of his behavior, finding him guilty and sentencing him to life in prison.

As the above evidence demonstrates, although Southern Black women could accuse their rapists in Civil War courts-martial, they still faced obstacles. In Tennessee, white soldiers initially refused to take testimony from Black victims or allow them to testify during a trial. In Virginia, more cases made it to trial, but attitudes about Black women and girls' supposed sexual promiscuity could make their testimony seem unreliable unless substantiated by white officers and Black Federals. During Sherman's March, enslaved women and girls tried to prevent sexual assault by blocking soldiers from entering their cabins. Sexual assaults that made it to court-martial were so blatant and so brutal as to leave no doubt that they were not consensual, and the women who reported it (or the white Federals who witnessed it) testified that the treatment was egregious. Historian Kaisha Esty observes that "white and northern Union soldiers' sexual expectations of Black women and girls were remarkably reflective of the attitudes of their white southern and pro-Confederate counterparts." African American women seem to have expected these attitudes and this treatment, but they did not accept it. From the earliest months of the war, they complained to the Federal command about the brutal treatment to which white soldiers sometimes subjected them. These women insisted that the army do something about soldiers who attacked loyal women. The army often responded to their concerns, but it did not always ameliorate the wrong.[37]

Black Men, White Women, and Sexual Assault After Emancipation

The leniency experienced by white soldiers accused of rape or attempted rape did not extend to Black men.[38] Nationwide attitudes regarding Black men as the only believable rapists of white women worked to their detriment. While slavery had sometimes spared Black men from spurious charges leveled by poor white women, Black Federals encountered white courts-martial inclined to believe any Southern white woman over an African American soldier. The bitter irony was that slavery had sometimes provided better protections for free and enslaved Black men accused of rape by white Southern women. Even though Black soldiers could now testify in their trials, they faced harsher punishments without powerful white enslavers to plead for leniency.

With emancipation came Black military service, and with Black military service came white Southern women who viewed the very presence of Black soldiers as an assault. Just outside of Nashville in November 1863, a white woman named Indiana Rose accused Pvt. George Nelson of the Thirteenth USCT of raping her. At the trial, the court did not press Rose on why it took her two days to report the assault or why she did not cry out for help given that the assault happened in a public place. The Northerners who made up the court were not in the habit of siding with Black men against the word of a poor white woman, as was sometimes the case in the antebellum South. Instead, the court assumed rape had occurred because Rose was white and Nelson was Black. The trial's other glaring irregularity is that Nelson objected to Thirteenth USCT Maj. William Innes serving on the court, asserting that he was prejudiced against him. Innes was removed from the court but then presented hearsay evidence, testifying that another soldier, Pvt. Lewis Hardin, told him that Nelson had been "one of the party." The court did not press Innes on whether Hardin meant one of the party present in the area or one of the party who ostensibly raped Indiana Rose. Based on scanty evidence, the court convicted Nelson of rape and sentenced him to death by hanging. No one—not the court and not the officers who approved the sentence—raised the glaring issues of hearsay and the lack of corroborating evidence.[39] Long-standing Northern attitudes associating Black men with the rape of white women led the court to sentence Nelson. Nelson's execution demonstrates that in the wake of emancipation, Southern Black men had more to fear from white Southern women than they had before the war.[40]

White Tennesseans continued to lodge flimsy rape charges against the men of the Thirteenth USCT in spring of 1864. Around the middle of May, civilian James Houlihan complained to Maj. William Innes (the same officer who provided hearsay evidence in Private Nelson's trial) that the previous evening a group of Black soldiers had descended on his home, roused his family from their beds, scared him off with a gun, and attempted to rape his daughter. Innes ordered Second Lieutenant Holinger to investigate, and a piece of cloth was traced back to Pvt. Robert Clark, whom Innes ordered arrested. When Clark stuck by his story that he bought the dress from a local white boy, Holinger used torture to extract the names of Clark's companions, ordering Clark to be spread-eagled and given nothing to eat. After an hour and a half of this treatment, Clark divulged the names, and Innes arrested and placed Clark and fellow privates Robert Clark, James Sibley, George Fowler, and Samuel Keith in irons.[41] The trial itself was a farce. Margaret Houlihan, the victim of attempted rape, did not testify, and neither the girl's mother nor brother could identify the prisoners as those who came to their house. The accused admitted they had left camp but only to visit the home of local Black women. Clark's counsel, Lt. R. D. Woolsey of the Twelfth USCT, enjoined the court to consider that "the accusation is brought against the prisoner by a resident of a disloyal state, and that the accused is not only odious to a large majority of the people from the fact that he is a soldier in the Union army, but he is doubly so by being a colored soldier."[42] The trial demonstrates that white Southerners interpreted the mere presence of Black Federals in or near their homes as assault. In addition, the soldiers' white officers treated them as though they were guilty, arresting them without positive identification by a victim, torturing them to extract confession, and subjecting them to ball and chain while awaiting trial. Some white Southerners reacted to emancipation by lodging spurious charges of rape, and some white officers gave too much weight to the accusations.[43]

Outside of Tennessee we have less direct evidence from Black defendants but overwhelming evidence of unequal punishments. In Virginia during the spring of 1864, the army executed Pvt. William Johnson of the Twenty-Third USCT for desertion and attempted rape of an unnamed white woman. Although the trial record has been lost, Gen. Benjamin Butler noted the disparity in his review of the Jennie Green and Andrew Smith case. Butler argued in his refusal to mitigate Smith's sentence: "A day or two since a negro man was hung in the presence of the army, for the attempted violation of the person of a white woman. Equal and exact justice would have taken this officer's *life*, but imprisonment in the Penitentiary for a long term of years, his loss of rank and position—if that imprisonment be without hope or possibility of pardon, as it should be—would be almost an equal example."[44] Butler's response is revealing: He believed "equal and exact justice" would execute a white officer for raping a young Black girl and execute a Black soldier for attempted rape of a white woman. Widespread Northern attitudes characterizing Black men as the only believable rapists of white women predisposed courts-martial to see Black Federals as guilty even as they extended leniency to white soldiers who raped Black girls. While Southern enslavers' pecuniary investment in slavery made them lenient toward Black men accused of

FIG 4.1. [Execution of Pvt. William Johnson, 23 regt., USCT]—The U.S. Army was much more likely to execute Black soldiers for rape. In this photograph, Pvt. William Johnson of the 23rd U.S. Colored Troops is hung in Petersburg, Virginia, after being convicted of desertion and attempted rape. (Library of Congress)

raping white women up until the very end of the war, white Federals had no financial or community ties to African American soldiers.[45] As a result, the unequal justice already commonplace in Northeastern and Midwestern states now fell harshly on Southern Black Federals.

Unequal justice also meant that some Black Federals accused of rape never had a trial. Stationed near Jacksonville, Florida, in spring of 1864, George E. Stephens recorded three instances of Black soldiers executed without trial for the crime of raping white women. Stephens was disturbed by the blatant inequality:

> I do not think a black man should be hung for a crime if a white man is not treated with the same punishment for a like crime. . . . If men are to be shot or hung without a legitimate trial under the civil or military law, the life of no man is protected or safe, and we are living under a tyr-

anny as inexorable as slavery itself. . . . We may as well look at facts which cannot admit of but one solution, viz.: the fixed determination of the people of the United States to maintain a line of demarkation [*sic*] between the white and black race, and to deny to the black equal rights and justice as enjoyed by the white.[46]

As Stephens noted, not only did Black men face harsher punishments, but sometimes they did not even get a trial in which they could defend themselves.[47] That the military behaved so callously toward the lives of self-emancipated Black men did not bode well for any African Americans, Northern or Southern. While Stephens had hoped that ending slavery would erase the "line of demarkation between the white and black race," drumhead courts-martial signaled the army's, and perhaps the nation's, intent to continue to exclude African Americans from equal rights and equal justice. Stephens's thoughts indicate that Northern and Southern African Americans had known all along that the fight was not simply about destroying slavery but eliminating the unequal and unjust treatment of Black Americans. When white officers of the U.S. military meted out unequal justice to Black Federals, the long fight for equal rights faced yet another setback.

As the war drew to a close, elite Confederate women joined poor white women in accusing Black Federals of rape. Southeast of Raleigh in Duplin County, North Carolina, two planter-class women accused two Black Federals of attempted rape. Out on a raid, the men had stumbled on the plantation of enslaver Dr. Matthew Moore, whose wife and young ward, Scynthia Linnear, remained at home. Pvt. George Morgan testified in his defense that he had been in the wrong place at the wrong time: While visiting the plantation's enslaved men and women, he heard a fuss at the main house; on entering, the women began screaming. Morgan, perhaps knowing he would not receive a fair trial, made sure that at his arrest seven Federal soldiers heard him question Linnear and Mrs. Moore, "Did I disturb you?" The court-martial seemed to presume him guilty, asking Linnear leading questions like "Did any of the men try to kiss you or hug you?" The prosecution fell apart when neither Linnear nor Moore could identify him. In fact, the women seemed offended by the question, tartly responding that they "did not know one n——r from the other."[48] Linnear and Moore took Morgan's presence in their house to be an attempt at sexual assault. They expected that the court-martial would take their word over that of a Black man and seemed offended that they would need to positively identify the man they had accused of a crime that merited the death penalty.

The women also accused Pvt. James White of "attempting to ravish the person of Mrs. Matthew Moore, and grasping her about the neck, hug, and attempt to kiss her, and presenting a pistol at her head, threaten that he would kill her unless she would let him go to bed with her." White and his compatriots testified that they had gone into the house to search for rebels. As soon as they entered, Linnear and Moore began yelling and screaming. In response, White had laughed, putting his hands on Moore to calm her, saying, "Hush! I am not going to hurt you." Moore did not take the stand—she was ill. In a highly suspect maneuver, Linnear testified for her. The young woman's story constantly changed: At first she wasn't sure White was the man who had attempted to rape Moore. Later she was certain. She was sure *someone* had attempted to rape Moore, and that White had put his hands on Moore's shoulder. This was enough to convict him of "assaulting and grossly insulting a woman." He was sentenced to forfeit all pay and be confined to hard labor for two years.[49] These elite women interpreted White's attempt to reassure them that he intended them no harm as an attempted rape. His very presence in the plantation house was an assault, pointing to the destruction of slavery and the authority that Black Federals now had over elite Southern women. Moore and Linnear could not countenance such an insult, and lodging charges was a way to reset the balance of power in their favor.

While Confederates had warned ad nauseam that Black Federals would bring widespread sexual assault, not one wartime rape confirmed these fears—that is, until a week after Richmond's capture. One evening, seven men of the Thirty-Eighth USCT left camp after taps. The party made their way to the home of Fannie and Washington Crawford, a newly married, poor farming family. Crawford, home alone with her blacksmith brother's seventeen-year-old daughter Eliza, refused to open the door and commenced screaming. Corporal John Sheppard fired off his revolver, perhaps hoping to cow the women into submission. This brouhaha sent four men back to camp. But Sheppard, Sgt. William Jackson, and Private Brooks stayed behind. Once inside, Jackson raped Crawford. Back at camp the next morning, the men boasted of their exploits. At Jackson's court-martial, fellow soldiers testified that the men told them "they got what they wanted of the women."[50] The court found Jackson guilty and sentenced him to be executed. His trial is evidence that at least one Black soldier used rape as a tool of war against a white woman. But his trial also demonstrates that his fellow Black soldiers found his behavior appalling. The court had also perhaps learned a lesson, for it stringently questioned the woman who accused him, at last seeming suspicious of poor white women who accused Black Federals of rape. One detail remained consistent: Jackson suffered a harsher punishment than any white soldier ever experienced for raping a Black woman.[51]

IN CONCLUSION, while Confederate rumors spread fear that Black Federals would launch a wholesale attack on elite Southern women, data from courts-martial reveals that the reverse happened. White Federals attacked African American women and girls at alarming rates, while only a handful of white Southern women accused Black Federals of sexual assault during the course of the war. These white women came overwhelmingly from poor farming backgrounds, and many lodged spurious charges because they interpreted the presence of African American soldiers in white homes to be an assault in and of itself. White officers, already inclined to believe Black men to be rapists, inflicted harsh punishments on them. For its part, the Black community warned about white Federals preying on African American women and girls, and wartime courts-martial for sexual assault bear up these fears. In refugee camps or in their homes, Black women and girls remained vulnerable to sexual assault by white Federals, some of whom used wartime rape as a reinforcement of racial subordination. Even so, Black women and girls went to great lengths to report their rapists, insisting that the Federal army recognize their loyalty by punishing soldiers who assaulted them. Although new military laws allowed their testimony, defendants challenged their ability to honestly testify, and courts let their assumptions of Black promiscuity influence trials' outcomes. Wartime rape illustrates the uneven progress of emancipation as Black women struggled for freedom from sexual assault and Black men struggled against false accusations rooted in their supposed hypersexuality.

A new wartime policy illustrates that the fight over emancipation took many forms. Along the Sea Islands of the Atlantic Coast, Black female civilians worked with white Federal commanders and Black regiments to wage war on Confederate strongholds, particularly plantations, freeing Black Unionists in the process. These raids, although effective, were highly controversial. Some Northern commanders and politicians sided with the

Confederate press, criticizing the attacks as waging war on supposedly peaceful white civilians. These controversies, combined with the ascendance of Western commanders Ulysses S. Grant, William Tecumseh Sherman, and Philip Sheridan, led to new raiding strategies. Eschewing collaboration with Black soldiers and Black civilians, these men waged war on the entire home front. Ending the war, not ending slavery, was their goal. These choices sidelined loyal Black women and created a much more difficult path to freedom.

CHAPTER FIVE

From Collaborative to Noncooperative Raiding

ALTHOUGH WILLIAM TECUMSEH SHERMAN'S 1864 Christmas gift to President Abraham Lincoln was the capture of Savannah, the city's residents received the much less welcome present of thousands of hungry Union soldiers bent on pillaging. Savannah's Black women, many of whom hired out their time or had earned their freedom and owned significant property, experienced the worst of the destruction.[1] Sarah Ann Black, a free woman who enjoyed a comfortable existence, watched it vanish within two days. Before the arrival of Union soldiers, Black firmly believed that "[the Yankees] were too good friends of us" to take African Americans' possessions. But when Black tried to reason with the white Federals who arrived at her home, insisting that she was loyal and the army should take supplies from Confederates, the men refused to believe that she owned her home and property. They told her that "white people had run off & left [her] to mind it," and Black blamed this attitude for the way in which Federals "lived off us just as if we were the commissary."[2]

Black's unsuccessful experience in negotiating the boundaries of Federal raiding policies signals the new approach to army policy brought east by William Tecumseh Sherman and Philip Sheridan in 1864. These generals eschewed the collaborative approach to raiding first practiced along the Sea Islands of the Atlantic Coast in the spring and summer of 1863. Rather than embracing raiding's emancipatory potential, Western commanders focused on bringing the war to the doors of all Southern women, regardless of political sympathies. These commanders insisted that their objective was to destroy Southern civilians' will to fight, not to welcome Black refugees into their lines or to enlist and arm Southern Black men.[3] In the last year of the war, Western Federals sought to bring all Southern women to heel.

Prior to the raids of 1864, Black female civilians, Black Federal soldiers, and abolitionist white commanders developed collaborative raids along the Sea Islands. In this region, large numbers of enslaved people and Confederates bent on running the blockade resulted in Federals conducting targeted raids, destroying rice and cotton and carrying off enslaved people to Federal lines. Emancipation and the Militia Act brought further change, as Black Federal soldiers partnered with Black women like Harriet Tubman and Elizabeth Garey to create new raiding strategies. Using knowledge of local geography and local Black communities, raids emancipated the enslaved, destroyed Confederate war resources, and struck fear into the hearts of rebels. Although successful, the raids also experienced extraordinary pushback from the Northern public, blinded by their racist attitudes toward Black soldiers. As a result, collaborative raiding faded by the end of the summer of 1863, as the Democratic and Confederate press successfully characterized these raids as unprovoked attacks on peaceful white civilians rather than strategic attacks against rebel war resources.

Raiding changed yet again with the adoption of the Lieber Code and the ascension of Grant, Sherman, and Sheridan to the highest levels of Federal command. With hard war now explicitly sanctioned, these men embraced some of the same strategies as the Sea Island raids to destroy Confederate war resources and strike fear into the hearts of rebels. But they did not prioritize collaboration with civilian women and emancipation was not their goal. Neither Grant, nor Sherman, nor Sheridan relied on intelligence or input from Black women. Instead, they waged war on all Southern women and refused to collaborate with African Americans.

Civilian women found these new forms of raiding to be unsettling. Destruction was not always targeted, and enlisted men often found it easier to requisition supplies from free Black women. Elite Confederate women suffered, but their lofty social position and vociferous complaining occasionally, even this late in the war, secured them guards.[4] And while the Lieber Code encouraged commanders to distinguish between "loyal" and "disloyal citizens," individual officers and enlisted men often ignored these injunctions.[5] Perhaps most egregious was Federals' treatment of free and enslaved Black women. While these women initially welcomed raiding as a declaration of war on plantation households, they quickly realized that some white Federals singled them out for inordinate property destruction. And since these armies at best discouraged, and at worst attacked, Black Southern women who tried to shelter within Federal lines, African Americans faced a difficult choice. Should they remain on plantations, savings depleted and fields destroyed? Or follow a hostile Federal army and hope that, eventually, commanders would be more sympathetic to their plight?

While collaborative raiding continued the long tradition of negotiation between Southern women and the Federal army over wartime policies, noncooperative raiding was the army's attempt to set itself as the driver of policy with civilians its passive victims. While Grant, Sherman, and Sheridan insisted that raiding was a humanitarian endeavor designed to bring a swift end to the war, the particular raiding strategies they embraced attempted to end Southern women's involvement in negotiating military policy. The army intended these new raiding policies to be entirely conceived of and implemented by the army, with civilian women its passive recipients. It hoped to signal that the Federal army had finally taken charge of military policy toward civilians, and that it refused attempts to negotiate or collaborate. It was not entirely successful. Although official policy and soldier accounts attempted to erase civilian women by using language focusing on living off of the country, Southern women continued to influence, negotiate, and resist the effects of raiding. Nowhere is this more clear than in loyal women's postwar Southern Claims Commission testimony, in which they highlighted their active involvement in raiding. Although Southern women were often unsuccessful in mitigating raiding's effects, their powerful testimony reveals them to be anything but war's passive victims. Even to the bitter end of the conflict, Southern women continued to actively engage the Federal army over its policies toward civilians.

Collaborative Raiding: Combahee and Darien, Summer 1863

The Federal outposts along the Sea Islands had revolutionary potential. Nearly everyone knew this to be true: the abolitionist commanding general, David Hunter; the general supervising the self-emancipated, Rufus Saxton; the resident camp spy, Harriet Tubman; and of course the men who made up the First and Second South Carolina regiments. These men and their families had endured years of uncertainty about their status and hostility from Confederates and Federals alike. But the Emancipation Proclamation had granted them legal freedom. They hoped to do the same for others. And since they maintained close ties with their friends and family still living under slavery in Confederate territory, these goals seemed achievable.

Collaborative raiding first emerged in this environment. Federal commanders, aided by intelligence provided by African Americans, waged swift attacks to capture Confederate war resources. By spring of 1863, the First and Second South Carolina occupied Jacksonville, Florida, from which Col. James Montgomery's men spread out in raids based on intelligence from Black sailors working on one of the Federal gunboats. They returned with nearly forty captive Confederate militia, nine and a half bales of cotton, and dozens of formerly enslaved people. Confederates worried that, if the campaign persisted, all of central Florida might fall under Federal control. Within days the regiments were back in Port Royal and Camp Saxton: All resources would be needed to capture Charleston. Jacksonville was a mere distraction, and the incendiarism engaged in by the Eighth Maine, Sixth Connecticut, and First South Carolina received widespread condemnation in Democratic and Republican newspapers.[6]

In spite of the setback in Jacksonville, the Department of the South's commanders knew there was something to these raids, and so they continued that summer. Montgomery was eager to continue his Florida successes, and he found an ally in fellow John Brown supporter Harriet Tubman. With her network of spies among the enslaved population, Tubman devised a new target: a raid up the Combahee River, just south of Charleston. Federals had so far been unsuccessful in breaching the heavy fortifications in Charleston Harbor. But the city and the surrounding countryside relied on the large-scale rice production of the Combahee region, and enslaved people made up the labor force. The raid was a smashing success: Tubman and Montgomery carried off 756 formerly enslaved people, destroyed fields of rice, cotton, and corn, and burned plantations. As Tubman herself proclaimed in a dictated letter to the *Boston Commonwealth*, "Nearly or quite all the able-bodied men [from the expedition] have joined the colored regiments." Newly arrived Fifty-Fourth Massachusetts soldier and war correspondent James Henry Gooding praised the attack for precisely this reason: Combahee helped fill the ranks of Black regiments.[7]

Combahee had also successfully targeted the Confederate elite. Gooding reported that "thirty-four large mansions, belonging to notorious rebels, were burned to the ground." Despite inflicting what scholar Willie Lee Rose estimates as $2 million in damage and earning accolades in Republican newspa-

FIG 5.1. *Harper's Weekly*, "Raid of Second South Carolina Volunteers (Col. Montgomery) Among the Rice Plantations on the Combahee, S.C."—Harriet Tubman's successful raid on the rice region south of Charleston gained notoriety throughout the North, as captured here in this image for *Harper's*. While the image shows burning plantations and fleeing African Americans, it credits Col. James Montgomery, rather than Tubman, for the raid. (Library of Congress)

pers, some found fault. Col. Thomas Wentworth Higginson, commanding the First South Carolina, faulted Montgomery for "burning private houses."[8] Higginson's perspective differed greatly from that of the Second South Carolina, the men who set the fires. To them, the plantations on which they had once been enslaved, and where they returned to free their families and friends, were not private homes at all. They were brutal workhouses, constructed and maintained by people held in bondage. And Higginson seemed to be alone in his critique. For many, particularly the Republican press, the benefits of the Combahee River Raid stifled worries about incendiarism.

Montgomery conducted one more raid aided by a Black woman. Nowhere near as famous and born free, Elizabeth Garey and her family had lived in Darien, Georgia, all of their lives. The prosperous family, with assets totaling $2,500, had much to lose if Federals raided and burned the town.

Nevertheless, Elizabeth sent word via her friend Sgt. Edward King in the First South Carolina that Darien would be a good target. Halfway between Savannah and Fernandina, Darien was infamous for running cotton and rice past the Federal blockade. Nearby Liberty County held the largest number of enslaved people in the state. And Confederate guerrillas roamed the area, making life miserable for free and enslaved Black people. That included the Gareys. Supported by rebel militia, Confederate neighbors persecuted the family for their Unionism, driving them out of their home and forcing them to seek shelter in abandoned houses along the coast. This is how one week after Combahee, the Second South Carolina steamed up the Altamaha River into Darien with the Fifty-Fourth Massachusetts in tow. Elizabeth instructed her son Charles to watch their property.[9] Federals needed to know which buildings to burn and which to spare.

The regiment did not spare any buildings. After landing, the men quickly loaded cotton and cattle onto gunboats. Then Montgomery issued orders to burn the town. His account does not survive, but his subordinate Col. Robert Gould Shaw recalled Montgomery asserting that the regiments were "outlawed, and therefore not bound by the rules of regular warfare." Seventeen-year-old Charles Garey attempted to spare his family's property. The young man mustered the courage to speak directly to Montgomery, telling him that he and his family remained loyal. The colonel was undeterred, assuring Charles that "he thought the loyal people would be paid" by the government after the war. Montgomery then recruited Charles to leave Darien for Beaufort, where he could enlist in the military. Charles agreed. As the day drew to a close, Elizabeth's son contemplated a new life while he watched as the soldiers "took buckets of tar . . . and pine knots and set fire to the buildings." The fires burned so brightly that Elizabeth and the rest of the Garey family watched "the property burning from . . . back in the woods."[10] Elizabeth never expressed regret for sending along the intelligence that led to the burning of Darien.

Much like Combahee, the Darien raid burned cotton, captured livestock, brought away free and enslaved Black people—some of whom enlisted in the military—and weakened another Confederate stronghold. But while Combahee's results had outweighed qualms about burning plantations, Darien's successes were much smaller in comparison. And so nearly everyone—abolitionist officers, the Democratic press, and Confederate propagandists—focused on incendiarism. Shaw was beside himself, worried about the "reputation of the black troops and of those connected with them" and questioning Montgomery's penchant for "wanton destruction." Higginson seemed almost gleeful when he wrote to his family, "The 54th chafe under the burning of Darien & their reproachful letters from home." He was only partly correct: The men chafed under the reproach because they believed it to be in bad faith. Gooding's report to the *New Bedford Mercury* blamed the Democratic press for the outroar, an attack designed to bring "'N—— worshipers' in contempt" in the hopes of "commanding the Powers that be to stop enlisting the 'impediments to civilization.'" Confederate newspapers and rebel commanders echoed the very criticisms of the Northern Democratic press. In a nearly three-page lecture on wartime conduct, Confederate general P. G. T. Beauregard blamed the "violations of long and thoroughly established laws of war" on "negroes . . . either fugitive slaves, or who had been carried away from their masters' plantations." Similar to the Democratic press, Beauregard argued that Darien represented the "atrocious consequences which have ever resulted from the employment of a merciless, servile race as soldiers." Conveniently forgotten in the uproar was Darien's long history of blockade running and harboring Confederate guerrillas. No one mentioned that, like Combahee, the raid was a collaboration between Black civilians and Black Federals. Nor did it spark a discussion about what sort of warfare Black Federals should engage in when Confederates treated them as insurrectionists rather than legitimate combatants. By this point, Quincy Gillmore, no friend to emancipation, had replaced the abolitionist Hunter. Gillmore defended Black troops but did not sanction collaborative, emancipationist raids. Raiding as collaboration between white commanders, Black Federals, and Black civilians was dead in the water by July 1863.[11]

Noncooperative Raiding: Virginia, Summer 1864

One year later, much had changed. Ulysses S. Grant now served as general-in-chief and commander of the Army of the Potomac. He elevated several other Western commanders, most notably William Tecumseh Sherman and Philip Sheridan. These men articulated new raiding policies based on the Lieber Code's injunction that "the more vigorously wars are pursued, the better it is for humanity." Sheridan stated his purpose in the Shenandoah Valley as "reducing [war's] advocates to poverty." Ending the war quickly would put Federals "on the side of humanity." Sheridan characterized all civilians as being advocates of war because they did not care about destruction "so long as [it] did not come to their doors." Sherman's attitudes displayed more nuance. While he tolerated civilians with "southern feelings," he made an exception for those who demonstrated a "love of murder, of war, desolation, [and] famine." Enlisted men from the Western theater embraced these changes. They believed that an army worrying about civilians was less effective at fighting, and so they scoffed at reports of starving civilians, cheered when the military ceased giving out rations, and encouraged living off the land in order to "starve the South into submission." By 1864, commanders, officers, and enlisted men from the Western theater had arrived in the East and agreed that civilians needed to be punished.[12]

Commanders initially attempted to set limits on raiding. Before Sheridan took control, Gen. David Hunter instructed Federal cavalry in the Shenandoah Valley that forage was to be "seized under the direction of officers duly authorized." Enlisted men paid these rules no mind. George Cooley acknowledged that he and a friend were "liable to be arrested for leaving the picket line," but even so the men "killed a secesh heifer." Cooley's language is particularly instructive: While earlier in the war enlisted men might have acknowledged that they took a cow from a secessionist civilian, the civilian now disappeared as the owner of the cow. Instead, the heifer itself had political loyalties, and because the heifer was a secessionist, Cooley and his compatriots were justified in its seizure.[13]

While enlisted men's commanders could not always stop soldiers from unauthorized raids, civilians—if acknowledged—still had some influence. Peter Gamache of Massachusetts watched as one poor fellow tried to take a cow that was tied in front of a house. Its owner, a young woman, "rushed out after the two," and upon catching up, "*held out her hand and the soldier* meekly handed her the rope." Confronted directly by a civilian woman, Gamache's companion caved. But when soldiers could get away with it, they disassociated the possessions they confiscated from their owners, making it seem as though they took property belonging to no one.[14]

Loyal African American residents soon realized that the officers and enlisted men of the Department of West Virginia would not even spare them from raiding as they worked to lay waste to the valley. Martha Jane Charity, married to Union soldier and free Black man William Charity, sought to make clear to the Federals who showed up at her house that she was a soldier's wife. Her protestations fell on deaf ears, and Federals took her mule "from the stable," not even relenting when she "followed as far as the picket line trying to get him back." Judith Hass, a free African American woman, felt that she had done her duty to the Federal army by giving soldiers food "cheerfully as long as [she] had it in [her] house," but these actions offered no immunity. During Hunter's raids, a soldier "came [into her kitchen] and told [her] that he wanted [the mare] and said if [she] didn't open the door he would break it open." As with Charity, Hass followed the soldier, "trying to recover [the horse,] but [she] failed." To add insult to injury, Federals visited her again the next day and took all her corn, "leaving [her] about three pecks for [her] support, which was all [she] had in the world." In Augusta County, free woman Mary Blackburn was caring for her sick husband when men of Hunter's command seized her horse, bridle, and saddle, and then her flour and bacon. Blackburn protested the seizure of her food, telling "one of [the soldiers] that I thought he might leave me a little flour."[15] Although African American women still attempted to shape raiding policies by highlighting their loyalty, their political sympathies no longer worked in their favor. Rather than treating Black women as allies, white Federals took the possessions of loyal and disloyal.

Once Sheridan took command, raiding cast a wider net. On September 8, he allowed the men of his command to seize "horses, mules, forage, and fresh beef, or, in the case of actual necessity, flour and bacon." Noticeably, the orders did not enjoin Sheridan's men to distinguish between loyal and disloyal civilians, and so the valley's poor white farming women found that their Unionism did them little good. Mary Jane Clem of Shenandoah County watched from her house during the summer of 1864 as Union soldiers entered her barn and took her and her sister-in-law's horses. The men worked so quickly that Clem did not even have time to complain. Widow Catharine Fravel, who baked bread and cared for sick Federals, hoped her generosity would be enough to protect her from further incursions. When Union cavalry began taking hundreds of pounds of her corn and one of the two pigs she raised "for family use," Fravel protested to an officer. Rather than receiving a safeguard, which might have happened in the past, the officer told her "they would take it any how."[16] While women's loyalty had sometimes spared them earlier in the war, Sheridan's men now had authorization to forage for necessities. Loyal women still attempted to shape policy by protesting the actions of officers and enlisted men, but soldiers now turned a deaf ear to women's protests.

When Confederate guerrilla John Singleton Mosby began harassing Sheridan's men, some soldiers began to extend Federals' destruction to elites. In Loudoun County visiting relatives, Confederate Lucy Rebecca Buck heard of no fewer than six neighbors who had their houses burned, recording later that "the Corps that passed us was Sheridan's." The destruction was so extensive that Sheridan issued orders condemning the "pillaging of houses and the destruction of private property," singling out stragglers as the culprits. Some enlisted men, incensed by rebel guerrilla activity, targeted the supporters of those guerrillas: elite Confederates like the Buck family.[17] Their intention was to destroy civilian support for Mosby's raiders.

Targeting rebel elites did not stop at incendiarism. Three weeks after the house burnings in Loudoun County, Sheridan's soldiers paid Buck and her family a visit, during which soldiers searched the house, confiscated horses, broke open trunks and desks, and demanded food. Federals faulted Mosby for making them dependent on civilians for food. Buck recalled them telling her that "Mosby's having taken their wagon trains had cut off their supplies and they were starved." If Sheridan's men hoped their actions would cow elite Confederates like Buck, they were disappointed. The Buck women repeatedly defied orders, refused to unlock trunks or hand over belongings, and referred to the men as "wretch[es]" and "miscreant[s]." Buck characterized them as robbers, asserting that their searches for government property and arms were merely a cover to steal "booty, money and the like." Elite rebels characterized Federals as "impudent" when soldiers conducted raids of their property, and their vociferous and strident refusals to comply hint at why some soldiers preferred confiscating poor white and Black women's possessions. Even when faced with armed enemy soldiers, wealthy Confederates thought nothing of lying, not complying, and characterizing Federals as uncivilized marauders.[18]

For their part, enlisted men in the Shenandoah Valley Campaign made destruction more palatable by making no mention of civilians in their letters and diaries. While they encountered Shenandoah residents, their accounts focused on the provisions they acquired.[19] Only a handful of soldiers recounted their experiences with civilians. Sgt. Ezra Walker of the 116th Ohio was gratified to find evidence of union sentiment upon entering the Valley. In Waterford, "ladies waved union flags and many of them wore them pinned on their dresses, they brought water out to the street for the men to drink and seemed to have a kind word for all." Just a few days later, the army passed through Middletown, whose ladies "commenced baking pies & bread which they either gave to the men or sold at a very reasonable price."[20] Walker was gratified by displays of loyal feeling and women's fulfillment of traditional roles: They encouraged, succored, and provisioned the army.

Walker's attitude quickly changed when Federals passed through Winchester to camp south of town. Confederate elites watched from their doorways, laughing that soldiers were once again trying to hold the town. Walker denied them the honorific of "ladies," referring to them instead as "*females*." The women's laughter was misplaced. By this point, Sheridan's men engaged in incendiarism. Walker saw "great columns of smoke rising" due to the cavalry "burning hay and grain to keep it from falling into the hands of the rebels." Walker was soon doing his part to subdue the rebellion. Claiming that there were "*all* rebels in our rear," he left camp to go "over to an orchard and got all the apples I could carry afterwards went for oats—queer way of doing that, to go to a mans [*sic*] farm or orchard and take what you can carry away without saying a word to him about it." Walker was not alone in linking rebel women's outrageous behavior with raiding from local civilians. These women might not be able to own property in their own right, but they could certainly be made to feel war's destructiveness when Federals felt emboldened to take whatever they wanted from private homes and farms.[21]

At least one Shenandoah Valley rebel suffered the consequences of her treason. Winchester's Laura Lee finally saw her luck run out in late 1864. After years of smuggling letters and supplies for the rebel army, Federals ordered her and her sister to remove themselves from the town. Lee was forced to comply, but not before characterizing the order as "inhuman" and "cruel."[22] Lee was wealthy and certainly had the resources to survive as a refugee—she had been preparing for such an eventuality all year. But the privileged woman was unused to being ordered to do anything, and being turned out of her home by the enemy was an insult. Lee's state of mind indicates that, far from repentant, elite rebel ladies continued to cling to recalcitrance.

Even women fortunate enough to receive safeguards did not benefit from them. Sgt. Ezra Walker walked right up to a house with a guard, "told him what I wanted and he told me where to go to keep out of sight . . . and afterwards made signs when to hide." To add to the destruction, cavalry members took time off from burning the valley to go foraging. William Allen Tall of the Second West Virginia Cavalry remarked that "while [the firing] lasted we have been living fine for a week on rosteng ears & aples. We have eaten up a good many corn fields." Tall felt no remorse for either the raiding or the incendiarism, commenting that "the people of the valley begin to feel the effect rebellion on ther land for the 2 armeys will nearly disstroy the country entirely."[23] While the Lieber Code enjoined armies engaged in civil war to "throw the burden of the war . . . on the disloyal citizens," Federals in the Shenandoah did no such thing, particularly after dealing with Mosby. They colluded with safeguards and raided and burned, regarding all civilians as disloyal, no matter their political sympathies.

Only one Federal soldier expressed remorse for some of the destruction. English immigrant Thomas Campbell, enlisted in the 122nd Ohio Infantry, grew concerned about how unequally his fellow soldiers applied raiding policies. In August, he came across "a family not far distant with 7 small children[, who] have been literally strip'd of everything. First came the rebs then our boys. Who took all left . . . They had not food enough in the house to give the children their breakfast. . . . What injustice. What wrongs are committed. Tis enough to make a man blush. For his kind." Campbell worried that the raiding's extensiveness would harm rather than help Federal endeavors because they risked alienating the entire civilian population. "Talk about cultivating a Union sentiment wherever we go," he griped that fall. "[Raiding] has the contrary ef fect [*sic*]." Campbell worried that Federals who raided from poor farming folk were no different from rebels. And that lack of difference would not win them any supporters to their cause.[24]

Campbell also feared that raiding made soldiers ungovernable, refusing to listen to orders and engaging in unsanctioned violence. In late September, "stringent orders were read to the troops, forbidding pillaging and foraging." But Federals felt no compunction to obey. "We had not been in camp an hour," Campbell noted incredulously, "before the boys com menced [*sic*] to bring in . . . anything they could lay their hands on." The men suffered no consequences because "the officers wink at it and take their share of what ever comes along."[25] In a large, diffuse, and occasionally undisciplined volunteer army, enlisted men could act contrary to orders as long as they had the blessing of regimental officers. And Campbell believed that raiding resulted in other abuses as well. Earlier that month he despaired that "a rape was com mitted [*sic*] by some of our men. on the per son [*sic*] of a handsome young lady. . . . She reported the outrage to Genl Ricketts. efforts [*sic*] have been made to ferret out the vile rascal. but without sucefs [*sic*]." He feared how the sexual violence and inability to find the perpetrator would reflect on all Fed-

FIG 5.2. Edwin Forbes, "Bummers (Foragers)"—Foraging parties usually consisted of several soldiers from a particular regiment tasked with rounding up provisions. In this unusual sketch, war correspondent Forbes shows a civilian woman standing in the door of her modest farmhouse, demonstrating that soldiers took from poor farming families as well as the wealthy and elite. (Library of Congress)

erals, noting that "such villains bring dis grace [*sic*] on the best & holiest causes."[26] While most of the men in Sheridan's command did not mention raiding's effect on civilians, Campbell grew concerned over its abuses. Federals did not spare poor families, they refused to listen to orders not to forage, and raiding allowed them unprecedented access to Southern women's homes. In at least one case, that had led to sexual violence. Raiding had the potential to undermine Federal claims that their cause was just because it resulted in abuses that were hard to justify.

Sheridan's destruction of the valley was complete by winter of 1864. His orders to Brig. Gen. Wesley Merritt made clear his intention to "clear the country of these parties that are bringing destruction upon the innocent, as well as their guilty supporters, by their cowardly acts," and ordered Merritt to "consume and destroy all forage and subsistence, burn all barns and mills and their contents, and drive off all stock in the region." Even seasoned Union soldiers accustomed to the army's devastation seemed awed by the sheer amount of damage. Thomas Campbell cited the success of Sheridan's September orders to destroy "all the wheat & barns containing it" in Harrisonburg and Staunton. As a result, "not a stack of wh[e]at or barn . . . [is] left standing" across twenty-five miles of Virginia countryside. Rather than pointless destruction, Campbell felt the measure justified, since "if left in our rear . . . twould be giving aid & comfort to the rebs," and so "the innocent suffer with the guilty." In December, New York cavalryman Henry Dove camped with Sheridan's men in Snicker's Gap during a scouting party and marveled that "Sheridan's cavalry have *burnt* everything for about 20 miles this side of the mountains," including "houses barns grain and all and drove off all the cattle and sheep." Dove admitted that "it looked hard to see every thing burning up," qualifying this moment of pity by telling his father, "but we could not help it."[27] Sheridan's enlisted men did not wring their hands over incendiarism, as some had done after Jacksonville, Combahee, and Darien. No one doubted that these men were civilized. The men of Sheridan's command had greater leeway to characterize their raiding as in accordance with military regulations. Abuses, such as initially sparing elite Confederates and taking from loyal Black women, were the work of stragglers. They largely went unacknowledged because Sheridan had neutralized Mosby and destroyed civilian resistance in the valley.

Before, During, and After Atlanta: Spring–Fall 1864

William Tecumseh Sherman hoped to finally bring the war to Georgia civilians during the Atlanta campaign. While not quite ready to sanction large-scale raiding, overstretched supply lines meant Federals had to live off the land at least a little in northwestern Georgia. Illinoisan John Boon cheerily wrote home about the "good . . . country" between Chattanooga and Rome, and how "the people were well fixed. They were too well fixed and that was what ailed them but they learned a dear lesson." Frederick Henry Kellogg of the Fifteenth Illinois felt no shame in telling his family about taking fresh meat from civilians. When his mother rebuked him for destroying rebel property, Kellogg informed her, "You ought to have been in the rear of the 17th army corps as we were two days. They left nothing in the houses and burnt nearly all the outbuildings and all the fences. We are not half so bad for we only take their corn and bacon and let our horses eat their wheat and oats, sometimes drive off their cattle and kill a pig occasionally."[28] With this new type of raiding, soldiers embraced living off of civilians and compared themselves favorably to Federals who engaged in incendiarism.

Given the location, the women experiencing raiding were primarily white and loyal. During and after the Battle of Resaca, Union soldiers swarmed Gordon County homes for food. Elizabeth Miller, a widow and mother of six, described how her place was "covered with soldiers" who soon "commenced killing my hogs." Miller was a Unionist and widely known for aiding Union men escaping Confederate service, but her complaints to officers went nowhere. The men insisted "they were out of supplies, and were compelled to subsist off of the country." Fellow Gordon County resident Eliza Robertson heard similar reasoning from Union soldiers who took her horse, chickens, sweet potatoes, and barrels of flour and syrup. "These troops said they were subsisting entirely off of the country. . . . I know they took everything to eat they could find in the country," Robertson stated. Wealthy plantation owner Anna Skelly fared little better. She vividly recalled, "You never saw such hungry people in your life—they just drove the hens off the roost & ate the same eggs—they drank from pails of milk—we had servants cooking all day baking bread cooking ham & c.—The day after they left we ate boiled corn & had nothing else to eat."[29] For all three women, it was some consolation that Federals treated them "with a good deal of respect." Miller went as far as to say that Union soldiers had protected her "other than the taking of my property." These loyal Georgians took Sherman's invasion as a sign that it was their turn to contribute to the war effort. They willingly contributed out of a sense of womanly obligation, and Union soldiers repaid them by behaving with decorum.[30]

The behavior of some of the men of Sherman's army after the capture of Rome demonstrates that hard fighting against the Confederate military and civilian behavior influenced soldiers' decisions to engage in destruction. Peter Funk, infantryman in the 150th New York of Hooker's Twentieth Army Corps, described how Rome's "residents fled in terror from the Yankees headed by Sherman, whose very name was a dread to them. Many of the houses were pillaged in a short time, some of the soldiers going so far as to set them on fire and ravaging things indiscriminately where . . . it would only cause suffering among the women and little ones." Eighty-Fifth Illinois soldier John Boon of Thomas's Fourteenth Corps took a different view of the destruction, commenting to his wife about how "the boys were soon all over the town. . . . I saw them carry off more than one thousand lbs. of tobacco. . . .

I got five lbs. of good smoking tobacco and . . . also got some good cigars."[31] The soldiers of Hooker's and Thomas's command who invaded Rome, after encountering stout resistance from Hood's Corps on short rations, assumed that residents fleeing in advance were rebels. As a result, some of these men did not restrain themselves from incendiarism and pillaging.

Soldiers did not always behave better when they encountered civilians who were unquestioningly loyal. While northwestern Georgia's enslaved women delighted in seeing enslavers' property destroyed, they were disappointed when soldiers also took their possessions. Rome County resident Callie Elder remembered how her father hid their enslaver's "fine stallion" and gold from Federals, both of which were quickly found. Elder was not troubled by her enslaver's loss of property, but she mourned when Federals took her grandmother's hard-earned money. The matriarch hid her ten-dollar gold piece in the milk she was churning, but soldiers "poured dat buttermilk out right dar onde porch and got grandma's money." Rather than treating them as allies, some of Sherman's men robbed Black women.[32] When it came to Black women, some of Sherman's white soldiers were animated by racism. They did not stop at taking "war resources" but also stole personal possessions and engaged in wasteful destruction.

As the army exited Rome, Sherman's men requisitioned more supplies from the local population, as quartermasters scoured the countryside for "seven days' forage and rations" and army commanders received orders to "subsist their troops independent of the railroad for twenty days . . . as we can safely rely on much meat, forage, and vegetables in the country to which we propose to go." Soldiers did receive one pound of bread and flour plus two days' allowance of salt per week, but orders stated that "all else must be gathered in the country." The language used in the orders, which focused on gathering "in the country," distanced the Federal military from its reliance on local civilians. The meat, vegetables, corn, and other products they gathered belonged to individual civilians. Rather than acknowledging that the property they took was the provenance of Southern civilians, military orders made it seem as though provisions existed in the region independent of human action.[33]

The military's orders had material impacts on the loyal women of Bartow County, who made it clear that Federal soldiers foraged from the farms and larders of civilian women. Unionist Sarah Scott, a mother of four, gave up some of her property but attempted to negotiate with Federals to "leave me a portion of it, for my family." Her appeal was in vain, for the soldiers "said they could not" because "their army was nearly destitute of rations." Not only that, Federals told Scott that it would do her and her family good to have her property taken because if Union soldiers did not take it, "others would take it." The elderly Mary McDonald, another Bartow resident, heard similar reasoning. Federals told her they had "orders to take everything—that they were intending to break down the rebellion." McDonald had a hard time believing that the property of an elderly woman—one horse, several cows and calves, hogs, oxen, sheep, flour, and salt—would dismantle the Confederacy. And so she pressed the soldiers who were taking her possessions on whether they really needed it. "Some of the soldiers . . . said they needed it and some said they did not need it," she recalled. Even McDonald's pointed questioning did not convince the men to leave her property behind. At times raiding created dependency on the U.S. Army. Federals took so much of Sarah Crow's property that she and her family followed the army when it fell back to Chattanooga in the fall.[34] In their postwar claims, Bartow County's poor Unionist women made clear that they attempted to negotiate with Federals but to no avail. While they tried to retain enough of their provisions to be self-sufficient, raiding was sometimes so thorough that it left them in a state of dependency.

The increase in raiding gave Federal soldiers a valid reason for scouring the countryside and inviting themselves into civilians' homes. Some soldiers took this as license to engage in sexual assault. Around Burnt Hickory, Pvts. William Cutsinger and Charles Billingsly of the Seventh Indiana Battery went to the home of James Smith and, pretending to be members of the provost guard, placed him under arrest and took him to camp. Cutsinger then went back to the Smith home and ordered James's wife Louisa to leave her children and follow him back to camp. From there he led her into a thicket, told her she must "obey his orders," and raped her. He then held Louisa down while Billingsly assaulted her. In all, the men raped Louisa five times. They did not try to hide their crimes. Cutsinger bragged about the attack to members of his company the very next day. When the court convicted both men and sentenced them to ten years in prison, they deserted to the Confederate army.[35] Sexual assault was certainly not part of Sherman's raiding strategy, and the men's defection to the rebels says quite a lot about their character. But raiding did involve squads of soldiers exerting authority over civilians, and some, like Cutsinger and Billingsly, abused the policy.

Poor farming women recognized the threat posed by Federal soldiers and resorted to insults and lectures. When a soldier tried to take Fulton County resident Nancy Jett's wagon, she protested. The Federal was unmoved, instructing her if she "didn't go in the house he shoot my brains out." Jett did not cower. "I told him to shoot I talk long as breth in me," but to no avail. The soldier ended up taking her wagon.[36] Jett's behavior demonstrates that poor white women, particularly rebels, refused to engage in polite negotiations or fictions of loyalty. Instead, they insulted, provoked, and harangued in attempts to keep their belongings. By this stage in the war, however, Federal soldiers ignored their bluster.

Jett was most comfortable resorting to violent language with Black Federals. When several African American soldiers visited her farm and asked for water, Jett refused and told them to "go to the d[evil]." The men returned her ire in kind. "It made me mad they talk so big they curse me and said they intend to report me," she wrote in a letter to her husband. Jett threatened the men with violence: "I told them if I still had A gun I blow them threw." One Black soldier eventually came back and searched the house, which angered Jett even more. This time she found an ally in a white Federal. The man took exception to an African American searching a white woman's house and offered to "give me ther pistle to shote him" if the Black Federal came back. While Jett still resented the U.S. Army's intrusions, she and the white Federal resorted to threats of violence to keep African American soldiers at the bottom of the racial hierarchy.[37]

Jett went on to endure weeks of Yankee foraging parties. She told her Confederate soldier husband that the army "took everything" so that she "hant A ear of corn left." But she did not want him to worry. Nearly all of their worldly possessions might be gone, but the Federal government provided rations. "I have live well sence the yanky bin her we send Any kind of vegible they give flower meal meet cracker shuger coffee." When Jett's foodstuffs ran low, she and her female neighbors simply went "to the camps to get something to eat." In spite of their rebel sympathies, Jett and her female friends benefited from the army's largesse. Federals might take all of their possessions, but they would not allow Confederate soldiers' wives to starve.[38]

The siege of Atlanta left soldiers with time on their hands, and some of them used that time to subject civilians to sexual assault. Pvt. Albert Lane of the 100th Ohio repeatedly visited the Cobb County home of John and Roanda Dickerson, eventually striking up conversation with their seventeen-

FIG 5.3. Edwin Forbes, "Virginians going to the commissary for rations"—While sketched in Virginia, Forbes's illustration demonstrates that Federals mainly fed white Southern civilians. The African American man appears to be held in bondage by the wealthy women in the ox-drawn cart. (Library of Congress)

year-old daughter Louisa. Although all family members made it clear to Lane that his visits made them uncomfortable and they wanted him to leave, Lane instead got into bed with the young woman, telling her mother that he had orders from an officer to "take girls from twelve years old and upwards to camp whether they were willing to go in or not." Lane finally left after John ordered him out of the house. But he did not go far. When Louisa went outside to relieve herself before settling in for the night, Lane caught hold of her and assaulted her. When Roanda tried to intervene, Lane called her a "god damned old bitch" and told her to "go into the house and stop your noise or I will stomp you into hell" and then threatened to shoot John. This caused Roanda to faint, and while John tended to her, Lane sexually assaulted Louisa.[39] Soldiers not actively engaged in marching or fighting could escape camp, invent army orders, and prey on civilian families. In an army of this size, and with soldiers allowed into civilian houses, it was difficult to prevent abuses.

Raiding policies took a turn with the capture of Atlanta. By evacuating civilians from the city, Sherman could engage in more complete destruction. It relieved his command of the need for "provost guards" who would have to "liste[n] to . . . complaints and . . . grievances . . . that are not military." It would also save supplies, as "the residence here of a poor population would compel us . . . to feed them or see them starve under our eyes."[40] Whether friend or foe, civilian women proved an encumbrance that only prolonged war. By sending women out of the city and thus making them a problem to be dealt with by others, Sherman could use his resources to subdue the Confederate army rather than attend to the wants and needs of women and children.

But civilians remained in Atlanta. The vast majority of them were Black women and children who either refused to leave with their enslavers or did not have the luxury of fleeing. The city's destruction fell upon them. Cognizant of their presence or not, Federals began dismantling women's houses soon after entering.[41] Free Black woman Polly Beadle was visiting a friend in early September when her neighbor ran up, exclaiming, "Lord Polly look up!" Beadle rushed home to find Union soldiers demolishing the fence around her house. The soldiers took her "dwelling house, stable, well house & fence to their camp, and made tents of the lumber. . . . They took everything we had. . . . We had nothing to eat & no house left" after the soldiers finished their work. Elsewhere in Fulton County, Saletia Kennedy watched as squads of soldiers pillaged her farm. Even the commissioner of claims admitted that Federals had "plundered a good deal."[42] Enlisted men's racism may have been what fueled their attack on Beadle's and Kennedy's homes.

Soldier letters and diaries from the Atlanta campaign said nary a word about Atlanta's Black population. Instead, the men focused on the experience of white residents. Thomas Speed walked the city streets after occupation, describing "a city of deserted houses . . . People of refinement[,] taste and wealth . . . have exiled themselves . . . and left [their homes] to be destroyed by our soldiers."[43] Other soldiers assured themselves that poor white civilians fared better, not worse, once the U.S. Army arrived. Wisconsin soldier Burr Murdock reported that "when we came in town the people was badly scared" because "the rebs told them we would burn the town." But soon civilians warmed up to them, since "we use them a great deal better than their own soldiers did." Charles Edward Bates commented on the dreadful condition of women and children refugees, describing scenes of "clothing in rags, children by millions, food scarce, almost a famine in fact it was a hard sight."[44]

The men in Sherman's command made no mention of their compatriots' poor treatment of Black women, instead focusing on the Confederate army's poor treatment of white women and children.

Throughout fall of 1864, Federals continued to only notice the suffering of white civilians. When the army returned west in October 1864, Ohioan William W. Osborn observed the devastated countryside surrounding Adairsville, declaring that the civilians "are in a suffering condition. Nothing to eat only what the soldiers give them." Fellow Ohioan Alfred Wilcox, on the march in Summerville, noted the depleted countryside where he saw "no houses that contained citizens except one and in that the women and children were gathering potatoes to keep them from the soldiers."[45] But down near Atlanta, Federals continued to pillage from African Americans. In November, soldiers engaged in a prelude to the March to the Sea by ransacking the property of Monemia Johnson and her husband. Johnson's postwar claim for her destroyed property totaled a staggering $2,592. Once again, the Claims Commission admitted that Federals had engaged in "pillage."[46] Sherman's army did not need the supplies, for they had enough to share with northwestern Georgia's white women. Their pillaging of the Johnson family was motivated by racism.

Unequal Destruction on the March to the Sea, Winter 1864

With the destruction of Atlanta complete, Federals brought raiding in earnest to the rest of Georgia. Destruction took on a different character now that soldiers received short rations and relied on foraging for their food. Even so, commanders sought to impose limits. Brig. Gen. Giles Smith instructed the Seventeenth Corps to "keep constantly in mind that we are not warring upon women and children." Foraging parties should "take such articles as are needed" and were forbidden to enter houses or to set fire to "a building or any other property, without orders." The very next day, Maj. Gen. J. C. Davis, commanding the Fourteenth Corps, reproved his men for the "increase of straggling and marauding." "Even in the midst of an enemy's country," Davis declared, "the dictates of humanity must at least be observed. . . . No good can result . . . from indiscriminate destruction of property or the burning of the homes of women and children."[47] While the march through Georgia declared war on Southern civilians' homes, commanders attempted to prevent unnecessary destruction. It remained to be seen whether officers and enlisted men would abide by these dictates.

FIG 5.4. Alfred Waud, "Stripping a rail fence for fires"—A common lament among female civilians—especially farming women—was that the Federal army dismantled their fences during raids. In this image, Waud depicted just such an occurrence. (Library of Congress)

It did not take long for Sherman's men to put raiding into effect. Just outside of Atlanta in Walton County, formerly enslaved woman Julia Cole recalled how "dem sojers went in de smokehouses and stores evvy-where and tuk what dey wanted." Just a few miles away in the town of Madison, plantation owner and widow Dolly Lunt Burge tried in vain to claim a guard. Before she could do so, "like Demons [the Federals] rush[ed] in." Even with a guard, soldiers "came up behind [the house] tore down all [my] garden palings, made a road through my back yard & lot field, driving their stock & riding through, tearing down my fences & desolating my home. Wantonly doing it when there was no necessity for it." Both enslaved women and plantation owners recalled Federals de-scending on them like locusts, taking what they wanted with such rapid-ity that women had no time to negotiate.[48]

Enlisted men feasted off of the bounty of Georgia civilians. William Baugh claimed that he "never lived so well in my life, as I did the last month," describing how he was "getting fat as butter." The overabundance came because soldiers "foraged them from the people." Alfred Wilcox reflected on raids in Oxford by describing soldiers who were "perfectly ignorant . . . that there is anyone else in the country to eat anything or use anything but ourselves." He was quite honest that raiding adversely affected the poor. "Anything we want we take wherever we find it no matter who owns it," he admitted. "The poor lose everything, the rich nearly all." When raiding, Sherman's soldiers did not take race, class, or political sympathies into account. As Wilcox explained, "War necessarily causes suffering and if we conduct it so as not to hurt anybody we shall not accomplish our purpose. Let the people feel the weight of the war and they will be anxious to have it end." The difficulty was that raiding hurt some more than others. While elites retained some provisions, poor white and Black women, as Wilcox himself admitted, fared the worst.[49]

Initially, central Georgia's African American women aided soldiers when they raided their enslavers' possessions. A group of Black women in Oxford directed Federals to where Confederates hid good horses and even offered to show them the exact location. Lester Dewitt Taylor remarked how local inhabitants "buried gold, silver, clothing, meal," all to no avail since "the negroes often tell us where to dig to find them." Near Fernsbridge, two Black women told Federals where white residents had hidden their belongings. Upon investigating, the soldiers found "dishes, 4 gallons of strained honey, [and] very nice dresses and clothes."[50] African Americans demonstrated their loyalty to the Union by betraying their enslavers and offering support to Federals who sought to deprive elite rebels of their possessions. They hoped to be treated with respect in return.

Federals often did not return the favor. Some soldiers even coerced African Americans into helping them with their raids. Della Briscoe of Putnam County recalled how U.S. soldiers tied her father's hands behind his back and forced him to show the soldiers where her enslaver had hidden his mares. This was after soldiers had "tore up the interior" of the house and eaten all they wanted from the farm. Rachel Adams insisted that Federals stole nearly everything her enslaver had, which only made her life and the lives of her fellow bondpeople more difficult. "Dat didn't look right, did it?" she tartly observed. Rather than an army of liberators, enslaved Georgians found that Sherman's men behaved like a marauding horde, ignoring the ways in which their destruction hurt their African American allies as well as their rebel enemies.[51]

In their words and behavior, Sherman's men resisted working as an army of emancipation. In Oxford, Alfred Wilcox encountered "several darkey women and men" who wished to follow the army. Rather than welcoming them, Wilcox discouraged the women from following. In spite of reluctant soldiers, "Wagon loads of men women and children" followed the army, bringing "horses, mules and ox teams and wagons." The scenes brought Wilcox no joy. He sourly remarked in his diary, "Before we get to Savannah we shall be over encumbered by them." Some Federals even bragged about how poorly they treated enslaved people. William Osborn recorded how he and his fellow soldiers stopped at a beautiful plantation. Rather than bothering the house's inhabitants, Osborn and his companions stole peanuts from "the N——s" and commenced roasting them in front of them.[52] The actions of Sherman's men seemed calculated to alienate African Americans. When soldiers could not see a direct benefit to themselves or the army, they treated African Americans as a hindrance at best and as inferior at worst.

Enlisted men often did not dwell on the raiding visited on African Americans. Instead, they focused on their pillaging of elite rebels. When the men reached the state capital of Milledgeville, all hell broke loose. William Osborn recounted how soldiers visited a planter's "beautiful Mansion. And in it was a Nice Piano and beautiful furniture and fine looking Girls—and some of our troops went into the House and broke up the furniture and destroyed the Piano and went as far as to take the Ribbons off of diplomas belonging to the girls who was Graduates of some Institution." Alfred Wilcox blamed Louisville's destruction on the fact that "there was no guard placed" so stragglers "sacked the town going into every house and taking or destroying every thing they pleased. Some one set a house on fire and it spread . . . and turned several families out of doors." The farther the army marched, the more opportunity it provided for soldiers in the front and the rear to engage in unlicensed destruction. Rather than making an example of these men, Sherman disavowed them.[53]

Once Federals reached wealthy Liberty County, they had a chance to plague elite Rebels and welcome enslaved people into their lines. They chose not to do so. When soldiers first arrived at the wealthy Pond plantation, they did not immediately go to the plantation house. Instead, they went straight to the cabins of enslaved people. Formerly enslaved woman Sylvia Baker recalled how she "cooked and worked for [the soldiers] till they went away." Perhaps she was happy to do so at first as a display of her loyalty. But she was upset when this was not enough for Federals, who "went on and took all the property from us," meaning the plantation's enslaved people. It was only after soldiers had appropriated Baker's labor and taken the property of enslaved people that they descended on Baker's enslavers. Baker found their behavior insulting, stating in a postwar claim: "They made no difference they took it all clean from white as well as from the blacks." Some Liberty County residents had amassed significant property. Jane Holmes's labor had built up property valued at $500. The soldiers took it all. She watched them come "right down the field" to her house and "they kept on coming in gangs till they had taken all the property." Soldiers took all of Linda Jones's chickens, hogs, corn, and rice. Underlining how much she lost that day, Jones testified, "They went on there & took all the property."[54] In Liberty County, Sherman's men behaved exactly the opposite of armies of liberation. Rather than recognizing the loyalty of African American women and leaving them some of their hard-earned property, the soldiers made no distinction between the meager possessions of loyal enslaved women and the abundant wealth of Confederate enslavers.

After stealing from enslaved women, Federals visited elite Confederates. The prominent Pond and Jones families found Federals' search for weapons to be the height of impudence. At the Pond plantation, soldiers searched "all the rooms . . . [taking] all the silverware and jewelry . . . and everything to eat that could be found." The relieved women of the house noted that Federals refrained from entering bedchambers. Numerous soldiers also visited the Jones and Mallard families and searched their homes from top to bottom. Although the soldiers only took a small gold pen from among the women's personal possessions—a fact they credited to their constant presence—Federals took nearly all their food. The soldiers told the women that the small sack of meal and rice remained "to keep us from starving. . . . At other times they told us they meant to starve us to death." When the women appealed for a guard, the men refused. Raiding would be meaningless if the wealthy could obtain guards for their property. While elite Confederate women viewed themselves as entitled to protection, some of Sherman's men refused to even shield rebels from raiding.[55]

Federal soldiers did not behave themselves once they arrived in Savannah. Here they continued to prey on Black women, who attempted to protect their significant property to no avail. Free woman Celia Boisfeillet tried to display her loyalty by aiding the Federal army but "did not have a chance to do anything for [them]" because "when they came here they helped themselves." Boisfeillet tried to reason with the soldiers, asking them to leave some of her possessions behind, telling them it was "hard to be stripped of every thing." The soldiers replied to her exactly as they had to Sarah Ann Black, accusing her of "hiding the things for the rebels or some white man." Rachel Bromfield had a similar interaction. Federals informed her as they took her property from her house that "it was secession property." When Bromfield challenged the men to ask her white neighbors who the property belonged to, they made no response and "went on & took it," even as the Federal prisoners Bromfield harbored tried to reason with them. Rather than taking the possessions of Savannah's wealthy Confederate residents, Sherman's men singled out Black women. In spite of a mountain of evidence to the contrary, soldiers redefined these women's property as belonging to white residents. They could have chosen to visit war's hardships on wealthy rebels. Instead, Sherman's men made it clear to Black women that they would not extend to them the same courtesy as they extended to Savannah's white women.[56]

Federals made no mention of their destruction of Black women's property in Liberty and Chatham Counties. Some even went so far as to avow, as did Ohioan Lester Dewitt Taylor, that "all private property as well as public" was respected in Savannah. In this way, soldiers stole from enslaved and free Black women and then denied that they had done so. Their reshaping of the historical record made it seem as though they had visited war's hardships equally on Georgia's civilians. In their postwar testimony before the Southern Claims Commission, the Peach State's Black women set the record straight, insisting that they had tried—and failed—to redirect white soldiers' foraging to the disloyal rather than the loyal.[57]

Depredations and Restraint: The March Through the Carolinas, Winter 1865

If raiding ever wore kid gloves, they came off once Sherman's army entered South Carolina. Sherman's orders in the "cradle of secession" stated that he "want[ed] the people of the south to realize that fact that they shall not dictate laws of war or peace to us." The Federal army, he argued, "[has] a perfect war right to the products of the country we overrun. . . . Let the whole people know that the war is now against them, because their armies . . . do not . . . defend their women and children and prevent us reaching their homes." Sherman's words should give us pause, not because of his methods but because of the women and children he left out of his directives. Like the men in his army, Sherman referred to white women and children, those people left defenseless by the Confederate army. His orders were entirely silent about African American women and children, almost as if they did not exist. And therein lay the problem: In a state whose Black population neared 60 percent, Sherman's directives only extended to a minority of civilians.[58]

By this point, South Carolina's Black women knew that they would bear the brunt of war's brutality unless they intervened. Perhaps they had heard through the grapevine telegraph of how Sherman's soldiers had conducted themselves in Liberty and Chatham Counties. However they heard, they left nothing to chance. Amie Lumpkin, who lived near Columbia, described how she and other enslaved people prevented their enslavers' houses from being burned by "stand[ing] by de side of de road" and entreating Union soldiers "not te burn our white folks' house."[59] Their pleas worked, demonstrating that even this late in the war, the active involvement of Southern women could still shape military policy toward civilians.

While enslaved women spared plantation houses, Federals' arrival meant a lack of food and shelter. Rosa Starks remembered that soldiers left "one thousand" enslaved African Americans "cold and hungry." In Woodward, Josephine Stewart recalled that Federals' destruction resulted in everyone on the plantation being put on "short rations." Winnsboro resident Mary Woodward was incensed by a more personal Yankee thievery, as one soldier "took my lovely beads and put them 'round his horse's neck . . . leavin' me sobbin'." "They say you must love your enemies . . . but I never have pray for dat Yankee scamp," Woodward confessed.[60] The treatment enslaved women experienced at the hands of Sherman's men did not endear the U.S. Army to them. With beloved possessions stolen and the pangs of hungry bellies, African American women viewed Federals more as their enemies than their friends.

Federals' callous attitudes toward Black women were on full display when the Fifteenth and Seventeenth Corps, infamous for their destruction, arrived in Beaufort. Their presence in a town occupied by the U.S. Army since November 1861 seems curious, and they did not acquit themselves well while they were there. People who had self-emancipated early in the war and built up a living for themselves found that soldiers evaporated their possessions.

Freedwoman Harriet Smith recalled bitterly that Sherman's men "did not spare either white nor black." Rose Goethe "found [Union soldiers] in my house which they had broken open." "They cleaned me out entirely," Goethe remarked. Federals took "every beast" and all of the corn that Mary Orr owned. Orr had to beg soldiers for her clothes, which they only "gave . . . back to me" because of her pleas.[61] The most notorious corps in Sherman's army visited special destruction on loyal Southern women. The only explanation is that these men delighted in preying on freed African Americans, doing so to remind them of their place in the country's racial hierarchy.

As Federals worked their way up the coast, they took so much from some self-emancipated Black women that the women became dependent on the government for survival. Freeborn Agnes Jackson had so far lived free from interference from either Federals or Confederates, but when Sherman's men arrived in the vicinity, she experienced repeated raids. They became so intrusive that she "begged for protection" from "a gentleman who I judged to be a high officer." The officer refused to grant her a safeguard, instead telling her that she was not safe in her home but "would have to go across the river to Beaufort." Federals went so far as to take possession of her house, forcing Jackson to gather up her three young daughters and set out on foot to seek refuge on Port Royal Island.[62] Similar to the loyal white women in northwestern Georgia, Jackson tried to remain self-sufficient and independent throughout the war, and her application for protection was designed to keep her and her family from dependence on the government. Some soldiers made that impossible, taking so much from her that she was forced to leave her home.

Ties to the Federal army did not dissuade soldiers from taking freeborn Lavinia Cohen's property. Even though her husband had provided important information about Confederate numbers and movements to the U.S. military, Sherman's men paid no mind. Cohen and her husband were so destitute after the raid that they appealed to Federal headquarters at Hilton Head Island to "furnis[h]" them with "some provisions as we had been entirely broke up by the first lot that came through." Sherman's army rendered even manifestly loyal African Americans to a level of dependency on the Federal military, meaning a Black couple who had been free for decades now competed with newly freed people on the Sea Islands for limited resources.[63]

South Carolina's white Unionist women fared better with Federals. Nancy Sandifer of Barnwell County watched Union soldiers take all of her fowl, destroy her beehives, and requisition her corn and fodder. And yet Sandifer asked for and obtained a guard to watch over her house. Ann Mew, an elderly woman who lived on the Coosawhatchie River, had much of her property taken but felt satisfied after complaining to the officer in charge. "He protected us personally," she recalled, "and prohibited the soldiers from swearing and told them that we were ladies and that they must not take my clothes." Even desperately poor white Unionist women fared better than African Americans, because soldiers recognized them as women and extended to them some protection. When individual officers determined which Southern civilians received safeguards, racist hostility played a role in who obtained protection and who was left on their own.

Elite Confederate women convinced themselves that they suffered the worst of Sherman's destruction. Aiken resident Pauline DeCaradeuc readied herself for Yankee raids, describing how she and her family were in "most fearful times." DeCaradeuc simply knew that her family's wealth would make them a target. In some ways, she was correct. Soldiers repeatedly visited the DeCaradeuc plantation over two days. The men called them "d[amne]d rebels" and demanded "liquor . . . gold . . . [and] silver," broke open every "door, drawer, [and] trunk," smashed mirrors and furniture, and threw clothing all over the floors. DeCaradeuc's mother's entreaty to a Federal officer did no good: Although the man claimed to be "disgusted with all this [destruction]," he walked into another room, "broke open" a trunk, and "began stuffing his pockets." DeCaradeuc viewed the raids as revenge for Confederates firing "the first gun on Sumter," which meant Federals felt compelled to "arrest and shoot every influential citizen . . . every mover of secession." But Sherman's men made no arrests and shot no influential secessionists. They did destroy many of the DeCaradeucs' possessions, but that was all. The DeCaradeucs had certainly never been treated so insolently. But compared to some women, whose livelihoods were ruined and who were turned out of their houses, the wealthy plantation owners fared well.[64]

Although they would never admit it, some elite Confederates benefited from Federals' presence. Women living on the outskirts of Columbia housed Union generals and benefited from guards over their property. Plantation mistress Mary Maxcy Leverett endured one day of destruction by Union soldiers before one of Sherman's generals made her house his headquarters. Leverett responded by lambasting Federals for "warring on women & children." "I pointed to the ruined town," she described of one exchange, "and asked if *this* was what *they* styled 'civilized warfare'? and told them not a nation in Europe in the nineteenth-century would be guilty of such an outrage." Leverett and other elite, educated Confederates like her surely knew that such claims were demonstrably false. But rhetoric accusing Federals of unprecedented outrages served the rebel cause. Leverett characterized Sherman's army as "composed almost wholly of North Western men & they are a regularly educated set of thieves, burglars, robbers & house burners—& are accomplished villains."[65] Far from appreciating the protection, Leverett used her proximity to Federal soldiers to excoriate them for their style of warfare. They neither stole from her, robbed her, nor burned her home, but this behavior did not change her opinion of them one bit.

Other wealthy rebels seemed more cognizant that Federals let them off easy. Grace Brown Elmore was spared much destruction, thanks to a visit by General Sherman. His men confined themselves mostly to taking her food. Even so, Elmore marveled at the meanness of Federals: not to her, but to her enslaved people. "The negroes were not saved, their clothes, their bread, all that they owned was taken," Elmore recorded. As Elmore well understood, her wealth and status spared her from much destruction. Sherman's men felt no such compunction when it came to enslaved South Carolinians, a group of people to whom they meted out unequal destruction.[66]

Enslaved women on Columbia's outskirts had bitter memories of Federals. Rather than armies of liberation, they encountered soldiers who treated them worse than their rebel enslavers. Victoria Adams was held in bondage on a plantation in Fairfield County. When the Union army visited, the soldiers "'stroyed most everything we had 'cept a little vittles; took all de stock and take them wid them." To add insult to injury, Federals "burned all de buildings 'cept de one de massa and missus was livin' in." The men then asked Adams if she wanted to be free. "I never say I did; I tell them I want to stay wid my missus and they went on and let me alone." Based on how the U.S. Army had acted, Adams felt uncomfortable answering their question about freedom and preferred to remain where she was. For Adams, raiding's legacy was hunger and exposure to the elements.[67]

Union soldiers' behavior changed dramatically once the army entered North Carolina. Sherman and his command issued orders "not to destroy" civilian property. And officers and enlisted men seemed less inclined to wreak destruction. As John Boon explained, "the state was the last one to secede and then not until she was forced out." For these reasons, Boon had not seen "half a dozen houses fired in this state." Lester Dewitt Taylor seemed encouraged that once the army entered Fayetteville, "there was a large turn out of citizens to view us on our entrance than at any place in Geo[rgia] or S.C."[68] The presence of white Unionists and orders from on high kept Federals a bit more in line in the Tar Heel State.

Better behavior did not mean that soldiers refrained from unwarranted destruction. John A. Boon went to a house that had been burned and found "gold and silver melted together," the amount of which was estimated by "a Negro woman" as being "$32,000. . . . It is made into rings by some of the boys." Elliott McKeever, who raged at a mother's house being burned to the ground, felt no qualms about going "right on to the corncrib" at another house to "get my sack filled. There were two women and some children huddled in the back in the room as I passed but I did not stop." While Lester Taylor was encouraged by the presence of white Unionists, he and his compatriots ensured that "the territory through which we passed . . . was more than made desolate; we left scarcely nothing except N[egro] huts."[69] While soldiers went a bit easier on North Carolina, they still had to live off the land. Rather than widespread incendiarism, they confined themselves to taking foodstuffs.

White Unionist women noticed the change in tactics. Near Fayetteville, Mary Carver complained directly to General Howard about the taking of her property. Howard responded by giving Carver as many provisions "as my son and myself could carry home." The elderly Abigail Eldridge had a more difficult time obtaining redress. Even though she objected to "the men taking my property," she could get "no satisfaction from them." In Johnston County, "poor lone widow" Jane Royals watched as soldiers "went to the lot and took [her] horse and to the smoke house and took [her] meat." Sarah Bailey, residing near Raleigh, begged Union soldiers not to take her property, and only received assurances from a Union soldier that "protections would be made to care of [her]." Although Federals seemed more restrained in North Carolina, they continued to take provisions and supplied rations when women had nothing left.[70]

Free Black women had much of their property taken and protested in vain. Elsie Drake watched as Union soldiers took not only food but also water buckets, bed quilts, blankets, and shawls. Drake noted that the soldiers "just came in my house and took any they pleased." Ann Revels was treated much more courteously, going so far as to describe one Federal as "gentlemanly" because he told her that he "must have [her property] for his men must be fed" and "that [she] *must* not think hard of him for taking it." The soldiers even offered a guard but refused to protect anything but the house. That some Federals behaved courteously toward North Carolina's African American women demonstrates that while most of Sherman's men treated Black women with contempt, individuals could make different choices.

The Tar Heel State's Black women approved of raiding when soldiers restricted their ire toward treasonous enslavers. Eveline Morgan of Wedgeboro, North Carolina, watched as the Yankees came through after her enslaver had fled, "breaking into things . . . and throw[ing] things around." Morgan blamed the destruction on the fact that her "old master was a senator; they wanted to git him. They sure did cuss him. . . . They was after senators and high-ups like that," she explained. Angeline Martin felt that she fared better once Federals came to town. Her owners fled the Yankees, leaving her and her parents on the homestead. Martin recalled how the "Yankees come [to her owner's house] and used it for headquarters. . . . They didn't burn up nothin' just kill the hogs and chickens and give us plenty."[71] Enslaved women sanctioned Federals living off the land when destruction was confined to the luxurious possessions of their enslavers.

Union soldiers' ravenous appetites stood out to North Carolina's enslaved women. Tempie Herndon Durham explained simply that Yankees were "all de time hungry," and many women remembered the soldiers' penchant for the smokehouse. Fannie Dunn found raiding to be entirely frustrating, because "one Yankee would come along an' give us" something to eat "an' another would come on behind him an' take it." Indeed, enslaved women seemed fed up with U.S. soldiers who not only commanded but expected obedience from them. In response, some women allied themselves with enslavers rather than Federals. Susan High's mother saved her enslaver from being killed by Yankees when he refused to disclose where his valuables were located. Sherman's march brought hunger, difficult decisions, and impossible situations to the doors of North Carolina's enslaved women. They would have to make freedom for themselves after war's end.[72]

Sherman's men continued their disparate treatment of Southern civilians as they made their way through the Carolinas. While some elite Confederates did experience property destruction, others benefited from the presence of Federals through generals who used their homes as headquarters. Particularly around Beaufort, soldiers subjected a group of people who had been free since almost the beginning of the war to widespread property destruction, creating straightened circumstances and dependency on the Federal government. While soldiers restrained themselves from incendiarism in North Carolina, they continued raiding from both white and Black civilians. By this point in the war, soldiers believed that paying attention to loyalty and listening to civilian women's complaints would only prolong the conflict.

"War Corrupts the Pure and Innocent": Surrender, Spring 1865

Raiding continued in Virginia during the last weeks and months of Federal campaigns. In many places, soldiers used raiding as retaliation against Confederates. Near Nottoway, rumors of Confederate deserters who attacked Federals were enough for the army to raid the region and set "almost every house on fire." In the Richmond environs, W. W. Parker delighted in destroying the home of Libby Prison's owner, describing it as a "perfect desolation." Rufus Smith, in camp at Chesterfield Court House, summarized that by May, "The Whites were all sick of the war . . . and they are now as humble as the blacks are themselves."[73] Federals congratulated themselves for asserting their superiority over rebel civilians and Virginia's African Americans, and they believed that raiding had accomplished its goal of striking fear and dread into the hearts of all Southerners.

Federals did not spare the loyal. Ellen Carpenter, the sister of a U.S. Navy officer and an invalid, could not secure protection of her property. While the army was encamped on her brother's plantation in Spotsylvania County, soldiers took food, horses, cattle, sheep, corn, and even cured tobacco. Carpenter's status distanced her from dealing with raiding personally: When she heard that soldiers intended to force open the door to the cornhouse, Carpenter had one of her enslaved men send out the key. When she tried to halt the proceedings by explaining that the corn and other food were needed to feed her family and enslaved people, the soldiers appeared unmoved, simply telling her to obtain a quartermaster's receipt. Although Carpenter's wealth and bondpeople distanced her from direct contact with Federal soldiers, her loyalty and relation to a navy officer did not benefit her. Soldiers did not destroy her plantation, but her attempts to save her property were unsuccessful.[74]

Poor loyal women continued to labor for the army even as soldiers raided their homes and gardens. Octavia New of Charles City did not have time to notice the men who took her horses, pigs, geese, turkeys, and fifteen bushels of potatoes, because she was "cooking for the soldiers" at the time. By March 1865, Lydia Fishburn had already supplied Union soldiers on two other occasions. When Sheridan's men stopped by her home toward the close of the war, she had nothing left to give them but "pantry stores," including bacon, butter, lard, sorghum, and vinegar. Although Fishburn complained, it did no good, for the soldiers told her they needed "the provisions to eat."[75] In contrast to elite women, poor loyal women provided Federals with their physical labor and their material possessions. While the women hoped for a gendered exchange—they cooked, laundered, and sewed while Federals spared their pantry—soldiers no longer listened to women's attempts to bargain or negotiate.

RAIDING BEGAN AS a collaboration between Black women, abolitionist white commanders, and Black Federal soldiers. Along the Sea Islands of South Carolina and Georgia, the U.S. Army and Southern women worked together to liberate enslaved people, attack Confederate war resources, and destroy plantations. But white abolitionist officers' worries about pushback combined with pressure from Democratic and Confederate newspapers to discourage these collaborative raids. When Grant, Sherman, and Sheridan came east in 1864, they brought raiding with them but eschewed collaboration and negotiation with Southern women. Rather than armies of liberation who targeted Confederates, Western commanders and enlisted men insisted that raiding treat all civilians, loyal and disloyal, Black and white, as war's passive victims. While this style of raiding did not mandate unequal treatment, it ignored African American women as allies to such an extent that individual officers and enlisted men could choose to focus war's destruction on them. While elite women certainly suffered, enslaved women suffered even more, particularly during Sherman's campaigns, a fact noticed even by enslavers. The army's raiding policies in the last years of the war sought to cast the military as the driver of policy and civilian women as war's passive victims. It did not fully succeed. Southern women continued to vigorously participate in shaping Federal military policy toward civilians, a fact they made quite clear in postwar testimony before the Southern Claims Commission.

Conclusion

JUST AS THE FEDERAL MILITARY attempted to sideline Southern women through raiding policies, civilians in the immediate postwar period wrote Southern women—Black women in particular—out of the war. Postwar literature on wartime service categorized women's involvement as loyal Northern white women versus rebel Southern women. Brockett and Vaughan's 1867 *Woman's Work in the Civil War* entirely excluded African American women, focusing on white Northern women with small sections about loyal white Southern women. That same year, elite Confederate Sallie Ann Brock published *Richmond During the War*, dedicated to her "southern sisters, who, in the cause of the late Southern Confederacy . . . 'did all that woman ever dares.'"[1] Women had either been loyal, Northern, and white, or rebel Southern ladies. Where were the stories of free Black women providing intelligence? Enslaved women risking life and limb to reach Federal lines? White Unionist enslavers who became rebels after emancipation? Poor Confederate women who demanded support from the Union army? These more complex stories, stories that revealed women's active political involvement in preserving their homes in a war over slavery, were much harder to access, buried in military reports and personal letters and diaries.

It was not until six years after the war that hundreds of Southern women would speak out about their active involvement in the war. They did so in testimony before a committee established by Congress, the Southern Claims Commission, to compensate loyal Southerners for contributions to the war effort. But by this point, the nation was in the throes of Reconstruction. Mountains of written testimony presented to a congressional committee went largely unnoticed. And yet it is within these files that Southern women spoke clearly and authoritatively about their wartime contributions and the ways in which they shaped and negotiated Federal military policy.[2]

Elizabeth Garey seized the chance to tell her story and make clear her manifold contributions to the success of the U.S. Army. She quickly filed a large claim of $3,400 for the destruction of her house and requisition of her cow, food stockpiles, furniture, kitchen supplies, and crockery. But Garey also clearly stated that her contributions well surpassed material goods, highlighting how she had personally, and at great cost to herself and her family, passed along information about blockade running and Confederate militia and troop locations. In the opinion of the special commissioner, she had "aid[ed] the movements of the army by imparting information and . . . saving many valuable lives." Both of her adult sons had served in the navy. Her claim was so compelling that the special commissioner pleaded for the commission to make an exception to its rules. He admitted that most of the claim was for "property *destroyed* . . . few of the 3,400 for property taken & used by the Army," the usual standard for reimbursement. "I have allowed the hearing . . . for the reason that the case is one of peculiar hardship—to very excellent loyal people. It would be a human act and a commendable one for Congress to make a donation of 5 or 10 thousand dollars to that family." But Congress had been disinclined to even accept claims from Black Unionists. Its decision to rule out property destruction for compensation disadvantaged free and enslaved Black Southerners, who experienced destruction out of proportion with their numbers. Commissioners gave Elizabeth Garey the paltry sum of thirty-four dollars. The amount did not even compensate her for the loss of her cow.[3] The inequity African American women experienced during the raids at the end of the Civil War continued in the postwar period. Black women like Elizabeth Garey risked their lives to provide intelligence and collaborate on raids yet received neither recognition nor adequate compensation. The Claims Commission continued the federal military's unequal treatment of Southern Black women.

Elizabeth Garey's experience with the Southern Claims Commission demonstrates that the Civil War ended like it began—with little acknowledgment of the war's effect on Southern women and children. At the beginning of the conflict, the army preoccupied itself with white male Southern civilians, concerned that any provocation would motivate them to enlist en masse in the Confederate army. The policy of conciliation resulted from such fears. When politicians and military men spared a thought for Southern women, it was for white women, whom they believed in need of the army's protection. The military gave little thought to Black women, certain that bonded people would not play a role in the grand drama of civil war.

And yet Southern civilians played a crucial role in the conflict from the very beginning. Confederate ladies opposed the Union and supported rebels in both word and deed. White Unionists expected a gendered exchange, one in which Federals would protect them and their human property in recognition of their loyalty. And Black women insisted that they could be useful to the army and help end the war, if only the military would recognize their loyalty. Policies of conciliation could not withstand this onslaught.

Southern women's actions pushed the U.S. Army toward harsher war policies. Small numbers of white Unionists and the very obvious advantage that enslaved women provided to rebels made everyone from commanders to enlisted men question why exactly the army protected slavery. But it was the brazen deception of rebel ladies that motivated Federals to act. These women did not need protection when they unapologetically used their gender as a shield for treasonous activities. By mid-1862, the army began to change its policies toward civilians, in part due to the deception of rebel ladies.

New policies of confiscation, foraging, and emancipation brought war into Southern women's homes. In the Eastern theater, the army punished rebel women for their treason by encouraging enslaved people into its lines, following the mandates of the Confiscation Acts. In the Western theater, conciliationist commanders and large numbers of proslavery soldiers balked at interfering with slavery. When they did, they ignored confiscation's injunctions that the policy was voluntary, forcing Black women to labor for them and illegally removing others from their lines, characterizing them as a nuisance. Even with harsher war policies, Southern women insisted on negotiating the ways in which Federals implemented hard war. Rebels argued and accused, white and free Black Unionists framed policies as a gendered exchange, and enslaved Black women resisted Federals who appropriated their labor and wasted their property. In sum, Federals did not enact harsher war policies on a passive civilian population but struggled with civilian women regarding who had control over domestic spaces.

The most transformative military policy of all, emancipation, coincided with a sharp increase in Southern women accusing Federal soldiers of sexual assault. Wartime rumor in the wake of the destruction of slavery spread malicious gossip warning of Black Federals preying on white women. In reality, wartime sexual assault was usually perpetrated by white Federals on enslaved and free Black women and girls, who brought accusations against their rapists and pushed the army toward laws of war that prosecuted soldiers who committed crimes against civilians. Even as Black women insisted that the army hold soldiers who sexually assaulted them responsible, Black Federals had to defend themselves against spurious charges by poor white women. In a sharp break with the antebellum status quo, Black women and girls gained more rights even as Black men lost the protections of a slave system that regarded them as valuable laborers.

Emancipation also created new alliances between Black female civilians, Black Federals, and white commanders. The policy of raiding originated along the Sea Islands as a collaborative policy designed to target Confederate plantations and liberate enslaved people. But it lost this focus on liberation when Western commanders moved east. Now in charge of the entire Federal military, Ulysses S. Grant handed down orders to destroy Confederate war resources and ruin rebel morale. Raids under Sheridan and Sherman not only spurned cooperation with loyal women but rejected emancipation. Sherman in particular was indifferent if not hostile toward Black women and children, and his enlisted men often singled out enslaved and free African American women for particularly devastating destruction. In the last year of the war, Federal commanders spurned negotiation with Southern women. They attempted to put themselves firmly in control of military policy, insisting that the Federal army needed to subdue both the rebel military and Southern women. They were not entirely successful. As testimony from the Southern Claims Commission makes clear, Southern women continued to influence military policy toward civilians until the very last days of the conflict.

Emblematic of these intrepid Southern women is Elizabeth Garey, who demonstrates civilian women's crucial wartime contributions. She did not remain on the sidelines waiting for the Federal military to win the war. Instead, she actively involved herself, providing intelligence that led to the burning of Darien and the destruction of rice and cotton crucial to the Confederate war effort. The assistance provided by Southern women like Garey undoubtedly benefited the U.S. Army and contributed to its success. By paying attention to their stories, it is clear that Southern women drove policy and influenced the Federal army in ways it never imagined and, in the postwar period, in ways it often refused to acknowledge.

ACKNOWLEDGMENTS

THIS BOOK has taken me on an incredible journey, from its origins in Joshua Rothman's spring 2010 research seminar to its finished form. Throughout this long (and sometimes torturous) process, I have benefited from the help and support of numerous people.

This manuscript and I began our journey in the History Department at the University of Alabama, where George Rable asked a question that started it all: Why hadn't historians written about the interactions of U.S. soldiers and Southern women? I took this question and ran with it, and George has cheered me on and steered me right ever since. His humility, patience, and generosity never cease to amaze. My dissertation committee, Lesley Gordon, Mark Grimsley, Holly Grout, and Joshua Rothman, provided excellent feedback in the transition from dissertation to manuscript. A special thank-you to research support from the Filson Historical Society, U.S. Army Heritage and Education Center, and Virginia Museum of History and Culture.

I will never forget the collegial atmosphere and supportive community of Kalamazoo College. Special thanks to Dennis Frost for his excellent mentorship, and to Joshua and Rose Hartman, Ivett López Malagamba, Stephen Oloo, Michael Powers, Kathryn Sederberg, Darshana Udayanganie, and McKenzie West for their camaraderie and companionship.

From Michigan, the manuscript and I ended up in Texas. A Junior Faculty Summer Research Grant from the University of Houston–Victoria provided needed support in summer of 2021. Colleagues Kevin Auer, Esther Liberman Cuenca, Nicole Eugene, Craig Goodman, Saidat Ilo, Anthony Madrid, Amina Patton, and Nadya Pittendrigh provided pep talks and a supportive environment. Friends Justin, Sam, and Michael Bell; Joe, Tess, Jane, and Kate Locke; and Sharon Stubblefield and Dan Jeziro commiserated during hard times and celebrated during victories.

Now I find myself in the Magnolia State, not two hundred miles from where it all began. It is here that I found the right fit at the University of Georgia Press. Thanks to Mick Gusinde-Duffy for decisive answers and quick email responses. Series editors Steve Berry, Amy Murrell Taylor, and Fay Yarbrough have lent much of their collective wisdom to this project and came up with the excellent title. Special thanks to Amy for her guidance during the revisions process, and to the two anonymous reviewers for their helpful feedback. The University of Southern Mississippi has given me the time and clarity needed to put the finishing touches on this work. My former school director, Matthew Casey, and mentors Courtney Luckhardt and Joe Peterson deserve a special shout-out for their listening ears and good advice. The Orazio A. Ciccarelli Fund for faculty development provided much appreciated financial support. Colleagues in the Dale Center for the Study of War and Society, including Kyle Zelner, Andy Wiest, Heather Stur, Kevin Greene, and Ken Swope, got me oriented and answered many, many questions. Thank you to Rebecca Tuuri and Deanne Stephens for their encouragement. Robby Desmond, *Chicago Manual of Style* wizard, helped me out when I was in a bind. My colleagues and friends in the Humanities Writing Group deserve a special thank-you: Reynolds Bodenhammer, Eliza Holmes, Erika Luckert, Katya Maslakowski, Jason McCormick, Bafumiki Mocheregwa, and Christopher Spaide. Once this is out, the party is at my house.

Civil War colleagues and friends provided excellent feedback and wise advice, including Angela Diaz, Jonathan Lande, and Evan Rothera. To Megan Bever, Laura June Davis, Angela Esco Elder, Lindsay Smith Privette, Lauren Thompson, and Dave Thomson: This work would not be nearly as fun or rewarding without the six of you. I'm so glad we have each other.

None of this would have been possible without the love and support of my family. To Alison, Jim, Maria, and Alix, I love you more than words can express. To Nita, Steve, Ali Grace, Cody, Curtis, Ruthie, and Caleb, y'all are so much more than in-laws.

This book is dedicated to my best friend and life partner, Stephen. Some days I can't believe how lucky I am to have so much love and laughter in my life. I'm beyond grateful for you, our cats, and the home we've built.

NOTES

Introduction

1. Emilio, *History of the Fifty-Fourth Regiment*, 41–42; Duncan, *Blue-Eyed Child of Fortune*, 342–44, 348; U.S. War Department, *War of the Rebellion: A Compilation of the Official Records of the Union and Confederate Armies* (hereafter *Official Records* or *OR*), ser. 1, 14:466–67; Foote, *Rites of Retaliation*, 68–78; Higginson, *Complete Civil War Journal*, 288–89.

2. Stephens, *Voice of Thunder*, 241–42; Emilio, *History of the Fifty-Fourth Regiment*, 44; Gooding, *On the Altar of Freedom*, 30; Dyer, *Compendium of the War*, 365, 700; Egerton, *Thunder at the Gates*, 100–106; 1860 U.S. Federal Census—Slave Schedule, M653. *OR*, ser. 1, 14:318 demonstrates that Darien citizens worked closely with the rebel military.

3. Foote, *Rites of Retaliation*, 68–78.

4. Testimonies of Elizabeth Garey and Charles A. Garey, Claim of Elizabeth Geary [*sic*], Chatham County, Georgia, Records of the Accounting Officers of the Department of the Treasury, Southern Claims Commission, Record Group 217, National Archives, Washington, D.C. (hereafter SCC-NA); *Savannah Republican*, June 19, 1863; *Savannah Daily Morning News*, June 16, 1863; 1860 U.S. Federal Census, M653; *OR*, ser. 1, 14:191, 6:278, 305; Rable, *God's Almost Chosen Peoples*, 241–42.

5. Susie King Taylor, *Reminiscences of My Life*, 9, 38.

6. Testimonies of Elizabeth Garey and Charles A. Garey, Claim of Elizabeth Geary [*sic*], SCC-NA; 1860 U.S. Census; *OR*, ser. 1, 14:318–19.

7. Glymph, "Archives of a Different Sort."

8. Blair, *With Malice Toward Some*; Grimsley, *Hard Hand of War*; Manning, *Troubled Refuge*; Mathisen, *Loyal Republic*; Neely, *Civil War and the Limits*; Royster, *Destructive War*.

9. For the memory of the Revolutionary War in the Federal military, see Grimsley, *Hard Hand of War*, 18–19, 20; for its memory among Southern white women, see Glymph, *Women's Fight*, 11, 21, 213–17; for female civilians as white, see *Women's Fight*, 89.

10. See "wartime citizenship" in Manning, *Troubled Refuge*, 205–7; Mathisen, *Loyal Republic*, 87–117.

11. Sutherland, *Savage Conflict*, 109; see also 95, 97.

12. Whites, *Gender Matters*, 45–64; Whites, "'Corresponding with the Enemy,'" 103–16; Streater, "'She Rebels' on the Supply Line," 88–102; Beilein, *Bushwackers*.

13. Campbell, *When Sherman Marched North*; Frank, *Civilian War*; Whites and Long, *Occupied Women*.

14. Foucault, *History of Sexuality*, 11–12. These insights are informed by Foucault's insistence that power is local.

15. Enslaving women elevated themselves as "models of domestic virtue" while eliding the way they and their homes "depended on the work of slave women." Glymph, *Out of the House of Bondage*, 6.

16. Enslavers frequently used the language of domesticity to justify the backbreaking household labor of enslaved women and girls. Bercaw, *Gendered Freedoms*, 2–6; Frankel, *Freedom's Women*, 1–13; Glymph, *Out of the House of Bondage*, 2, 21, 38, 42–43, 66–67; Jennifer Morgan, *Laboring Women*, 36, 40, 49, 69, 75–77, 100–102, 105–6, 135.

17. Campbell, *When Sherman Marched North*; Frank, *Civilian War*.

18. The plantation household was "a workplace, not a haven from the economic world," and was not "private or made so by the nature of the labor performed within it or the sex of the managers." Glymph, *Out of the House of Bondage*, 3.

19. Ash, *Firebrand of Liberty*; Brasher, *Peninsula Campaign*; Cimprich, *Navigating Liberty*; Lang, *In the Wake of War*; Manning, *Troubled Refuge*; Robinson, *Bitter Fruits of Bondage*; Amy Murrell Taylor, *Embattled Freedom*.

20. Romeo, *Gender and the Jubilee*; Glymph, *Out of the House of Bondage*.

21. For domesticity, see Bynum, *Unruly Women*; Cott, *Bonds of Womanhood*; Halttunen, *Confidence Men and Painted Women*; Jeffry, *Frontier Women*; Kasson, *Rudeness and Civility*; Stansell, *City of Women*; Wells, *Origins of the Southern Middle Class*; Welter, "Cult of True Womanhood."

22. Fields and Fields argue that one of the great tricks of racists is to disguise racism as race, making "racism . . . something Afro-Americans are, rather than something racists do." Fields and Fields, *Racecraft*, 96–97.

23. Scholarship establishes the Southern household as a place of political, economic, and reproductive significance. I expand on this work by exploring white and Black Southern women's choice to emphasize home over household. Bardaglio, *Reconstructing the Household*; Scott, *Southern Lady*; Fox-Genovese, *Within the Plantation Household*; Glymph, *Out of the House of Bondage*.

24. Glymph, *Out of the House of Bondage*, 7.

25. Fox-Genovese, *Within the Plantation Household*, 35, 65.

26. Fields and Fields, *Racecraft*, 84.

27. Fields and Fields argue that "Euro-Americans resolved the contradiction between slavery and liberty by defining Afro-Americans as a race; Afro-Americans resolved the contradiction more straightforwardly by calling for the abolition of slavery." Fields and Fields, *Racecraft*, 141; for antislavery politics, see Glymph, *Women's Fight*, 89.

28. Kerber, *Women of the Republic*, 36.

29. Quotation from Brill, *Weaker Sex in War*, 10; see also Elder, *Love and Duty*; Giesberg, *Army at Home*; Glymph, *Women's Fight*; McCurry, *Confederate Reckoning*; McCurry, *Women's War*.

30. Nineteenth-century women and men did not inhabit two "separate spheres" but the same world divided along lines of gender and race. Attie, *Patriotic Toil*; Boydston, *Home and Work*; Bynum, *Unruly Women*; Faust, *Mothers of Invention*; Giesberg, *Army at Home*; McCurry, *Masters of Small Worlds*; Varon, *We Mean to Be Counted*; Whites, *Gender Matters*.

31. Browning, *Shifting Loyalties*; Campbell, *When Sherman Marched North*; Frank, *Civilian War*; Romeo, *Gender and the Jubilee*.

32. Camp, *Closer to Freedom*; Glymph, *Out of the House of Bondage*, 14–15n38; Fulton, *Speaking Power*.

33. For similar methodology, see Rable, *God's Almost Chosen Peoples*.

34. Grimsley, *Hard Hand of War*, 14–16; Lang, *In the Wake of War*; Royster, *Destructive War*, 83; Sheehan-Dean, *Calculus of Violence*, 31–32; Witt, *Lincoln's Code*, 16–19, 51, 70–72.

35. Banner, *American Beauty*, 50–56; Halttunen, *Confidence Men and Painted Women*; Kasson, *Rudeness and Civility*; Mammina, "Domesticity in Conflict."

36. Bercaw, *Gendered Freedoms*; Glymph, *Women's Fight*; McCurry, *Confederate Reckoning*; Oakes, *Freedom National*.

37. Lorien Foote makes the excellent case for Civil War historians to think beyond the term "home front," which she argues is a modern anachronism that poorly describes the complex conditions of the conflict. See Foote, "Rethinking the Confederate Home Front."

Chapter One. Southern Women and the Chaos of Conciliation

1. *OR*, ser. 1, pt. 1, 16:59; see also *OR*, ser. 1, 7:669. Outside of a few elite Southern men who advised Buell and defended him during his trial, the voices of civilians are absent. See *OR*, ser. 1, pt. 1, 16:479–82, 484; *OR*, ser. 1, pt. 1, 16:497, 502–3.

2. *OR*, ser. 1, pt. 1, 16:8–9; Mortenson, *Politician in Uniform*, 102–3.

3. Scott, *Memoirs of Lieut.-General Scott*, 2:611; Grimsley, *Hard Hand of War*, 23–28; for the decentralization of the U.S. Army, see Sheehan-Dean, *Calculus of Violence*, 5; Grimsley, *Hard Hand of War*, 35.

4. Scott, *Memoirs of Lieut.-General Scott*, 2:625–28.

5. These findings are based on data gleaned from the *Official Records*. A keyword search of the *OR* returned seventy-nine results in which commanders used "citizens" in close proximity to "woman," "women," "lady," or "ladies." Of seventy-nine results, "citizen" was synonymous with men fifty times, in which citizens, women, and children were separate categories. Only twenty-nine times did "citizen" indicate both men and women, and this usage only occurred in the war's latter years.

6. Lincoln himself articulated all of these principles in his "Proclamation Calling Militia and Convening Congress" on April 15, 1861. Lincoln, *Collected Works*, 4:332; see *OR*, ser. 1, pt. 1, 51:331–32, 334, 369–70.

7. Grimsley, *Hard Hand of War*, 14, 16–17.

8. Lincoln, *Collected Works*, 4:150; Ash, *When the Yankees Came*; Grimsley, *Hard Hand of War*, 14–16; Lang, *In the Wake of War*; Royster, *Destructive War*, 83; Sheehan-Dean, *Calculus of Violence*, 31–32; Witt, *Lincoln's Code*, 16–19, 51, 70–72; for Northern politicians and "latent Unionism," see Varon, *Armies of Deliverance*, 4–5; for married women's citizenship filtered through their husbands, see Kerber, *No Constitutional Right*, 3–46.

9. For the protection of white women and children, see *OR*, ser. 2, 1:185; cf. *OR*, ser. 1, 2:805. Confederates hoped to motivate women to involve themselves in the conflict. Grimsley notes that Federals looked to the example of the Revolutionary War as suggesting that "successful warmaking should concentrate on the battlefield" and that "Americans believed that independence had been won mainly by efforts of the Continental Army." Grimsley, *Hard Hand of War*, 17, 19, 20.

10. Lincoln, *Collected Works*, 4:157, 280; Scott, *Memoirs of Lieut.-General Scott*, 2:625–28.

11. In his order calling up the militia, Lincoln ordered that "the utmost care will be observed . . . to avoid any . . . interference with property," banning the military from engaging with enslaved people. Lincoln, *Collected Works*, 4:332. The Confederacy made similar miscalculations. McCurry, *Confederate Reckoning*; Elshtain, *Women and War*, 3–6, 94–101.

12. Lincoln, *Collected Works*, 4:157; Scott, *Memoirs of Lieut.-General Scott*, 2:626–28 [emphasis in original]; Lincoln, *Collected Works*, 4:280.

13. *OR*, ser. 1, 1:360; Lincoln, *Collected Works*, 4:332; 1860 U.S. Census, M653; 1860 Slave Schedules, M653. Key West's free inhabitants numbered 2,407 while its enslaved population was 435.

14. *OR*, ser. 1, 1:375; *OR*, ser. 1, 1:413; Welcher, *Union Army*, 1:15. Lincoln authorized Scott to suspend the writ of habeas corpus in Baltimore on April 25, 1861. It seems likely that he also authorized its suspension in Key West. See Lincoln, *Collected Works*, 4:344.

15. *OR*, ser. 1, 1:362; Lincoln, *Collected Works*, 4:251–52; Clavin, *Aiming for Pensacola*, 147; Camp, *Closer to Freedom*, 123–24; Sheehan-Dean, *Calculus of Violence*, 39; "Fort Pickens," National Park Service; 1860 Slave Schedule. Pensacola's enslaved population was 957.

16. Stephens, *Voice of Thunder*, 14–15, 126–27, and see also 15n54; Manning, *Troubled Refuge*, 14–15.

17. While white women were technically citizens of the nation, the government recognized that women had a divided loyalty since they owed allegiance first to their families and then to the state. See Kerber, *No Constitutional Right*; Isenberg, *Sex and Citizenship*.

18. *OR*, ser. 1, 2:662; Welcher, *Union Army*, 1:73; see also Marshall, *Private and Official Correspondence*, 1:83.

19. McCurry, *Confederate Reckoning*, 218–226; Foner, *Fiery Trial*, 171–73. For Northern expectations of and policies toward African American Southerners, see Goodheart, *1861*; Brasher, *Peninsula Campaign*, 30–49.

20. Underwood, *Josie Underwood's Civil War Diary*, 79, 81, emphasis in original; Hoobler, "Civil War Diary of Louisa Brown Pearl," 315; Ellen Wallace diary, April 19, 1861, in 1861–1863, box 2, folder 2, Kentucky Historical Society; Robinson, *Bitter Fruits of Bondage*, 38–40, 59–60. Regarding Underwood's upbringing, see *Josie Underwood's Civil War Diary*, 2–6; Crofts, *Reluctant Confederates*; Fehrenbacher, *Slaveholding Republic*. For laws of war, see Witt, *Lincoln's Code*, 29–32, 70–77, 199–200.

21. Underwood, *Josie Underwood's Civil War Diary*, 99, 105; Ellen Wallace diary, August 28?, 1861, and September 18, 1861; Mahon, *Winchester Divided*, 7; McCurry, *Confederate Reckoning*, 117–32.

22. Welch quoted in Fritz, *Voices in the Storm*, 44; *OR*, ser. 1, pt. 1, 22:83; Light, *War at Our Doors*, 28; Edwards, *Scarlett Doesn't Live Here Anymore*, 80; Ott, *Confederate Daughters*, 35–72; Jabour, *Scarlett's Sisters*, 239–80; Phillips, "Brothers' War?," 68, 71–73; Rothman, *Slave Country*.

23. Maury, "Civil War Diary," 9–10.

24. Washington, *Up from Slavery*, 7; Franks quoted in Robinson, *Bitter Fruits of Bondage*, 41–42; see also Dwight, *Life and Letters*, 299; Mary Wooldridge in Rawick, *American Slave*, 16:107.

25. Jennie Small in Rawick, *American Slave*, 16:81; Owens, *Green County Soldiers*, 91; Susie King Taylor, *Reminiscences of My Life*, 7–8; Hahn, *Nation Under Our Feet*, 63–65.

26. *OR*, ser. 1, 2:654–55; Welcher, *Union Army*, 1:71; Grimsley, *Hard Hand of War*, 39. For military commissions, see Ramold, *Baring the Iron Hand*; Witt, *Lincoln's Code*, 24–27, 98–99, 123–28, 130, 132.

27. *OR*, ser. 1, 2:112–113; Welcher, *Union Army*, 1:73; for Confederate rumors, see *OR*, ser. 1, 9:363–364. U.S. Army officials contrasted their mild treatment of noncombatants with the extreme measures of the Confederate army. McCurry, *Confederate Reckoning*, 87, 90, 116, 117; Inscoe and McKinney, *Heart of Confederate Appalachia*, 200; Storey, *Loyalty and Loss*, 106–8; Mitchell, *Vacant Chair*, 72–74, 86, 87.

28. *OR*, ser. 1, pt. 1, 51:425–26; Welcher, *Union Army*, 2:126.

29. George McClellan to Mary Ellen Marcy McClellan, July 12, 1861, in *McClellan's Own Story*, 62. See also *OR*, ser. 1, 2:48–49, 123; John H. Shober letter, September 19, 1861, Accession 45073, Personal Papers Collection, Library of Virginia (hereafter PPC); Welcher, *Union Army*, 1:79; McCurry, *Confederate Reckoning*, 87, 90, 116, 117; Inscoe and McKinney, *Heart of Confederate Appalachia*, 200; Storey, *Loyalty and Loss*, 106–8; Mitchell, *Vacant Chair*, 72–74, 86, 87.

30. Dwight, *Life and Letters*, 56.

31. See Testimony of Anna Maria Armstrong, Claim of Benjamin Armstrong, Spotsylvania County, Virginia, and Claim of Elizabeth Mummaw, Frederick County, Virginia, SCC-NA. Armstrong was threatened with imprisonment for her Unionist sentiments, and Mummaw narrowly avoided having her house burned down. Dwight, *Life and Letters*, 82.

32. James L. Rea to "Dearest Mary," July 11, 1861, box 95, folder 21A, Civil War Documents Collection, U.S. Army Heritage and Education Center (hereafter CWDC); Dwight, *Life and Letters*, 38; Welcher, *Union Army*, 1:10.

33. Stephens, *Voice of Thunder*, 133–134; Glymph, *Women's Fight*, 106.

34. Marshall, *Private and Official Correspondence*, 112–13, 114, 116–17, 117–18, 186–87; *OR*, ser. 3, 1:243; Mathisen, *Loyal Republic*, 3–8, 87–117.

35. Marshall, *Private and Official Correspondence*, 187; Glymph, "Noncombatant Military Laborers," 25–29; Kendi, *Stamped from the Beginning*, 80–84, 88–89, 100–103. For Black women's labor, see Jacqueline Jones, *Labor of Love*.

36. Stephens, *Voice of Thunder*, 133–34; Glymph, *Women's Fight*, 106.

37. George A. Wilson to "Dear Friends," August 24, 1861, box 124, folder 15, CWDC; *OR*, ser. 1, 2:440–41, 448; Varon, *Armies of Deliverance*, 41–42. Just days later, Frémont issued his infamous proclamation. *OR*, ser. 1, 2:466–67; Lincoln, *Collected Works*, 4:506.

38. Wilson to "Dear Friends"; Varon, *Armies of Deliverance*, 41–42.

39. *OR*, ser. 1, 3:254.

40. Richard Bruner in Rawick, *American Slave*, 10:60; *OR*, ser. 1, 2:485–86; Manning, *Troubled Refuge*, 14–15.

41. Shaw, *History of the Tenth Regiment*, 125, 126; Alfred Pirtle letter, March 1[?], 1862, in Alfred Pirtle letters, 1862–1863, Filson Historical Society (hereafter APL).

42. Wills, *Army Life of an Illinois Soldier*, 29.

43. *OR*, ser. 2, 1:770–71; Hunter, *Bound in Wedlock*, 137, 143, 147.

44. David Samson to "Friend," October 31, 1861, box 102, folder 4, CWDC; *OR*, ser. 1, 5:611–12; Varon, *Armies of Deliverance*, 41–42; Sheehan-Dean, *Calculus of Violence*, 5.

45. *OR*, ser. 1, 6:4–5; Glymph, *Women's Fight*, 19–53.

46. *OR*, ser. 1, 6:6; Foote, *Rites of Retaliation*, 18–20.

47. Stinson P. Everill to "Friend Sadie," December 6, 1861, Accession 50039, PPC.

48. Hoobler, "Civil War Diary of Louisa Brown Pearl," 317–18; Underwood, *Josie Underwood's Civil War Diary*, 155–67; McCurry, *Confederate Reckoning*, 117–32.

49. *OR*, ser. 1, 7:497–98.

50. *OR*, ser. 1, 8:475–76, 476–77, 481; Sheehan-Dean, *Calculus of Violence*, 109.

51. Ready, *Diary of Alice Ready*, 45. See also Mahon, *Winchester Divided*, 11; Thornton, *Politics and Power*, xviii; Sommerville, *Rape and Race*, 5–7, 11, 22, 27; Stansell, *City of Women*, 25–27, 98–99; Kerber, *No Constitutional Right*, 13–15.

52. Shaw, *History of the Tenth Regiment*, 163; Hardin, *Private War*, 33.

53. *OR*, ser. 1, 7:425, 669.

54. Shaw, *History of the Tenth Regiment*, 163; Foroughi, *Go If You Think It Your Duty*, 68.

55. Hazen, *Narrative of Military Service*, 18.

56. Hardin, *Private War*, 38.

57. Alfred Pirtle to "Dear Ma," March 1 [7?], 1862, APL.

58. Gibson, *Seventy-Eighth Pennsylvania*, 37.

59. Foroughi, *Go If You Think It Your Duty*, 68.

60. Carney, *Kate Carney Diary*, 376. See also Hardin, *Private War*, 38; McCurry, *Confederate Reckoning*, 86.

61. Ready, *Diary of Alice Ready*, 84; Jabour, *Scarlett's Sisters*, 19, 38; Glymph, *Out of the House of Bondage*, 45; Hardin, *Private War*, 38, 42. Some Confederate women believed that their comrades took rude behavior toward Union soldiers a bit too far. See Sarah Morgan, *Civil War Diary of a Southern Woman*, 76, 121–22.

62. Hinkley, *Narrative of Service*, 17.

63. Mahon, *Winchester Divided*, 22.

64. Mahon, *Winchester Divided*, 19, 22.

65. Mahon, *Winchester Divided*, 21. The Lee Sisters may have also felt emboldened by the presence of Confederate guerrillas in the area. Sutherland, *Savage Conflict*, 84–93.

66. John Viles to Frank, March 18, 1862, John Viles letters, Accession 45072, PPC; *OR*, ser. 1, 5:747.

67. Mahon, *Winchester Divided*, 23; *OR*, ser. 1, 5:747.

68. Dwight, *Life and Letters*, 201–2.

69. Mahon, *Winchester Divided*, 21; Stephens, *Voice of Thunder*, 198–99.

70. Stephens, *Voice of Thunder*, 186, 205; Schwalm, *Hard Fight for We*, 97. See also Underwood, *Josie Underwood's Civil War Diary*, 179.

71. Testimony of Charlotte Hine in Trial of Col. John Basil Turchin, KK122, Records of the Office of the Judge Advocate General (U.S. Army), National Archives, Washington, D.C. (hereafter JAG); King, "'Prematurely Knowing of Evil Things,'" 174.

72. During Turchin's court-martial, Hine testified that she had been "so much alarmed" when the Federals raped the enslaved young woman that "although I wanted to protect my property I was afraid to stay," and she absconded across the river. Testimony of Charlotte Hine; Morris, *Southern Slavery and the Law*, 64–66; Edwards, "Status Without Rights"; Bardaglio, *Reconstructing the Household*, 66–68; Block, *Rape and Sexual Power*, 177–79, 208.

73. Testimony of Col. Carter Gazlay, 37th Indiana, in Trial of Col. John Basil Turchin.

74. Testimony of Col. Carter Gazlay and Acting Asst. Adjt. Gen. Chauncey Miller in Trial of Col. John Basil Turchin; Litwack, *North of Slavery*, 93–96; Block, *Rape and Sexual Power*, 208; Harris, *In the Shadow of Slavery*, 195–96.

75. *OR*, ser. 1, pt. 2, 16:273; Trial of Col. John Basil Turchin; cf. Gen. Ormsby M. Mitchel's response to Athens citizens in *OR*, ser. 1, pt. 3, 10:212–13; cf. his acknowledgement that "the negroes are our only friends," *OR*, ser. 1, pt. 2, 10:162.

76. *OR*, ser. 1, pt. 2, 16:319.

77. *OR*, ser. 1, pt. 1, 16:140, 145.

Chapter Two. Social Relationships and the Turn Toward Hard War

1. Welter, "Cult of True Womanhood"; Scott, *Southern Lady*, 4–5; Jabour, *Scarlett's Sisters*, 19, 38, 45; Glymph, *Out of the House of Bondage*, 4–6. For Federals as occupiers, see Whites and Long, *Occupied Women*, 1–13.

2. Shaw, *History of the Tenth Regiment*, 165; "An Interview with Mrs. Polk," *Nashville Daily Times and True Union*, March 3, 1864, quoted in Amy S. Greenberg, *Lady First*, 226; for a fulsome account of Polk's wartime views, see 209–44; Curry, *Four Years in the Saddle*, 34; Kerber, *Women of the Republic*, 235, 283; Cott, *Bonds of Womanhood*, 70–71.

3. Halttunen, *Confidence Men and Painted Women*, xv–xvii, 39, 92–118; Kasson, *Rudeness and Civility*, 96–109.

4. Kimmel, *Manhood in America*, 23, 26, 43, 44, 54–55; Rotundo, *American Manhood*, 19.

5. By "ladies" and "gentlemen," I refer to nineteenth-century labels for wealthy white women and men from good families, who displayed through their clothing, accoutrements, and good manners their membership in the upper class. See Jabour, *Scarlett's Sisters*, 19–45; Scott, *Southern Lady*, 3–21. Glymph notes that for ladies, work outside the home was a "disqualifying act" (*Out of the House of Bondage*, 4).

6. Halttunen, *Confidence Men and Painted Women*, 57–58, 60; Kasson, *Rudeness and Civility*, 100–109.

7. Harris, *In the Shadow of Slavery*, 98–99; Kerber, *Women of the Republic*, 1–12, 283–86; Stansell, *City of Women*, 19–30; Bloch, *Gender and Morality*, 46–47; Cott, *Bonds of Womanhood*, 98–99.

8. Susie King Taylor, *Reminiscences of My Life*, 15.

9. Welter, "Cult of True Womanhood"; Varon, *We Mean to Be Counted*, 137–38, 152, 154.

10. For young Confederate women's political sympathies, see Jabour, *Scarlett's Sisters*, 239–80; Ott, *Confederate Daughters*, 35–72, 129–65.

11. Sheehan-Dean, *Calculus of Violence*, 92–93, 111.

12. Kasson, *Rudeness and Civility*, 92–111; Halttunen, *Confidence Men and Painted Women*, 40; Banner, *American Beauty*, 50.

13. Patsy Hyde in Rawick, *American Slave*, 16:33, 18–19, 68, and see also Candis Goodwin and Millie Simpkins, 16:18–19, 68, and Hattie Clayton and Dellie Lewis 6:77, 255–57; Stephens, *Voice of Thunder*, 138; see also Halttunen, *Confidence Men and Painted Women*, 37.

14. Celia Henderson, Hannah Davidson, and Jennie Small in Rawick, *American Slave*, 16:42–43, 26, 80–81. Enslaved African Americans had their own ideas of what it meant to be a man or a woman. Deborah G. White, *Ar'n't I a Woman?*, 105–19; Glymph, *Out of the House of Bondage*, 90–91.

15. Millie Simpkins in Rawick, *American Slave*, 16:68.

16. Lucy Brooks in Rawick, *American Slave*, 16:2; Kendi, *Stamped from the Beginning*, 121–25; Jennifer Morgan, *Laboring Women*, 12–37.

17. William A. Smith to "My Dear Wife," August 9, 1862, box 109, folder 11, CWDC; Higginson, *Complete Civil War Journal*, 58; Banner, *American Beauty*, 46–48, 50; Kasson, *Rudeness and Civility*, 127.

18. Douglass Ritchie Bushnell to Wife, August 6, 1862, box 19, folder 10, CWDC, emphasis in original; Hunter, *Bound in Wedlock*, 157; Fields and Fields, *Racecraft*, 17.

19. See chapter 1, "The Chaos of Conciliation"; *OR*, ser. 1, pt. 2, 10:15.

20. McGee, *History of the 72d Indiana*, 60; Glymph, *Women's Fight*, 88–89; see also Robertson, "Indiana Soldier in Love and War," 208; Haines, *In the Country of the Enemy*, 75; Jenkin Lloyd Jones, *Artilleryman's Diary*, 44.

21. Foroughi, *Go If You Think It Your Duty*, 157; Bradley, *Star Corps*, 265. George Stephens shared these assessments. Stephens, *Voice of Thunder*, 138; see also McGee, *History of the 72d Indiana*, 73; Milton T. Carey to Cornelia Carey, March 27, 1862, in Milton T. Carey Papers, 1862–1865, Filson Historical Society; Eby, *Observations of an Illinois Boy*, 70. Regarding free labor, see Olmstead, *Cotton Kingdom*; Floan, *South in Northern Eyes*; Foner, *Free Soil*; Giesberg, *Army at Home*, 17–44, 68–91. Regarding indictments of slavery, see Ford, *Deliver Us from Evil*, 506; Mitchell, *Civil War Soldiers*, 109; *Springfield Republican* quoted in Bradley, *Star Corps*, 157.

22. Musser, *Soldier Boy*, 90; see also Jenkin Lloyd Jones, *Artilleryman's Diary*, 118; McGee, *History of the 72d Indiana*, 337; Halttunen, *Confidence Men and Painted Women*, 57–59, 71. For Midwestern domesticity, see Jeffrey, *Frontier Women*, 55–56, 78–80, 85; Banner, *American Beauty*, 59. For Southern expectations, see Jabour, *Scarlett's Sisters*, 38–39. Regarding educated women as good wives and mothers, see Kerber, *Women of the Republic*, 206–7, 210, 228–31. For the sparseness of public education in the South, see Farnham, *Education of the Southern Belle*; Hyde, *Schooling in the Antebellum South*, 117, 125, 128.

23. Mahon, *Winchester Divided*, 22; Peter, *Union Woman*, 33, 73, 3; Underwood, *Josie Underwood's Civil War Diary*, 165, 169. For nineteenth-century ideas linking outward appearance and inner character, see Kasson, *Rudeness and Civility*, 92–99. For appearance and virtue, see Halttunen, *Confidence Men and Painted Women*, 39–52.

24. Haines, *In the Country of the Enemy*, 82; Baer, *Shadows on My Heart*, 118. Regarding links between elite women's beauty, physical appearance, body movements, and facial expressions, see Banner, *American Beauty*, 48.

25. Charles Lutz to Brother, June 15, 1862, box 73, folder 13, CWDC; Grant proposed exactly this remedy for West Tennessee residents who made specious reports about their neighbors to Federal authorities. See *OR*, ser. 1, pt. 2, 17:51. See also Charles Brandegee to Father, January 18, 1862, box 14, folder 1, and Lewis Bayard Smith to Mother, August 19, 1862, box 109, folder 1, both CWDC.

26. James H. Bayne to Parents, January 22, 1863, box 6, folder 15, CWDC; Sarah Morgan, *Civil War Diary of a Southern Woman*, 68; see also Ashkenazi, *Civil War Diary of Clara Solomon*, 355; Ready, *Diary of Alice Ready*, 39, 51, 63.

27. Baer, *Shadows on My Heart*, 40; Hardin, *Private War*, 43, 92; see also Sarah Morgan, *Civil War Diary of a Southern Woman*, 169; Ready, *Diary of Alice Ready*, 51, 65, 69; Kate Carney, *Kate Carney Diary*, 431; Ashkenazi, *Civil War Diary of Clara Solomon*, 360; Uffelman et al., *Diary of Nannie Haskins Williams*, 2, 102; Kate Fos-

ter diary, entry for July 25, 1863, Catherine (Kate) Olivia Foster diary, folder 1, Mississippi Department of Archives and History (hereafter KFD); Halttunen, *Confidence Men and Painted Women*, 30–31, and regarding rules of behavior, see 114–17.

28. Sarah Morgan, *Civil War Diary of a Southern Woman*, 122, 163, and see also 68–69, 129, 158; Ashkenazi, *Civil War Diary of Clara Solomon*, 369; Mahon, *Winchester Divided*, 31–32; Jones-Rogers, *They Were Her Property*, 1–24; Halttunen, *Confidence Men and Painted Women*, 114–17; Kasson, *Rudeness and Civility*, 123–24, 128–30.

29. Hunter, *Bound in Wedlock*, 87–106; Litwack, *North of Slavery*, 247, 263–64.

30. Susie King Taylor, *Reminiscences of My Life*, 11; Camp, *Closer to Freedom*, 6–7, 25, 32–33, 118.

31. Susie King Taylor, *Reminiscences of My Life*, 15.

32. Trial of 1 Lieut. Francis W. Usher, KK398; Trial of 1 Lieut. James L. Goddard, II948; Trial of Maj. James M. Ruggles, KK61; Trial of 2 Lieut. Richard Lewis, MM197, all in JAG; Ramold, *Baring the Iron Hand*.

33. Brown, *Good Wives, Nasty Wenches*, 104.

34. KFD, entry for July 28, 1863; Carney, *Kate Carney Diary*, 377; Ready, *Diary of Alice Ready*.

35. Alfred Pirtle to Ma, June 22, 1862, APL; Thomas Speed to Ma, January 29, 1865, Thomas Speed letter book, Filson Historical Society; see also Andrew J. Lorish to "My dear friends," October 19, 1862, box 72, folder 12, and George A. Wilson to "Dear Sister," July 14, 1862, box 124, folder 15, both CWDC.

36. Alfred Pirtle to "Sis," July 12, 1863, APL; Lewis Bayard Smith to Mother, August 19, 1862, box 109, folder 1, CWDC; see also Alfred Pirtle letters of June 21, 27, and August 22, 1862, APL; Hinkley, *Narrative of Service*, 111; Jenkin Lloyd Jones, *Artilleryman's Diary*, 220; Getz, "Between the Lines," 65, 66, 67; Kasson, *Rudeness and Civility*, 169; Cott, *Bonds of Womanhood*, 64–65, 74.

37. Peter, *Union Woman*, 170, 173; Underwood, *Josie Underwood's Civil War Diary*, 170, 176; Claim of Mrs. Aaron V. Brown, Davidson County, Tennessee, SCC-NA; 1850 U.S. Federal Census—Slave Schedules, M432; see also Wells, *Origins of the Southern Middle Class*.

38. Greenland to "Friend Dolf," February 1, 1863, and see also Jack to "Daul," March 10, 1863, both in box 106, folder 8, CWDC; William Mickle to Parents, August 3, 1863, Accession 50590, PPC; see also Jenkin Lloyd Jones, *Artilleryman's Diary*, 231; John C. Baum to Parents, December 25, 1863, box 6, folder 13, CWDC. For genteel culture, see Kasson, *Rudeness and Civility*, 169–81; Halttunen, *Confidence Men and Painted Women*, 59, 102–3, 107–8.

39. Freland N. Holman to [unidentified], July 17, 1862, box 56, folder 15, CWDC; Alfred Pirtle to "Ma," May 4, 1862, APL; Douglas Ritchie Bushnell to "dear Wife,"

May 7, 1862, box 19, folder 10, CWDC; Jackson, *Colonel's Diary*, 185, 194, 208; Dwight, *Life and Letters*, 38; Andrew J. Lorish to "Brother," November 16, 1863, box 72, folder 12, CWDC.

40. Eby, *Observations of an Illinois Boy*, 56; Haines, *In the Country of the Enemy*, 75; Bynum, *Unruly Women*, 6–7; Stansell, *City of Women*, 12, 24.

41. Alfred Pirtle to "Sis," May 28, 1862, APL; Richard H. Watson to Jennie, February 6, 1862, box 120, folder 14, CWDC, emphasis in original; Jackson, *Colonel's Diary*, 185, 194, 208; Halttunen, *Confidence Men and Painted Women*, 59–60.

42. Alfred Pirtle to Ma, June 27, 1862, APL.

43. Baer, *Shadows on My Heart*, 61, and see also 71, 59. Louise Humphreys Carter refused to greet an old family friend because he joined the Union army. Louise Humphreys Carter Reminiscences, 7–8, Accession 50621, PPC; Cott, *Bonds of Womanhood*, 69; Halttunen, *Confidence Men and Painted Women*, 59.

44. Ready, *Diary of Alice Ready*, 70, 62, 63; Ashkenazi, *Civil War Diary of Clara Solomon*, 355, 396; Baer, *Shadows on My Heart*, 55; Cross and Cross, *Glencoe Diary*, 93; Carney, *Kate Carney Diary*, 376. See also *Kate Carney Diary*, 367, 379, 429, 436; Elizabeth Maxwell Alsop Wynne diary, entry for June 6, 1862, in Wynne Family Papers, 1809–1967, section 4, Virginia Museum of History and Culture; Varon, *We Mean to Be Counted*, 138, 152; Glymph, *Out of the House of Bondage*, 63–96; Jones-Rogers, *They Were Her Property*, 57–77.

45. Maury, "Civil War Diary," 77; Carney, *Kate Carney Diary*, 398, 392; Baer, *Shadows on My Heart*, 106, and see also 72, 73, 98; Varon, *We Mean to Be Counted*, 137–38, 152, 154. See also Hardin, *Private War*, 45–47; Ready, *Diary of Alice Ready*, 64; Carney, *Kate Carney Diary*, 407, 415; Glymph, *Out of the House of Bondage*, 36; Jones-Rogers, *They Were Her Property*, 61–63.

46. Carney, *Kate Carney Diary*, 432; Uffelman et al., *Diary of Nannie Haskins Williams*, 2; Baer, *Shadows on My Heart*, 40, 94, 98; Cross and Cross, *Glencoe Diary*, 103; Maury, "Civil War Diary," 74; Ready, *Diary of Alice Ready*, 65, 49, 64; Hardin, *Private War*, 62; Glymph, *Out of the House of Bondage*, 33–49; Jones-Rogers, *They Were Her Property*, 204.

47. Underwood, *Josie Underwood's Civil War Diary*, 170–71; Uffelman et al., *Diary of Nannie Haskins Williams*, 22, 44, 46; Baer, *Shadows on My Heart*, 125, 128; see also Carney, *Kate Carney Diary*, 401. Regarding women's role of "enforc[ing] the hundreds of rules governing polite social intercourse," see Halttunen, *Confidence Men and Painted Women*, 59–60.

48. William Alcott quoted in Halttunen, *Confidence Men and Painted Women*, 51.

49. Claim of Elizabeth F. Tucker, Fayette County, Tennessee, SCC-NA.

50. William S. Rosecrans to Ellen Tompkins, January 1871; Jacob D. Cox to Ellen Tompkins, December 7, 1870; Petition of Ellen Tompkins to Secretary of War,

November 26, 1869, all in Tompkins Family Papers, 1800–1871, section 9, Virginia Museum of History and Culture; Kerber, *Women of the Republic*, 36, 51–53; Kerber, *No Constitutional Right to Be Ladies*, 4–39; Isenberg, *Sex and Citizenship*, 10–11, 34.

51. Light, *War at Our Doors*, 49; Ready, *Diary of Alice Ready*, 56; Carney, *Kate Carney Diary*, 378–79, 393; see also Maury, "Civil War Diary," 81; Elizabeth Maxwell Alsop Wynne diary, June 25, July 14, August 22, 1862.

52. *OR*, ser. 2, 5:320. Dick brought at least one case from this information. Citizen Edward Bredell, LL609, JAG; Maj. Edward B. Eno to Brig. Gen. James B. Totten, July 20, 1862, *OR*, ser. 1, 13:482; see also William A. Smith to Wife, March 5, 1862, box 109, folder 11, CWDC; Peter, *Union Woman*, 3, 86–87, 92, 111, 116, 121; Whites, "'Corresponding with the Enemy,'" 103–16.

53. Curry, *Four Years in the Saddle*, 100; Bickham, *Rosecrans Campaign*, 58, 64, 66, 134; Durham, *Nashville: The Occupied City*, 200–201; *OR*, ser. 1, vol. 20, pt. 2, 193; Gullickson, "La Petroleuse," 242, 250, 260–61; Mitchell, *Vacant Chair*, 90; see also Jackson, *Colonel's Diary*, 98; James H. Bayne to Parents, September 16, 1862, box 6, folder 15, CWDC.

54. Halttunen, *Confidence Men and Painted Women*, xv; Bynum, *Unruly Women*, 69.

55. *OR*, ser. 1, 15:426, 510; Leonard, "What Lafayette Bailey's Letters Lacked," 72–75; Eby, *Observations of an Illinois Boy*, 56; Isenberg, *Sex and Citizenship*, 45–47; Long, "(Mis)Remembering General Order No. 28," 17–32; McCurry, *Confederate Reckoning*, 104–44; Sheehan-Dean, *Calculus of Violence*, 111–12.

Chapter Three. Domestic Struggles over Confiscation, Foraging, and Emancipation

1. Sam Word in Rawick, *American Slave*, 11:240; Dyer, *Compendium of the War*, 673.

2. "Second Confiscation Act" and "Militia Act of 1862," Freedmen and Southern Society Project; *OR*, ser. 1, pt. 2, 12:50; *OR*, ser. 1, pt. 3, 11:362; Siddali, *From Property to Person*, 120–226; Oakes, *Freedom National*, 224–39, 360–62; Manning, *Troubled Refuge*, 188–89; Amy Murrell Taylor, *Embattled Freedom*, 50–52, 57–60.

3. Foroughi, *Go If You Think It Your Duty*, 60–61; *OR*, ser. 1, 7:669.

4. Peter, *Union Woman*, 75, 78, 73; Underwood, *Josie Underwood's Civil War Diary*, 162.

5. Underwood, *Josie Underwood's Civil War Diary*, 162–63; for a formerly enslaved woman reflecting on similar scenes in West Virginia, see Nan Stewart in Rawick, *American Slave*, 16:68; for Federals asking for food in Virginia, see

George Hill Jr. to Brothers, April 10, 1862, box 55, folder 16, CWDC; Margaret Tilloston Kemble Nourse diary, May 29, 1862; Isenberg, *Sex and Citizenship*, 34–35; Mitchell, *Vacant Chair*, 72–74, 90, 91–96; Glymph, *Out of the House of Bondage*, 86–87.

6. Hardin, *Private War*, 41; *OR*, ser. 1, 7:669.

7. Carney, *Kate Carney Diary*, 440; Hardin, *Private War*, 39–40; Elizabeth McGavock Harding to William Giles Harding, May 11, 1862, William Giles Harding Papers, series II, Vanderbilt University (hereafter WGHP); Cashin, *War Stuff*, 64–68; see also Light, *War at Our Doors*, 43; Ready, *Diary of Alice Ready*, 82.

8. Stephens, *Voice of Thunder*, 146, 169, 138–39; *OR*, ser. 1, 5:6; Glymph, *Out of the House of Bondage*, 111–12; Penningroth, *Claims of Kinfolk*, 107.

9. Margaret Tilloston Kemble Nourse diary, April 6, 9, 12, 17, 1862; *OR*, ser. 1, pt. 1, 12:53.

10. Light, *War at Our Doors*, 32, 43, 41; *OR*, ser. 1, pt. 1, 12:53.

11. Mahon, *Winchester Divided*, 25; *OR*, ser. 1, 5:747.

12. Mahon, *Winchester Divided*, 26, 33, 66; *OR*, ser. 1, pt. 1, 12:555.

13. Mahon, *Winchester Divided*, 43, 44; *OR*, ser. 1, pt. 3, 12:338, 343; Blair, *With Malice Toward Some*, 6, 129, 149–50; Royster, *Destructive War*, 86–87.

14. Baer, *Shadows on My Heart*, 42, 53, 59, 60, emphasis in original.

15. Baer, *Shadows on My Heart*, 68–69; *OR*, ser. 1, pt. 3, 12:299.

16. Baer, *Shadows on My Heart*, 61.

17. Baer, *Shadows on My Heart*, 75.

18. Maury, "Civil War Diary," 70; *OR*, ser. 1, pt. 1, 12:53.

19. Maury, "Civil War Diary," 70, 74, 80.

20. Stephens, *Voice of Thunder*, 199; Fields and Fields, *Racecraft*, 128–29, 142.

21. Ashkenazi, *Civil War Diary of Clara Solomon*, 384.

22. Ashkenazi, *Civil War Diary of Clara Solomon*, 384.

23. Baer, *Shadows on My Heart*, 53.

24. Baer, *Shadows on My Heart*, 107; *OR*, ser. 1, pt. 3, 12:407; Glymph, *Out of the House of Bondage*, 100.

25. Baer, *Shadows on My Heart*, 122, 123; *OR*, ser. 1, pt. 2, 12:50.

26. Claim of Ann C. Brandt, Culpeper County, Virginia, SCC-NA; see also Margaret Tilloston Kemble Nourse diary, June 27, 1862.

27. Claims of Susan P. W. Hall and Sarah E. Thomas, Culpeper County, Virginia, SCC-NA; see also Claim of Mary L. Payne, Culpeper County, Virginia, SCC-NA.

28. Elizabeth Maxwell Alsop diary, July 24, 1862; *OR*, ser. 1, pt. 2, 12:104–6.

29. Elizabeth Maxwell Alsop diary, July 24, 1862; Glymph, *Out of the House of Bondage*, 100–101.

30. Margaret Tilloston Kemble Nourse diary, July 31, 1862; Ash, *When the Yankees Came*, 116, 120; Browning, *Shifting Loyalties*, 166–72; Davis, "Don't Let Nobody Bother Yo' Principle," 18–19; Glymph, *Out of the House of Bondage*, 65, 66, 76.

31. Maury, "Civil War Diary," 85; Light, *War at Our Doors*, 41; "Second Confiscation Act" and "Militia Act of 1862," Freedmen and Southern Society Project; *OR*, ser. 1, pt. 3, 11:362; Glymph, *Out of the House of Bondage*, 109–10; Siddali, *From Property to Person*, 120–226.

32. Margaret Tilloston Kemble Nourse diary, August 21, 22, 23, and 27, 1862; *OR*, ser. 1, pt. 2, 12:52.

33. Claim of Charlotte S. Read, Fairfax County, Virginia, SCC-NA; McPherson, *Battle Cry of Freedom*, 531–33.

34. Stephens, *Voice of Thunder*, 208; Berlin et al., *Destruction of Slavery*, 298–99; Glymph, *Out of the House of Bondage*, 108–9. A similar atrocity occurred on Hutchinson's Island, South Carolina, in June 1862. Berlin et al., *Destruction of Slavery*, 125–28; Fields and Fields, *Racecraft*, 138.

35. Claim of Mary C. Latham, Rappahannock County, Virginia, SCC-NA. Burnside ordered the commanders of his division to supply their men with "three days' cooked rations." By the time Pleasanton's cavalry visited Latham, they had most likely run out of food. *OR*, ser. 1, 21:63; McPherson, *Battle Cry of Freedom*, 570.

36. Claim of Martha Bailey, Culpeper County, Virginia, and see also deposition of Ann Elizabeth King in Claim of Sam King, Spotsylvania County, Virginia, both SCC-NA; McPherson, *Battle Cry of Freedom*, 570–71.

37. Stephens, *Voice of Thunder*, 214, 215; McPherson, *Battle Cry of Freedom*, 573–74.

38. Buell excluded Black men and women from his lines. See chapter 1, "The Chaos of Conciliation," 43.

39. Foroughi, *Go If You Think It Your Duty*, 60–61, 106; Cashin, *War Stuff*, 55–57; McGee, *History of the 72d Indiana*, 510.

40. Elizabeth McGavock Harding to William Giles Harding, August 5, 1862, WGHP.

41. Carney, *Kate Carney Diary*, 425–26, 429.

42. Anderson, *Brokenburn*, 128, 181; Ash, *When the Yankees Came*, 92–93.

43. Carney, *Kate Carney Diary*, 440; French, *L. Virginia French's War Journal*, 23, 25; *OR*, ser. 1, 10:46–50; see also Uffelman et al., *Diary of Nannie Haskins Williams*, 10.

44. *OR*, ser. 1, pt. 2, 10:115, 31; Ready, *Diary of Alice Ready*, 70; see also Elizabeth McGavock Harding to William Giles Harding, August 14, 1862, WGHP.

45. Morris, *Southern Slavery and the Law*, 340–46.

46. Elizabeth McGavock Harding to William Giles Harding, June 3 and August 25, 1862, WGHP; Carney, *Kate Carney Diary*, 415; Glymph, *Women's Fight*,

32–42; Glymph, *Out of the House of Bondage*, 99. The same delusions were evident among Maryland slaveholders. See Berlin et al., *Black Military Experience*, 214.

47. Glymph, *Out of the House of Bondage*, 99; Edwards, *Scarlett Doesn't Live Here Anymore*, 78–79; Glymph, *Women's Fight*, 22.

48. French, *L. Virginia French's War Journal*, 17, 18; Glymph, *Out of the House of Bondage*, 107.

49. French, *L. Virginia French's War Journal*, 23.

50. The exception to the policy is David Hunter, commanding the Department of the South, who instituted a forcible draft of enslaved men in spring of 1863. *OR*, ser. 1, 14:1020–21; Foote, *Rites of Retaliation*, 20–21.

51. In Rawick, *American Slave*, see Julia Casey, 16:3; Minnie Fulks, 16:14; Fannie Berry, 6:3; Millie Simpkins and Elizabeth Sparks, 16:18–19, 68, 52–53; Nellie Smith, 12:309–310; see also Berry, *Price for Their Pound of Flesh*, 58–90; Penningroth, *Claims of Kinfolk*, 45–109.

52. *OR*, ser. 1, pt. 2, 17:15–16; *OR*, ser. 1, 8:370.

53. Passages from Rawick, *American Slave*: Josie Martin, 10:51–52; Harriet Casey, 10:75; Manda Walker, 3:170; Lucy Brooks, 16:2; Nellie Smith, 13:310; Ellen Thomas, 6:376–378; Lucinda Miller, 3:192; Kisey McKimm, 16:65.

54. Adeline Taylor in account of Henry Nelson, in Rawick, *American Slave*, 10:201; Jenkin Lloyd Jones, *Artilleryman's Diary*, 170; Amy Murrell Taylor, *Embattled Freedom*, 50–52; Nelson, *Ruin Nation*, 95; Penningroth, *Claims of Kinfolk*, 114–15.

55. *OR*, ser. 1, 13:202–3; "Second Confiscation Act," Freedmen and Southern Society Project.

56. Cordelia Lewis Scales to "Loulie," October 29, 1862, Cordelia Lewis Scales Letters, folder 1, Mississippi Department of Archives and History (hereafter CLSL); McPherson, *Battle Cry of Freedom*, 577.

57. Cordelia Lewis Scales to "Loulie," October 29, 1862.

58. Peter, *Union Woman*, 75, 78, 73; *OR*, ser. 1, pt. 2, 20:162; Cashin, *War Stuff*, 68–75.

59. Peter, *Union Woman*, 79; Kentucky Marriages, 1797–1865; 1860 U.S. Federal Census, M653; U.S., Confederate Officers Card Index, 1861–1865. Gibson served as a captain in John Morgan's cavalry.

60. Peter, *Union Woman*, 80; *OR*, ser. 1, pt. 2, 20:63; 1860 U.S. Census; U.S., Confederate Officers Card Index, 1861–1865. Before becoming a brigadier general, Preston served as a colonel on A. S. Johnston's staff. See Streater, "'She Rebels' on the Supply Line," 88–102.

61. Peter, *Union Woman*, 82.

62. Peter, *Union Woman*, 86; *OR*, ser. 1, pt. 2, 20:91; Howard, *Black Liberation in Kentucky*, 20–21; see also Teters, *Practical Liberators*, 3–4.

63. Mahon, *Winchester Divided*, 79; Glymph, *Out of the House of Bondage*, 109, 119.

64. Dwight, *Life and Letters*, 51, 199–200; Savilla Burrell in Rawick, *American Slave*, 14:151; Douglass, "Meaning of July Fourth"; Glymph, *Women's Fight*, 89.

65. Virginia Hammett diary, February 8, 1863, Virginia Museum of History and Culture; 1850 U.S. Census, M432; 1850 U.S. Federal Census—Slave Schedules, M432; 1860 U.S. Census. Hammett's father held one eighteen-year-old woman in bondage in 1850.

66. Virginia Hammett diary, February 22, 1863, and undated (perhaps February 23 or 24, 1863); *OR*, ser. 1, pt. 2, 25:66–67.

67. Virginia Hammett diary, March 9 and April 10, 1863.

68. Baer, *Shadows on My Heart*, 208; 1860 U.S. Slave Schedule.

69. Harriotte Hopkins Lee Taliaferro to Major Thomas Seddon Taliaferro Sr., undated, Taliaferro Family Papers, section 10, Virginia Museum of History and Culture.

70. Taliaferro to Taliaferro Sr., undated.

71. George E. Harvey to Uncle and Frank, July 13, 1863, Accession 51382, PPC.

72. Testimony of Catherine Alford in Claim of Robert Alford, Spotsylvania County, Virginia, SCC-NA; Rosen, *Terror in the Heart of Freedom*, 225.

73. *OR*, ser. 1, pt. 2, 23:55–57.

74. McGee, *History of the 72d Indiana*, 103; Cordelia Lewis Scales to Loulie, January 27, 1863, CLSL.

75. Bradley, *Star Corps*, 49; see also Jefferson Whitcomb diary, August 16 and 19, 1862, in 1862 July 25–1864 January 1, Virginia Museum of History and Culture.

76. Oliver Boucher to "Madam," June 22, 1863, box 12, folder 11, CWDC; Cashin, *War Stuff*, 57–64; Kerber, *Women of the Republic*, 54–55; see also George Hill Jr. to "Brother," April 10, 1862, box 55, folder 16, CWDC.

77. *OR*, ser. 1, pt. 3, 24:156–57; KFD, July 14, 16, 24, and 25, 1863.

78. KFD, July 16 and 28, 1863; see also Jessie K. Clark to Claudia Boddie, September 25, 1863, Clark-Boddie Family Papers, box 1, Mississippi Department of Archives and History.

79. Candis Goodwin in Rawick, *American Slave*, 16:18–19; Berlin et al., *Black Military Experience*, 138; in Rawick, *American Slave*: Avelina McConico 10:9–10; Maggie Snow and Charlie Snow, 10:205; Nannie Eaves, 16:60; Matilda Miller, 10:91; Lande, "Trials of Freedom," 703–4; Hahn, *Nation Under Our Feet*, 90, 92–95; Sheehan-Dean, *Calculus of Violence*, 292–93. White Federals and enslavers also noted these tactics. See Foroughi, *Go If You Think It Your Duty*, 169; French, *L. Virginia French's War Journal*, 108; Peter, *Union Woman*, 177.

80. In Rawick, *American Slave*: Mattie Mooreman, 10:131; Mary Ella Grandberry, 6:163; Martha Colquitt and Alice Hutcheson, 12:247, 283; Ike McCoy and Mattie Mooreman, 6:12–13, 131; Sallie Paul, 3:234.

81. Peter, *Union Woman*, 154.

82. Peter, *Union Woman*, 151; for the controversy between Fry and Boyle, see *OR*, ser. 1, pt. 3, 30:23, 64; *OR*, ser. 1, pt. 1, 31:723–24, 755.

83. Peter, *Union Woman*, 177.

Chapter Four. Wartime Sexual Assault and the Progress of Emancipation

1. Trial of Pvt. Charles Pratt, NN85, JAG.

2. Caruthers and Nicholson, *Statutes of Tennessee*, 318, 712; see also Sommerville, *Rape and Race*, 66.

3. Trial of Pvt. James Meoliff, 11780; Trials of Pvt. John Gray and Sgt. Henry Snow, 11773; Trial of Col. Richard White, KK259; Trial of Pvt. William Elliott, MM150; Trial of Sgt. Thomas Graham, MM699, all in JAG. Other scholars examining Black women's use of the court-martial system against their rapists include Esty, "I Told Him to Let Me Alone," and Feimster, "Rape and Mutiny at Fort Jackson."

4. Pratt was charged with the Ninety-Ninth Article of War, or "conduct prejudicial to good order and military discipline," and only the specifications to the charge listed the attempted rape as one of his crimes.

5. Witt, *Lincoln's Code*, 123–28, 264; for an example of this reticence, see Trial of Col. John Basil Turchin, KK122, JAG.

6. Throughout the slaveholding states, rape statutes often specified that victims could only be white. See Sommerville, *Rape and Race*, 64–70; Morris, *Southern Slavery and the Law*, 66–69. Since many Midwestern states did not allow Black testimony against white defendants, a white man who raped a Black woman with no white witnesses could expect to not be prosecuted. Litwack, *North of Slavery*, 93–96; Hahn, *Nation Under Our Feet*, 57–58, 63–65, 87; Sheehan-Dean, *Calculus of Violence*, 307.

7. LeConte, *When the World Ended*, 80–81; Faust, *Creation of Confederate Nationalism*, 60–61; Block, *Rape and Sexual Power*, 208, and see also 2–6, 166–67, 238; Hodes, *White Women, Black Men*, 145–46; McCurry, *Confederate Reckoning*, 238–39; Sommerville, *Rape and Race*, 8–11, 28–29, 32, 38, 124–25; Sheehan-Dean, *Calculus of Violence*, 309.

8. Hodes, *White Women, Black Men*, 1–2, 7; Sommerville, *Rape and Race*, 3, 103; Esty, "I Told Him to Let Me Alone," 34–35; Feimster, "Rape and Mutiny at Fort Jackson," 11–12.

9. Although Northern legal codes did not exclude Black women as victims of sexual assault, widespread cultural attitudes spread the "myth of the black-on-white rapist," as historian Sharon Block notes (*Rape and Sexual Power*, 177–79).

10. An Act for Establishing the Rules and Articles for the Government of the Armies of the United States, ch. 20, art. LXV, LXXVII, LXIX, LXXXII, 2 Stat. 367–369 (1806); 65th Article of War, 77th Article of War, 69th Article of War, and 82nd Articles of War, *Armies of the United States*; Benét, *Treatise on Military Law*, 17, 19, 22–24, 46–47, 52–58, 61–62; Ramold, *Baring the Iron Hand*, 317–18; for a comprehensive description, see Foote, *Gentlemen and the Roughs*, 11–16.

11. Benét, *Treatise on Military Law*, 62–65, 68–70, 89, 94, 108–11, 115; Act for Establishing the Rules and Articles for the Government of the Armies of the United States, ch. 20, art. LXX–LXXI, 2 Stat. 368 (1806); Article 1139, *Army Regulations*, 168; Foote, *Gentlemen and the Roughs*, 15; Ramold, *Baring the Iron Hand*, 318–19.

12. Benét, *Treatise on Military Law*, 42–45, 125–29, 137–40, 143, 146–48, 151, 152–53, 159; An Act for Establishing the Rules and Articles for the Government of the Armies of the United States, ch. 20, art. LXXXVII, LXXXIX, XC, 2 Stat. 369–70 (1806); Judge Advocate De Witt Clinton in review of sentence of 1st Lieut. Charles Wenz, MM2780, JAG; Foote, *Gentlemen and the Roughs*, 14–15; Ramold, *Baring the Iron Hand*, 319–20, 323.

13. *OR*, ser. 1, pt. 3, 40:743; *OR*, ser. 1, pt. 1, 37:163; *OR*, ser. 1, pt. 2, 26:33–4; *OR*, ser. 1, pt. 1, 39:230; Hodes, *White Women, Black Men*, 145–46; Sommerville, *Rape and Race*, 124–25; Sheehan-Dean, *Calculus of Violence*, 309.

14. In 1860, the total Southern population stood at 12.24 million people. Enslaved and free Black people made up 4.5 million. Based on these figures, we can estimate the total number of Southern white women at 3.87 million while Black women and girls numbered only 2.25 million. See Conlin, *Constitutional Origins*, 255; Hodes, *White Women, Black Men*, 141; Sheehan-Dean, *Calculus of Violence*, 306–7.

15. "Army in September 1865," Mapping Occupation; Trial of Pvt. Peter Small, OO1313, JAG. See also Pvts. Pompey Harkell, Providence James, Adron Benjamin, and Oretus Miller, MM3643, JAG. The soldiers were accused of raping sixteen-year-old Nancy Frost at Fort Macon, North Carolina. None were convicted. Similarly, Pvt. Charles Aiken of the Forty-Fifth USCT and Pvt. William Burden of the Fifty-Seventh USCT were accused of a number of crimes, including attempted rape (in the case of Aiken) and rape (in the case of Burden). Neither was convicted on the charge of attempted rape or rape. Trial of Pvt. Charles Aiken, MM3144 and Trial of Pvt. William Burden, MM3730, JAG.

16. Trials of Pvts. Benjamin Redding and James Grippen, MM3184, and Trials of Pvts. Gabriel Richardson, Henry Davis, and Howard Dixon, MM3197; Trial of Pvt. Evan Williams, OO1416, all JAG.

17. Instances of wartime rape that did not make it to trial can be found in Claim of Mary C. Latham, Rappahannock County, Virginia, SCC-NA; *OR*, ser. 1, 15:525; "A Warning to Intermeddlers," *New Orleans Daily Picayune*, July 19, 1862; George H. Patch to Mother and Father, April 28, 1864, George H. Patch Papers, 1862–1864, Virginia Museum of History and Culture; Jackson, *Colonel's Diary*, 191; Schwalm, *Hard Fight for We*, 100, 102–3; for drumhead courts, see Ramold, *Baring the Iron Hand*, 324–25.

18. Trial of Pvt. John Gray and Sgt. Henry E. Snow, II773; Trial of Pvt. James Meoliff, II780, both JAG; OR, ser. 1, pt. 1, 12:52; Trial of Pvt. Lewis B. Trost, KK207; Testimony of Mrs. Mildred Ann Clayton and Mrs. Charlotte Hine in Trial of Col. John B. Turchin, KK122, both JAG; see *OR*, ser. 1, pt. 2, 16:273–77, 319.

19. Trial of Pvt. John Gray and Sgt. Henry E. Snow, II773; Trial of Pvt. James Meoliff, II780; Trial of Corp. William W. Chinock, LL192; Trial of Pvt. Lewis P. Trost, KK207; Trial of Col. Richard White, KK259, all JAG.

20. Hawks, *Woman Doctor's Civil War*, 34; *OR*, ser. 1, 14:384; Schwalm, *Hard Fight for We*, 100, 102–3.

21. An Act for Establishing the Rules and Articles for the Government of the Armies of the United States, ch. 20, art. XXXIII, 2 Stat. 364 (1806); Enrollment Act, Pub. L. No. 37–35, 12 Stat. 793 (1863); Witt, *Lincoln's Code*, 233, 264–67, 270–71; Ramold, *Baring the Iron Hand*, 310–15; Esty, "I Told Him to Let Me Alone," 34.

22. Trial of Pvt. Henry Murphy, LL298; Trial of Sgt. Thomas Graham, LL269; Trial of Pvt. William Swift, LL380, all in JAG; Litwack, *North of Slavery*, 93; Esty, "I Told Him to Let Me Alone," 36.

23. Trial of Pvt. Zeno Cliff, NN478; Trial of Pvt. Francis Bruss, LL966, both JAG. For other soldiers who blatantly assaulted women under the care of officers, see Trial of Pvt. Frank Hunter, LL2719; Trial of Sgt. William Walker, NN3107; Trial of Major Alexander S. Hill, LL1666, all in JAG.

24. Trial of Pvt. Isaac Cox, LL2755; see also Trials of Pvt. Joseph Hunter and Pvt. John Goodwin, LL2688; Trials of Pvt. John Gray and Pvt. Henry Snow, II773, all JAG; Amy Murrell Taylor, *Embattled Freedom*, 87.

25. See John and Fenton Frazer and Susan and Winny A. [probably Irene Ann] Satturwhite, 1860 U.S. Census, M653; Trial of Pvt. Lot Edwards, NN529, JAG; Amy Murrell Taylor, *Embattled Freedom*, 86–88.

26. Trial of Sgt. Samson M. Perkins, NN561, and Trial of Pvt. Lot Edwards, NN529, both in JAG. The trial of Sgt. Austin Wilkins is referenced in the Lot Edwards trial but I have been unable to locate the original. Amy Murrell Taylor, *Embattled Freedom,* 86. For an eerily similar attack, see Trial of Charles Sperry, NN2427; Trials of Pvts. Andrew Tully and John Martin, NN2998; Trial of Sgt. Lawson M. Perkins, NN561, all in JAG.

27. Objection of Pvt. Lot Edwards in Trial of Pvt. Lot Edwards, NN529.

28. Trials of Sgt. Owen Curren and Pvt. William Cahill, NN2468, JAG. Contrast Barnes's treatment with that of Margaret Brooks. Barber and Ritter, "Physical Abuse . . . and Rough Handling," 58–59. See Trials of Pvt. John Davis and Pvt. James Jackson, LL2193, Trial of Pvt. Robert Corey, NN2812, and Trial of Pvt. Richard Kennedy, LL2227, all in JAG.

29. Trial of Lieut. Andrew J. Smith, NN2099; Statement of Gen. Benjamin Butler in Trial of Lieut. Smith, NN2099.

30. Lincoln, *Collected Works*, 8:193; Sommerville, *Rape and Race*, 61; Esty, "I Told Him to Let Me Alone," 36; Sheehan-Dean, *Calculus of Violence*, 310–11.

31. Trial of Pvt. John F. Hall, MM1909, JAG.

32. Trial of Pvt. Charles Clark, OO654, JAG.

33. In Rawick, *American Slave*: Anna Parkes, 13:162; Bessie Myers, 10:175; Rachel Sullivan, 13:228.

34. In Rawick, *American Slave*: Celia Henderson, 16:42–43; Tena White, 3:196–98; Mamie Riley, 3:23; see also King, "Prematurely Knowing of Evil Things," 179, 174.

35. Trials of Pvts. Thomas Killgore and David Kinkle, MM2471, JAG.

36. Trial of Sgt. Enoch George, MM1917; see also LL310, NN2308, NN561, LL1933, in JAG; Jacobs, *Incidents in the Life*, 49.

37. Esty, "I Told Him to Let Me Alone," 36.

38. Sheehan-Dean, *Calculus of Violence*, 243.

39. Foner, *Fiery Trial*, 243; Trial of Pvt. George Nelson, NN2168; see also Trials of Corp. Daniel Tierce and Pvt. Lewis Hardin, NN3232 and NN3007, all JAG. The vast majority of accusations of Black men raping white women occurred after the war. While beyond the scope of this book, these trials raise the issue of rape accusations as retaliation for Black men's freedom. See Trials of Pvts. Gabriel Richardson, Hendry Davis, and Howard Dixon, MM3197; Trial of Pvt. Evan Williams, OO1416; Trial of Pvt. John Vincent, MM3032; Trial of Pvt. Charles Aiken, MM3140; Trial of Pvt. Robert Ireland, MM3140; Trials of Pvts. Benjamin Redding and James Grippen, MM3184; Trials of Pvts. Pompey Harkell, James Providence, Benjamin Adron, and Oretus Miller, MM3643, all JAG.

40. See Hodes, *White Women, Black Men*, 59–60, 63, 145–46; Sommerville, *Rape and Race*, 21, 40, 118–19.

41. Testimony of 2 Lieut. William H. Hollinger and Maj. William Innes in Trial of Pvt. James Sibley, LL2449, JAG.

42. Defense of Pvt. Robert Clark by Lieut. R. D. Woolsey in Trial of Pvt. Robert Clark, NN2760, JAG.

43. Lande, *Freedom Soldiers*.

44. Opinion of Gen. Benjamin Butler in Trial of Lieut. Andrew J. Smith, NN2099, JAG; the trial record for Private Johnson has been either misplaced or lost.

45. Block, *Rape and Sexual Power*, 208; Sommerville, *Rape and Race*, 40–41, 70, 124–25, 144–46.

46. Stephens, *Voice of Thunder*, 298–99.

47. Sheehan-Dean, *Calculus of Violence*, 310.

48. Trial of Pvt. George Morgan, MM2031, and Trial of Pvt. Nicholas Adams, OO556, both JAG. This claim seems highly suspicious from elite white women living in a county whose 1860 enslaved population numbered over 7,200 individuals (1860 Slave Schedule, M653).

49. Trial of James White, MM2031, JAG. See also Trial of Pvt. John Cornish, MM2106, JAG; Cornish was sentenced to be executed for attempted rape of a white woman.

50. Trial of Sgt. William Jackson, MM1984, JAG; Virginia, U.S., Marriage Registers, 1853–1935; 1870 U.S. Federal Census, M593.

51. The harshest punishment was of Sgt. Enoch George, Fifth Veterans Ohio, sentenced to "hard labor at military prison for life" after raping Nisa Grimes: MM1917, JAG.

Chapter Five. From Collaborative to Noncooperative Raiding

1. Chatham County had sixty-four approved claims, the second-largest number in the state. African Americans filed fifty-eight of them, equating to over 90 percent. Few, if any, white Savannah residents recounted Union soldiers' destruction of their property. Johnson, *Black Savannah*; Harris and Berry, "Slave Life in Savannah," 93–123; Sumler-Edmond, "Free Black Life in Savannah," 93–123, 124–39; Penningroth, *Claims of Kinfolk*, 70–78.

2. Claim of Sarah Ann Blade [Black], Chatham County, Georgia; see also Claims of Celia Boisfeillet, Rachel Bromfield, Diana Cummings, Harriet Dallas, Elizabeth Geary [*sic*], Mary Jess, Georgianna Kelley, Judy Rose, Charlotte Thompson, and Eliza Williams, SCC-NA. Eleven of the thirteen women with approved claims in Chatham County were Black (Penningroth, *Claims of Kinfolk*, 70–78).

3. McPherson, *Battle Cry of Freedom*, 718; Hattaway and Jones, *How the North Won*, 487–96; Grimsley, *Hard Hand of War*, 144–45, 162–66; Amy Murrell Taylor, *Embattled Freedom*, 132; Witt, *Lincoln's Code*, 377–78, and see also 231–39, 274–83; Royster, *Destructive War*, 340–41; Sutherland, *Savage Conflict*.

4. Frank, *Civilian War*, 6–7, 8, 27; Whites, "'Corresponding with the Enemy,'" 103–16.

5. *OR*, ser. 1, pt. 1, 42:445, 39:414, 36:801; Blair, *With Malice Toward Some*, 159; quotation from Lieber Code in Witt, *Lincoln's Code*, 393.

6. *OR*, ser. 1, 14:191–92, 838; Higginson, *Complete Civil War Journal*, 292; Ash, *Firebrand of Liberty*, 168–69, 171, 195; Foote, *Rites of Retaliation*, 44–45, 60–61, 64–65.

7. *OR*, ser. 1, 14:462; Humez, *Harriet Tubman*, 58; Bradford, *Scenes in the Life*, 86–87; Gooding, *On the Altar of Freedom*, 27–28; Fields-Black, *Combee*, 298–345.

8. Gooding, *On the Altar of Freedom*, 27–28; Fields-Black, *Combee*; Rose, *Rehearsal for Reconstruction*, 246, 247–48; Higginson, *Complete Civil War Journal*, 282; Foote, *Rites of Retaliation*, 68–70.

9. *OR*, ser. 1, 14:318; "The Ridge," National Park Service; Testimony of Elizabeth Garey and Charles A. Garey, Claim of Elizabeth Geary [*sic*], Chatham County, Georgia, SCC-NA; 1860 U.S. Census, M653; Susie King Taylor, *Reminiscences of My Life*, 9, 38; Fields-Black, *Combee*, 403.

10. Emilio, *History of the Fifty-Fourth Regiment*, 41–42; Testimony of Charles A. Garey and Elizabeth Garey in Claim of Elizabeth Geary [*sic*], SCC-NA; Duncan, *Blue-Eyed Child of Fortune*, 342–44, 348; *OR*, ser. 2, 4:954; *OR*, ser. 1, 14:318, 466–67; Witt, *Lincoln's Code*, 235–37.

11. Duncan, *Blue-Eyed Child of Fortune*, 343, 348; Higginson, *Complete Civil War Journal*, 292; Gooding, *On the Altar of Freedom*, 31; *OR*, ser. 1, 14:464; *OR*, ser. 1, pt. 2, 28:13, 21; Ash, *Firebrand of Liberty*, 196–97; Foote, *Rites of Retaliation*, 68–70; Fields-Black, *Combee*, 405–8.

12. Witt, *Lincoln's Code*, 379; *OR*, ser. 1, 36:801; *OR*, ser. 1, pt. 2, 39:136; Grimsley, *Hard Hand of War*, 172–73; Witt, *Lincoln's Code*, 231–37, 275–76, 278–79; Royster, *Destructive War*, 324; Gallagher, "Two Generals and a Valley," 14–15; Samuel Brooks to "Deair Wife," May 31, 1864, box 15, folder 14; George L. Cooley to Julia, May 29, 1864, box 26, folder 11; John A. Boon to Friends, January 15, 1864, box 11, folder 15; Ezra Kidder to unidentified, April 10 and 14, 1864, box 65, folder 14, all CWDC.

13. *OR*, ser. 1, pt. 1, 37:517–18, 607, 614; George L. Cooley to Julia, May 20, 1864, box 26, folder 11, CWDC.

14. Sergeant Peter Gamache, Memoir, 3, box 43, folder 19, CWDC.

15. Testimony of Martha Jane Charity in Claim of William Charity, Charles City County, Virginia; Claim of Judith Hass, Campbell County, Virginia; and Claim of Mary Blackburn, Augusta County, Virginia, all SCC-NA; William G. Thomas, "Nothing Ought to Astonish Us," 242–43.

16. *OR*, ser. 1, pt. 2, 43:50; Claims of Mary Jane Clem and Catharine Fravel, Shenandoah County, Virginia; Claim of Elizabeth Garber, Augusta County, Virginia, all SCC-NA.

17. Baer, *Shadows on My Heart*, 292, 296; *OR*, ser. 1, pt. 2, 43:58; see Grant quoted in Sheehan-Dean, *Calculus of Violence*, 330; William G. Thomas, "Nothing Ought to Astonish Us," 232–33; Bluhm, *Shenandoah Valley Campaign*, 46–47.

18. Baer, *Shadows on My Heart*, 292, 294–96, 297; William G. Thomas, "Nothing Ought to Astonish Us," 232–33; Bluhm, *Shenandoah Valley Campaign*, 46–47; Sheehan-Dean, *Calculus of Violence*, 331.

19. Henry C. Carr diary, June 8, 1864, box 21, folder 5; George L. Lacey to Parents, June 7, 1864, box 57, folder 6; Charles Shumway Culver diary, January 9 and 12, February 21, and March 4, 1865, box 30, folder 1; Silman Andre diary, May 14, 15, 17, 20, 22, and June 21, 1864, box 2, folder 11; Jasper B. Cheney to Mother, July 19, 1864, box 22, folder 18; Henry C. Carr diary, May 31, June 8, June 25, and September 6, 1864, box 21, folder 5; Samuel Brooks to "My Dear Wife," November 17, 1864, box 15, folder 14; Dayton E. Flint to Parents, January 26, 1865, box 40, folder 7; Albert H. Artman diary, October 10, 12, 13, 30, and November 8, 1864, box 3, folder 7; Allen Baker Jr. diary, August 10, 11, 19, 20, 28, September 1, 14, 15, 18, 15, and October 23, 1864, box 4, folder 8; Charles Chapin diary, May 18, 1864, box 22, folder 2; all CWDC.

20. Quarter Master Sergeant Ezra L. Walker diary, July 16 and 31, 1864, box 119, folder 10, CWDC.

21. Quarter Master Sergeant Ezra L. Walker diary, August 17 and 18, 1864; Thomas Campbell diary, August 11 and 17, September 26, 1864, box 20, folder 4, both CWDC.

22. Mahon, *Winchester Divided*, 176, 179, 180, 181–84.

23. Quarter Master Ezra L. Walker diary, August 19, 1864; William Allen Tall to unknown, August 25, 1864, box 113, folder 15, both CWDC.

24. Thomas Campbell diary, August 15 and September 29, 1864.

25. Thomas Campbell diary, August 28 and 29, 1864.

26. Thomas Campbell diary, September 28, 29, and 7, 1864.

27. *OR*, ser. 1, pt. 1, 43:56; Thomas Campbell diary, September 30, 1864; Henry Dove to Father, December 5, 1864, Accession 45544, PPC; for references to burning during the spring, summer, and fall campaigns, see Thomas Campbell diary, May 21, 23, 26, June 17, 18, July 12, August 16, and October 5, 1864; Andrew J. Lorish to "My dear Brother Sister & Neice," September 11, 1864, box 72, folder 12; Henry H. Houghton Memoirs, n.p., box 57, folder 5; Samuel Brooks to "Deair Wife," May 31, 1864, box 15, folder 14; Albert H. Artman diary, September 29 and October 1, 8, 1864; Allen Baker Jr. diary, September 17, 27, October 3, 4, 1864; Napoleon Bonaparte Hudson to Brother, March 12, 1864, box 57, folder 16, all CWDC; Cashin, *War Stuff*, 145–52; William G. Thomas, "Nothing Ought to Astonish Us," 240–41; Grimsley, *Hard Hand of War*, 185; Sheehan-Dean, *Calculus of Violence*, 332–34.

28. *OR*, ser. 1, pt. 4, 38:159; John A. Boon to Friends, May 19, 1864; Frederic "Fred" Henry Kellogg to Mother, April 16, June 20, 1864, box 64, folder 5, both CWDC; Castel, *Decision in the West*, 186, 196, 206–7, 218; Royster, *Destructive War*, 322.

29. Claims of Elizabeth Miller, Eliza Robertson, and Anna Skelly, trustee, Gordon County, Georgia, SCC-NA; Castel, *Decision in the West*, 186.

30. Claim of Elizabeth Miller, Gordon County, Georgia, SCC-NA.

31. *OR*, ser. 1, pt. 4, 38:193; John A. Boon to Friends, May 19, 1864; Peter W. Funk diary, May 20, 1864, box 43, folder 14, both CWDC; Castel, *Decision in the West*, 214–15, 218; some corps commanders took a harder line against pillaging than others. See *OR*, ser. 1, pt. 4, 38:128, 273; Foote, *Rites of Retaliation*, 175–206.

32. Callie Elder, in Rawick, *American Slave*, 12:313; Witt, *Lincoln's Code*, 380–81.

33. *OR*, ser. 1, pt. 1, 38:860.

34. Claims of Sarah Scott, Mary McDonald, and Sarah Crow, all Bartow County, Georgia, SCC-NA; see Testimony of Martha Barrett in Claim of Nancy Russell, Bartow County, Georgia, SCC-NA; Castel, *Decision in the West*, 214–15, 218.

35. Trials of Pvts. William Cutsinger and Charles Billingsly, NN2165, JAG; 1880 U.S. Federal Census, T9; Sheehan-Dean, *Calculus of Violence*, 312.

36. Nancy Jett to Richard Burch Jett, September 2, 1864, Richard Burch Jett Papers, 1863–1887, Stuart A. Rose Manuscript, Archives, and Rare Book Library, Emory University (hereafter RBJP).

37. Nancy Jett to Richard Burch Jett, September 2, 1864.

38. Nancy Jett to Richard Burch Jett, September 2, 1864; Hunter, *Bound in Wedlock*, 139, 179.

39. Trial of Pvt. Albert Lane, LL3150, JAG. Lane was court-martialed, found guilty, and sentenced to ten years in prison.

40. *OR*, ser. 1, pt. 1, 36:801, 416, 414; Castel, *Decision in the West*, 548–49; Sheehan-Dean, *Calculus of Violence*, 304–5.

41. Clayton, *Requiem for a Lost City*, 132–35; Myers, *Children of Pride*, 1191; Galloway, *Dear Old Roswell*; Frank, *Civilian War*, 53–56.

42. Claim of Henry and Polly Beadles [*sic*], and Claim of Saletia A. Kennedy, Fulton County, Georgia, SCC-NA; Cashin, *War Stuff*, 141–45.

43. Thomas Speed to Mr. & Mrs. Thomas Spencer Speed, September 13, 1864, Thomas Speed letter book, 1863–1896, Filson Historical Society; Jackson, *Colonel's Diary*, 151; Castel, *Decision in the West*, 548–49.

44. Burr Murdock to Sister, September 9, 1864, box 83, folder 14, CWDC; Charles Edward Bates to Parents, July 19, 1864, Charles Edward Bates Papers, 1858–1865, section 7, Virginia Museum of History and Culture; Castel, *Decision in the West*, 528–29.

45. William W. Osborn diary, October 14 and 18, 1864, box 87, folder 22; Alfred Wilcox diary, October 16 and 19, 1864, box 123, folder 8, both CWDC; Witt, *Lincoln's Code*, 276–77; Cashin, *War Stuff*, 140–41; by October Sherman had sanctioned foraging. Glatthaar, *March to the Sea*, 120.

46. Claim of Monemia Johnson, Cobb County, Georgia, SCC-NA; Castel, *Decision in the West*, 553–55; Glatthaar, *March to the Sea*, 53–56, 138–39; Witt, *Lincoln's Code*, 282; cf. Sarah Gray in Rawick, *American Slave*, 12:79.

47. *OR*, ser. 1, 44:481, 489; Johann Heinrich Sudkamp diary, November 10, 1864, box 113, folder 4, CWDC; Castel, *Decision in the West*, 553–54; Glatthaar, *March to the Sea*, 119–33; Cashin, *War Stuff*, 133–41; Grimsley, *Hard Hand of War*, 175; Royster, *Destructive War*, 341; Witt, *Lincoln's Code*, 280–81.

48. Julia Cole in Rawick, *American Slave*, 12:235; Carter, *Diary of Dolly Lunt Burge*, 159–62.

49. William G. Baugh to Parents, November 7, 1864, and to Sister Lizzie, November 9, 1864, William G. Baugh Letters, 1864–1865, Stuart A. Rose Manuscript, Archives, and Rare Book Library, Emory University (hereafter WGBL); Aldred Wilcox diary, November 18 and 26, 1864, box 123, folder 8, CWDC; George F. Glossbrenner diary, November 24, 27, 28, December 1, 2, 3, 4, 5, 6, 7, 8, 12, 14, 15, 1864, box 47, folder 1; Lester Dewitt Taylor diary, November 27, 1864, box 114, folder 5; William W. Osborn diary, November 24, 1864, box 87, folder 22; John A. Boon to Family, December 17, 1864, box 11, folder 15, all CWDC.

50. Lester Dewitt Taylor diary, December 15, 1864; Alfred W. Wilcox diary, November 18 and 27, 1864; see John A. Boon to Family, December 17, 1864; all CWDC.

51. Della Briscoe, Julia Cole, and Rachel Adams in Rawick, *American Slave*, 12:125, 235, 7.

52. Alfred W. Wilcox diary, November 18 and 23, 1864; William Osborn diary, November 23, 1864, both CWDC; Campbell, *When Sherman Marched North*, 16–17, 65; Manning, *Troubled Refuge*, 75–76. Joseph Glatthaar cites partnerships between Sherman's soldiers and African Americans. African American women interpreted these interactions differently. See Glatthaar, *March to the Sea*, 53–65; Burke Davis, *Sherman's March*, 130–31.

53. William W. Osborn diary, November 23, 1864; Alfred Wilcox diary, November 24 and 28, 1864; Campbell, *When Sherman Marched North*, 9; Glatthaar, *March to the Sea*, 134–55; Sheehan-Dean, *Calculus of Violence*, 295–96.

54. MacKethan, *Recollections of a Southern Daughter*, 71; Claims of Sylvia Baker, Julia Holmes, and Cesar and Linda Jones, Liberty County, Georgia; see also Claims of Lydia Baker, Patsy Campbell, Eliza James, Lucy McIver, and Rachel Norman, all Liberty County, Georgia, in SCC-NA. Campbell notes that formerly enslaved people filed eighty-nine of ninety-two settled claims for wartime damages in the county.

Campbell, *When Sherman Marched North*, 16; Penningroth, *Claims of Kinfolk*, 70–78; Witt, *Lincoln's Code*, 392–93.

55. MacKethan, *Recollections of a Southern Daughter*, 71–76; Myers, *Children of Pride*, 1220–27; Frank, *Civilian War*, 102; Campbell, *When Sherman Marched North*, 15–16.

56. Claims of Celia Boisfeillet and Rachel Bromfield, Chatham County, Georgia, SCC-NA; see also Claims of Diana Cummings, Harriet Dallas, Elizabeth Geary [*sic*], Mary Jess, Georgianna Kelly, Judy Rose, Charlotte Thompson, and Eliza Williams, Chatham County, Georgia, all SCC-NA. For the wartime experience of Savannah's black women, see Jones, "Wartime Workers, Moneymakers," 140–60.

57. Lester Dewitt Taylor diary, December 23, 1864; Alfred Wilcox diary, December 6, 1864; see also William G. Baugh to Parents, December 25, 1864, WGBL; Sheehan-Dean, *Calculus of Violence*, 290–91.

58. *OR*, ser. 1, pt. 2, 47:543; Witt, *Lincoln's Code*, 275–84; Glatthaar, *March to the Sea*, 140–41.

59. Rawick, *American Slave*, 3:130.

60. Rawick, *American Slave*, 3:147, 154, 257; Manda Walker in Rawick, *American Slave*, 3:170; cf. Delia Thompson in Rawick, *American Slave*, 3:160; Campbell, *When Sherman Marched North*, 45, 47, 48.

61. Claims of Harriet Smith and Rose Goethe, and also Ann Goethe, Beaufort County, South Carolina, all SCC-NA; Campbell, *When Sherman Marched North*, 61; Glatthaar, *March to the Sea*, 55–57.

62. Claim of Agnes Jackson, Beaufort County, South Carolina, SCC-NA.

63. Claim of Lavinia Cohen, Beaufort County, South Carolina, SCC-NA.

64. Mary D. Robertson, *Confederate Lady Comes of Age*, 61, 65–69. For elite white Confederate women's understanding that the war now targeted them, see Frank, *Civilian War*, 31.

65. Frances Wallace Taylor et al., *Leverett Letters*, 389, 390, 391. Civil War scholars have recently placed the conflict in the context of other nineteenth-century wars, demonstrating important limits to destruction. Foote, *Rites of Retaliation*, 5–6; Sheehan-Dean, *Calculus of Violence*, 2, 6, 37, 39–42, 191–92.

66. Weiner, *Heritage of Woe*, 102–3; see also Smith et al., *Mason Smith Family Letters*, 174–77; Marzalek, *Diary of Miss Emma Holmes*, 400, 402; Frank, *Civilian War*, 47.

67. Victoria Adams in Rawick, *American Slave*, 2:12; Schwalm, *Hard Fight for We*, 123.

68. John A. Boon to Family, April 3, 1865; Lester Dewitt Taylor diary, March 12, 1865, both CWDC; Campbell, *When Sherman Marched North*, 75–76; Glatthaar, *March to the Sea*, 146–47.

69. William G. Baugh to Beloved Parents, March 14 and 27, 1865, WGBL; Lester Dewitt Taylor diary, March 12, 1865; Elliott B. McKeever Memoirs, n.p., box 78, folder 12, CWDC; for foraging in North and South Carolina, see Samuel E. Adams diary, box 1, folder 10; Nathan Atwood Gill diary, box 46, folder 1; and Abijah F. Gore diary, box 47, folder 11, all CWDC; Campbell, *When Sherman Marched North*, 78.

70. Claims of Mary Carver, Cumberland County, North Carolina; Abigail Eldridge and Jane Royals, Johnston County, North Carolina; Sarah A. Bailey and Polly Johnson, Wake County, North Carolina, all SCC-NA.

71. Bradley, *Star Corps*, 258; Cream Mack, Eveline Morgan, and Angeline Martin, all in Rawick, *American Slave*, 10:26, 136, 49.

72. Tempie Herndon Durham, Louisa Adams, Barbara Haywood, Chaney Lewis, Mary Anderson, Fannie Dunn, Sarah Louise Augustus, Sarah Demro, Lantea Adeline Hinton, and Susan High, in Rawick, *American Slave*, 14:2, 20, 51, 248, 271, 285, 386, 406, 418, 434.

73. *OR*, ser. 1, pt. 1, 42:445, 39:414, 36:801; W. W. Parker to "My Dear Wife," October 27, 1864, Accession 50677; Rufus A. Smith to Father, May 31, 1865, Rufus A. Smith Letters, 1864–1865, Accession 50546, PPC; see also Daniel E. Worthley to Sister, April 8, 1865, Accession 44131; Nathaniel Howard Talbot to "Dear Ones," April 10, 1865, Nathaniel Howard Talbot Letters, 1865, Accession 45225, both PPC.

74. Testimony of Ellen Carpenter in Claim of J. N. Carpenter, U.S. Navy, by his wife Mrs. Mary F. Carpenter of Washington, D.C., Spotsylvania County, Virginia; Testimony of Katherine Couse and Deposition of Ann Couse, Claim of Peter Course, Spotsylvania County, Virginia; Testimony of Harriet McGee and Deposition of Frances McGee in Claim of Absalom McGee, Spotsylvania County, Virginia; Claim of Ann Goodloe, Albemarle County, Virginia, all SCC-NA.

75. Claim of Octavia L. New, Charles City County, Virginia; Claim of Lydia Fishburn, Augusta County, Virginia, both SCC-NA; see also Cashin, "Widow in a Swamp," 171–84.

Conclusion

1. Brockett and Vaughan, *Woman's Work in the Civil War*; Brock, *Richmond During the War.*

2. Penningroth, *Claims of Kinfolk*, 114–15. Penningroth notes that initially the commission only intended to accept claims from white Unionists.

3. Claim of Elizabeth Geary [*sic*], Chatham County, Georgia, SCC-NA.

BIBLIOGRAPHY

Manuscript Collections

Stuart A. Rose Manuscript, Archives, and Rare Book Library, Emory University, Atlanta, Georgia

William G. Baugh letters, 1864–1865

Filson Historical Society, Louisville, Kentucky

Milton T. Carey Papers, 1862–1865
Alfred Pirtle Papers, 1847–1924
Thomas Speed letter book, 1863–1896

Kentucky Historical Society, Frankfort, Kentucky

Ellen Wallace diary, 1849, 1864–1865
Ellen Wallace diary, 1861–1863

Library of Virginia, Richmond

Louise Humphreys Carter reminiscences
Henry Dove letter
Stinson P. Everill letter
George E. Harvey letter
William Mickle letter
W. W. Parker letter
Rufus A. Smith letters
John Viles letters
Daniel E. Worthley letter, 1865 April 8

Mississippi Department of Archives and History, Jackson

Clark-Boddie Family Papers
Catherine (Kate) Olivia Foster diary
Cordelia Lewis Scales letters

National Archives and Records Administration, Washington, D.C.

RECORD GROUP 153: RECORDS OF THE OFFICE OF THE JUDGE ADVOCATE GENERAL, U.S. ARMY

Entry 153.2.3 Court-Martial Case Files and Related Records

RECORD GROUP 217: RECORDS OF THE ACCOUNTING OFFICERS OF THE DEPARTMENT OF THE TREASURY

Entry 217.8.5: Records of the Claims Division

U.S. Army Heritage and Education Center, Carlisle, Pennsylvania

Samuel E. Adams diary
Silman Andre diary
Albert H. Artman diary
Allen Baker Jr. diaries, part 2 of 3
James H. Bayne correspondence, parts 1 and 2
John C. Baum diaries
Boucher Family Papers parts 1 and 2
Charles Brandegee correspondence, parts 1–4
Samuel Brooks correspondence
Douglass Ritchie Bushnell correspondence
Thomas Campbell diaries, parts 1 through 3
Henry C. Carr diary
Charles Chapin diary
Jasper B. Cheney letters
George L. Cooley correspondence
Charles Shumway Culver diary
Dayton E. Flint letters
Peter W. Funk diary
Sergeant Peter Gamache report
Nathan Atwood Gill diary
George F. Glossbrenner diary
Abijah F. Gore diary
George Hill Jr. correspondence
Freland N. Holman correspondence
Napoleon Bonaparte Hudson letters
Frederic Henry Kellogg letters, parts 1 and 2
Ezra Kidder letters
George L. Lacey correspondence
Andrew J. Lorish letters
Charles Lutz correspondence, parts 1 and 2
Elliott B. McKeever account
Burr Murdock letters
William W. Osborn diary
James L. Rea correspondence
David Samson correspondence
George Simpson and James Randolph correspondence, parts 1 and 2

Lewis Bayard Smith letter book, part 1
William A. Smith correspondence
Johann Heinrich Sudkamp diary
William Allen Tall correspondence
Lester Dewitt Taylor diary
Watson Brothers correspondence, part 1 of 4
Alfred Wilcox diary
George A. Wilson correspondence

Jean and Alexander Heard Library, Vanderbilt University, Nashville, Tennessee

William Giles Harding Papers

Virginia Museum of History and Culture, Richmond

Charles Edward Bates letters, 1863–1864
Garnett Family Papers
Margaret Tilloston Kemble Nourse diary
George H. Patch Papers
Taliaferro Family Papers
Tompkins Family Papers
Jefferson Whitcomb diary
Wynne Family Papers

Newspapers and Periodicals

New Orleans Daily Picayune
Savannah Daily Morning News
Savannah Republican

Government Records

1850 United States Federal Census, (Washington, D.C.: National Archives and Records Administration, n.d.), accessed via Ancestry.com, M432.

1850 U.S. Federal Census—Slave Schedules (Washington, D.C.: National Archives and Records Administration, n.d.), accessed via Ancestry.com, M432.

1860 United States Federal Census (Washington, D.C.: National Archives and Records Administration, n.d.), accessed via Ancestry.com, M653.

1860 U.S. Federal Census—Slave Schedules (Washington, D.C., National Archives and Records Administration, n.d.), accessed via Ancestry.com, M653.

1870 United States Federal Census (Washington, D.C.: National Archives and Records Administration, n.d.), accessed via Ancestry.com, M593.

1880 United States Federal Census (Washington, D.C.: National Archives and Records Administration, n.d.), accessed via Ancestry.com, T9.

An Act for Establishing the Rules and Articles for the Government of the Armies of the United States, ch. 20, 2 Stat. 359 (1806).

Enrollment Act, Pub. L. No. 37–35, 12 Stat. 793 (1863).

Kentucky Marriages, 1797–1865, accessed via Ancestry.com.

United States War Department. *Revised United States Army Regulations of 1861 . . .* Washington, D.C.: Government Printing Office, 1863.

———. *War of the Rebellion: A Compilation of the Official Records of the Union and Confederate Armies.* 128 vols. Washington, D.C.: Government Printing Office, 1880–1901.

U.S., Confederate Officers Card Index, 1861–1865, accessed via Ancestry.com.

Virginia, U.S., Marriage Registers, 1853–1935, accessed via Ancestry.com.

Internet Sources

"Army in September 1865." Mapping Occupation. https://www.mappingoccupation.org/. Accessed June 5, 2025.

Douglass, Frederick. "The Meaning of July Fourth for the Negro." *Africans in America.* https://www.pbs.org/wgbh/aia/part4/4h2927t.html. Accessed June 12, 2024.

First Confiscation Act. Freedmen and Southern Society Project, University of Maryland. June 10, 2021. http://www.freedmen.umd.edu/conact1.htm.

"Fort Pickens." National Park Service. https://www.nps.gov/places/000/fort-pickens.htm. Accessed September 7, 2023.

Militia Act of 1862. Freedmen and Southern Society Project, University of Maryland. June 10, 2021. http://www.freedmen.umd.edu/milact.htm.

"The Ridge." *National Register of Historic Places.* https://npgallery.nps.gov/NRHP/AssetDetail?assetID=1bb280c6-63d7-4807-96e7-fc8724c996bb. Accessed April 2, 2021.

Second Confiscation Act. Freedmen and Southern Society Project, University of Maryland. June 10, 2021. http://www.freedmen.umd.edu/conact2.htm.

Published Primary Accounts

Anderson, John Q., ed. *Brokenburn: The Journal of Kate Stone, 1861–1868.* Baton Rouge: Louisiana State University, 1955.

Andrews, Eliza Frances. *The War-Time Journal of a Georgia Girl, 1864–1865*. New York: Appleton-Century-Crofts, 1908.

Ashkenazi, Elliot, ed. *The Civil War Diary of Clara Solomon: Growing Up in New Orleans, 1861–1862*. Baton Rouge: Louisiana State University, 1995.

Baer, Elizabeth R., ed. *Shadows on My Heart: The Civil War Diary of Lucy Rebecca Buck of Virginia*. Athens: University of Georgia, 1997.

Benét, S. V., Bvt. Lieut.-Col. *A Treatise on Military Law and the Practice of Courts-Martial*. 6th ed. New York: D. Van Nostrand, 1868.

Berlin, Ira, Barbara J. Fields, Thavolia Glymph, Joseph P. Reidy, and Leslie S. Rowland, eds. *The Destruction of Slavery*. Freedom: A Documentary History of Emancipation, 1861–1867. Cambridge: Cambridge University Press, 1985.

Berlin, Ira, Steven F. Miller, Joseph R. Reidy, and Leslie S. Rowland, eds. *The Wartime Genesis of Free Labor: The Upper South*. Freedom: A Documentary History of Emancipation, 1861–1867. Cambridge: Cambridge University Press, 1993.

Berlin, Ira, Joseph P. Reidy, and Leslie S. Rowland, eds. *The Black Military Experience*. Freedom: A Documentary History of Emancipation, 1861–1867. Cambridge: Cambridge University Press, 1982.

Bickham, William D. *Rosecrans Campaign with the Fourteenth Army Corps, or the Army of the Cumberland*. Cincinnati: Moore, Wilstach, Keys, 1863.

Bradford, Sarah H. *Scenes in the Life of Harriet Tubman*. Auburn, N.Y.: W. J. Moses, 1869.

Bradley, George S. *The Star Corps, or, Notes of an Army Chaplain During Sherman's Famous "March to the Sea."* Milwaukee: Jermain & Brightman, 1865.

Brock, Sallie A. *Richmond During the War: Four Years of Personal Observation*. New York: G. W. Carleton, 1867.

Brockett, L. P., M.D., and Mrs. Mary C. Vaughan. *Woman's Work in the Civil War: A Record of Heroism, Patriotism, and Patience*. Philadelphia: Zeigler, McCurdy, 1867.

Butler, Benjamin Franklin. *Private and Official Correspondence of Major General Benjamin F. Butler, During the Period of the Civil War*. Norwood, Mass.: Plimpton Press, 1917.

Carney, Kate. *Kate Carney Diary*. New Canaan, Conn.: Readex Film Products, 1990.

Carter, Christine Jacobson, ed. *The Diary of Dolly Lunt Burge, 1848–1879*. Athens: University of Georgia Press, 1997.

Caruthers, R. L., and A. O. P. Nicholson, comps. *A Compilation of the Statutes of Tennessee . . .* Nashville: Steam Press of James Smith, 1836.

Chesnut, Mary Miller Boykin. *Mary Chesnut's Civil War.* Edited by C. Vann Woodward. New Haven, Conn.: Yale University Press, 1981.

Clayton, Sarah "Sallie" Conley. *Requiem for a Lost City: A Memoir of Civil War Atlanta and the Old South.* Edited by Robert Scott Davis Jr. Macon, Ga.: Mercer University Press, 1999.

Cross, Eleanor P., and Charles B. Cross Jr., eds. *Glencoe Diary: The War-Time Journal of Elizabeth Curtis Wallace.* Chesapeake, Va.: Norfolk County Historical Society, 1968.

Curry, William L. *Four Years in the Saddle: History of the First Regiment Ohio Volunteer Cavalry.* Columbus: Champlin, 1898.

Dodge, William Sumner. *History of the Old Second Division, Army of the Cumberland: Commanders: M'Cook, Sill, and Johnson.* Chicago: Church & Goodman, 1864.

Duncan, Russell, ed. *Blue-Eyed Child of Fortune: The Civil War Letters of Colonel Robert Gould Shaw.* Athens: University of Georgia Press, 1992.

Dwight, Wilder. *Life and Letters of Wilder Dwight, Lieut.-Col. Second Mass. Inf. Vols.* Boston: Ticknor & Fields, 1868.

Eby, Henry Harrison. *Observations of an Illinois Boy in Battle, Camp, and Prison, 1861–1865.* Mendota, Ill.: N.p., 1910.

Emilio, Luis Fennollosa. *History of the Fifty-Fourth Regiment of Massachusetts Volunteer Infantry, 1863–1865.* 2nd ed. Boston: Boston Book Co., 1894.

Foroughi, Andrea R. *Go If You Think It Your Duty: A Minnesota Couple's Civil War Letters.* St. Paul: Minnesota Historical Society, 2008.

French, Lucy Virginia. *L. Virginia French's War Journal, 1862–1865.* Edited by Jerry W. Smith. Chapel Hill: University of North Carolina Libraries, n.d.

Galloway, T. H., ed. *Dear Old Roswell: Civil War Letters of the King Family of Roswell, Georgia.* Macon, Ga.: Mercer University Press, 2003.

Getz, Elizabeth A. "Between the Lines: The Diary of a Unionist Woman at the Battle of Spotsylvania Court House." *Fredericksburg History and Biography* 1 (2002): 56–90.

Gibson, Joseph Thompson. *History of the Seventy-Eighth Pennsylvania Volunteer Infantry.* Pittsburgh: Pittsburgh Printing, 1905.

Gooding, James Henry. *On the Altar of Freedom: A Black Soldier's Civil War Letters from the Front.* Edited by Virginia Matzke Adams. Amherst: University of Massachusetts Press, 1991.

Haines, Zenas T. *In the Country of the Enemy: The Civil War Reports of a Massachusetts Corporal.* Edited by William C. Harris. Gainesville: University Press of Florida, 1999.

Hardin, Elizabeth Pendleton. *The Private War of Lizzie Hardin*. Edited by G. Glenn Clift. Louisville, Ky.: Dunne, 1963.
Hawks, Esther Hill. *A Woman Doctor's Civil War: Esther Hill Hawks' Diary*. Edited by Gerald Schwartz. Columbia: University of South Carolina Press, 1984.
Hazen, William Babcock. *A Narrative of Military Service*. Boston: Ticknor, 1885.
Higginson, Thomas Wentworth. *The Complete Civil War Journal and Selected Letters of Thomas Wentworth Higginson*. Edited by Christopher Looby. Chicago: University of Chicago Press, 2000.
Hinkley, Julian Wisner. *A Narrative of Service with the Third Wisconsin Infantry*. Madison: Wisconsin History Commission, 1912.
Hoobler, James, ed. "The Civil War Diary of Louisa Brown Pearl." *Tennessee Historical Quarterly* 38 (September 1979): 308–21.
Jackson, Oscar Lawrence. *The Colonel's Diary: Journals Kept Before and After the Civil War by the Late Oscar Lawrence Jackson*. N.p., 1922.
Jacobs, Harriet. *Incidents in the Life of a Slave Girl*. New York: Modern Library, 2021.
Jones, Jenkin Lloyd. *An Artilleryman's Diary*. Madison: Wisconsin History Association Commission, 1914.
LeConte, Emma. *When the World Ended: The Diary of Emma LeConte*. Edited by Earl Schenck Miers. Oxford: Oxford University Press, 1957.
Leonard, Sherli. "What Lafayette Bailey's Letters Lacked in Grammar They More Than Made Up for in Heartfelt Emotion." *America's Civil War* 11 (1985): 72–75.
Light, Rebecca Campbell, ed. *War at Our Doors: The Civil War Diaries and Letters of the Bernard Sisters of Virginia*. Fredericksburg: American History, 1998.
Lincoln, Abraham. *The Collected Works of Abraham Lincoln*. Edited by Roy P. Basler. 9 vols. New Brunswick, N.J.: Rutgers University Press, 1953.
MacKethan, Lucinda H., ed. *Recollections of a Southern Daughter: A Memoir by Cornelia Jones Pond of Liberty County*. Athens: University of Georgia Press, 1998.
Mahon, Michael G., ed. *Winchester Divided: The Civil War Diaries of Julia Chase and Laura Lee*. Mechanicsburg, Pa.: Stackpole Books, 2002.
Marshall, Jessie A., ed. *Private and Official Correspondence of General Benjamin F. Butler During the Period of the Civil War*. Norwood, Mass.: Plimpton Press, 1917.
Marzalek, John F., ed. *The Diary of Miss Emma Holmes, 1861–1866*. Baton Rouge: Louisiana State University Press, 1979.

Maury, Betty Herndon. "The Civil War Diary of Betty Herndon Maury." *Fredericksburg History and Biography* 9 (2010): 9–121.

McClellan, George B. *McClellan's Own Story: The War for the Union . . .* New York: Charles L. Webster, 1887.

McGee, Benjamin F. *History of the 72d Indiana Volunteer Infantry of the Mounted Lightning Brigade Volume*. Edited by William R. Jewell. Lafayette, Ind.: S. Vater, 1882.

Morgan, Sarah. *The Civil War Diary of a Southern Woman*. Edited by Charles East. New York: Simon & Schuster, 1991.

Musser, Charles O. *Soldier Boy: The Civil War Letters of Charles O. Musser, 29th Iowa*. Edited by Bobby Popchock. Iowa City: University of Iowa Press, 2008.

Myers, Robert Manson, ed. *The Children of Pride: A True Story of Georgia and the Civil War*. New Haven, Conn.: Yale University Press, 1972.

Olmstead, Frederick Law. *The Cotton Kingdom: A Traveller's Observations on Cotton and Slavery in the American Slave States, 1853–1861*. Edited by Arthur M. Schlesinger. New York: Da Capo Press, 1996.

Owens, Ira S. *Green County Soldiers in the Late War . . .* Dayton, Ohio: Christian Publishing House, 1884.

Peter, Frances. *A Union Woman in Civil War Kentucky: The Diary of Frances Peter*. Edited by John David Smith and William Cooper Jr. Lexington: University Press of Kentucky, 2000.

Rawick, George P., ed. *The American Slave: A Composite Autobiography*. 12 vols. Greenwood, Conn.: Greenwood Press, 1972.

Ready, Alice. *Diary of Alice Ready, 1860, 1862*. New Canaan, Conn.: Readex Film Products, 1990.

Robertson, James I., Jr. "An Indiana Soldier in Love and War: The Civil War Letters of John V. Hadley." *Indiana Magazine of History*, September 1963, 189–288.

Robertson, Mary D., ed. *A Confederate Lady Comes of Age: The Journal of Pauline DeCaradeuc Heyward, 1863–1888*. Columbia: University of South Carolina Press, 1992.

Scott, Winfield. *Memoirs of Lieut.-General Scott*. 2 vols. New York: Sheldon, 1864.

Shaw, James Birney. *History of the Tenth Regiment Indiana Volunteer Infantry*. Lafayette, Ind.: N.p., 1912.

Smith, Daniel E. Huger, Alice R. Huger Smith, and Arney R. Childs, eds. *Mason Smith Family Letters, 1860–1868*. Columbia: University of South Carolina Press, 1950.

Stephens, George E. *A Voice of Thunder: The Civil War Letters of George E. Stephens*. Edited by Donald Yacavone. Urbana: University of Illinois Press, 1997.

Taylor, Frances Wallace, Catherine Taylor Mathews, and J. Tracy Power, eds. *The Leverett Letters: Correspondence of a South Carolina Family, 1851–1868*. Columbia: University of South Carolina Press, 2000.

Taylor, Susie King. *Reminiscences of My Life in Camp: An African American Woman's Civil War Memoir*. Athens: University of Georgia Press, 2006.

Thomas, Ella Gertrude Clanton. *The Secret Eye: The Journal of Ella Gertrude Clanton Thomas, 1848–1889*. Edited by Virginia Ingraham Burr. Chapel Hill: University of North Carolina Press, 1990.

Uffelman, Minoa D., Ellen Kanervo, Phyllis Smith, and Eleanor Williams, eds. *The Diary of Nannie Haskins Williams: A Southern Woman's Story of Rebellion and Reconstruction, 1863–1890*. Knoxville: University of Tennessee Press, 2014.

Underwood, Josie. *Josie Underwood's Civil War Diary*. Edited by Nancy Disher Baird. Lexington: University Press of Kentucky, 2009.

Washington, Booker T. *Up from Slavery*. New York: Penguin, 1986.

Weiner, Marli F., ed. *Heritage of Woe: The Civil War Diary of Grace Brown Elmore, 1861–1868*. Athens: University of Georgia Press, 1997.

Wills, Charles Wright. *Army Life of an Illinois Soldier: Including a Day by Day Record of Sherman's March to the Sea*. Washington, D.C.: Globe, 1906.

Secondary Sources

Ash, Stephen. *Firebrand of Liberty: The Story of Two Black Regiments That Changed the Course of the Civil War*. New York: W. W. Norton, 2008.

———. *When the Yankees Came: Conflict and Chaos in the Occupied South, 1861–1865*. Chapel Hill: University of North Carolina Press, 1995.

Attie, Jeanie. *Patriotic Toil: Northern Women and the American Civil War*. Ithaca, N.Y.: Cornell University Press, 1998.

Bailyn, Bernard. *The Ideological Origins of the American Revolution*. Cambridge, Mass.: Belknap Press, 1967.

Ball, Erica L. *To Live an Antislavery Life: Personal Politics and the Antebellum Black Middle Class*. Athens: University of Georgia Press, 2012.

Banner, Lois W. *American Beauty*. New York: Alfred A. Knopf, 1983.

Barber, E. Susan, and Charles F. Ritter. "'Physical Abuse . . . and Rough Handling': Race, Gender, and Sexual Justice in the Occupied South." In Whites and Long, *Occupied Women*.

Bardaglio, Peter W. *Reconstructing the Household: Families, Sex, and the Law in the Nineteenth-Century South*. Chapel Hill: University of North Carolina Press, 2000.

Beilein, Joseph M., Jr. *Bushwhackers: Guerrilla Warfare, Manhood, and the Household in Civil War Missouri*. Kent, Ohio: Kent State University Press, 2016.

Bercaw, Nancy. *Gendered Freedoms: Race, Rights, and the Politics of Household in the Delta, 1861–1875*. Gainesville: University Press of Florida, 2003.

Berkin, Carole. *Revolutionary Mothers: Women in the Struggle for America's Independence*. New York: Vintage, 2006.

Berry, Daina Ramey. *The Price for Their Pound of Flesh: The Value of the Enslaved, from Womb to Grave, in the Building of a Nation*. Boston: Beacon, 2017.

Bever, Megan L. *At War with King Alcohol: Debating Drinking and Masculinity in the Civil War*. Chapel Hill: University of North Carolina Press, 2022.

Bever, Megan L., Lesley J. Gordon, and Laura Mammina, eds. *American Discord: The Republic and Its People in the Civil War Era*. Baton Rouge: Louisiana State University Press, 2020.

Blair, William. *With Malice Toward Some: Treason and Loyalty in the Civil War Era*. Chapel Hill: University of North Carolina Press, 2014.

Bloch, Ruth H. *Gender and Morality in Anglo-American Culture, 1650–1800*. Berkeley: University of California Press, 2003.

Block, Sharon. *Rape and Sexual Power in Early America*. Chapel Hill: University of North Carolina Press, 2006.

Bluhm, Raymond K., Jr. *The Shenandoah Valley Campaign, March–November 1864*. Washington, D.C.: Center of Military History, 2014.

Bond, Beverly G., and Sarah Wilkerson Freeman, eds. *Tennessee Women: Their Lives, Their Times*. Vol. 2. Athens: University of Georgia Press, 2015.

Boydston, Jeanne. *Home and Work: Housework, Wages, and the Ideology of Labor in the Early Republic*. Oxford: Oxford University Press, 1991.

Brasher, Glenn David. *The Peninsula Campaign and the Necessity of Emancipation: African Americans and the Fight for Freedom*. Chapel Hill: University of North Carolina Press, 2012.

Brill, Kristen. *The Weaker Sex in War: Gender and Nationalism in Civil War Virginia*. Charlottesville: University of Virginia Press, 2022.

Brown, Kathleen M. *Good Wives, Nasty Wenches, and Anxious Patriarchs: Gender, Race, and Power in Colonial Virginia*. Chapel Hill: University of North Carolina Press, 1996.

Browning, Judkin. *Shifting Loyalties: The Union Occupation of Eastern North Carolina*. Chapel Hill: University of North Carolina Press, 2011.

Butler, Judith. *Gender Trouble: Feminism and the Subversion of Identity*. New York: Routledge, 2006.

Bynum, Victoria E. *Unruly Women: The Politics of Social and Sexual Control in the Old South*. Chapel Hill: University of North Carolina Press, 1992.

Camp, Stephanie. *Closer to Freedom: Enslaved Women and Everyday Resistance in the Plantation South*. Chapel Hill: University of North Carolina Press, 2004.

Campbell, Jacqueline Glass. *When Sherman Marched North from the Sea: Resistance on the Confederate Home Front*. Chapel Hill: University of North Carolina Press, 2003.

Cashin, Joan E. *War Stuff: The Struggle for Human and Environmental Resources in the American Civil War*. Cambridge: Cambridge University Press, 2018.

———. "Widow in a Swamp: Gender, Unionism, and Literacy in the Occupied South During the Civil War." In Whites and Long, *Occupied Women*.

Castel, Albert. *Decision in the West: The Atlanta Campaign of 1864*. Lawrence: University Press of Kansas, 1992.

Cimprich, John. *Navigating Liberty: Black Refugees and Antislavery Reformers in the Civil War South*. Baton Rouge: Louisiana State University Press, 2023.

Clavin, Matthew J. *Aiming for Pensacola: Fugitive Slaves on the Atlantic and Southern Frontiers*. Cambridge, Mass.: Harvard University Press, 2015.

Clinton, Catherine, ed. *Southern Families at War: Loyalty and Conflict in the Civil War*. Oxford: Oxford University Press, 2000.

Clinton, Catherine, and Nina Silber, eds. *Battle Scars: Gender and Sexuality in the American Civil War*. Oxford: Oxford University Press, 2006.

Conlin, Michael F. *The Constitutional Origins of the American Civil War*. Cambridge: Cambridge University Press, 2019.

Cott, Nancy F. *The Bonds of Womanhood: "Woman's Sphere" in New England, 1780–1835*. New Haven, Conn.: Yale University Press, 1997.

Crabb, Alfred Leland. *Nashville: Personality of a City*. New York: Bobbs-Merrill, 1960.

Crofts, Daniel W. *Reluctant Confederates: Upper South Unionists in the Secession Crisis*. Chapel Hill: University of North Carolina Press, 1989.

Davis, Adrienne D. "'Don't Let Nobody Bother Yo' Principle': The Sexual Economy of American Slavery." In Davis, *Black Sexual Economies*.

Davis, Adrienne D., ed. *Black Sexual Economies: Race and Sex in a Culture of Capital*. Urbana: University of Illinois Press, 2019.

Davis, Burke. *Sherman's March*. New York: Random House, 1980.

Doyle, Don. *New Men, New Cities, New South*. Chapel Hill: University of North Carolina Press, 1990.

Durham, Walter T. *Nashville: The Occupied City*. Knoxville: University of Tennessee Press, 2008.

Dyer, Frederick H. *A Compendium of the War of the Rebellion* . . . Des Moines, Ia.: Dyer, 1908.

Edwards, Laura. *Scarlett Doesn't Live Here Anymore: Southern Women in the Civil War Era*. Urbana: University of Illinois Press, 2000.

———. "Status Without Rights: African Americans and the Tangled History of Law and Governance in the Nineteenth-Century U.S. South." *American Historical Review* 112, no. 2 (April 2007): 365–93.

Egerton, Douglas R. *Thunder at the Gates: The Black Civil War Regiments That Redeemed America*. New York: Basic Books, 2016.

Elder, Angela Esco. *Love and Duty: Confederate Widows and the Emotional Politics of Loss*. Chapel Hill: University of North Carolina Press, 2021.

Elshtain, Jean Bethke. *Women and War*. Chicago: University of Chicago Press, 1995.

Esty, Kaisha. "'I Told Him to Let Me Alone, That He Hurt Me': Black Women and Girls and the Battle over Labor and Sexual Consent in Union-Occupied Territory." *Labor* 19, no. 1 (March 2022): 32–51.

Farnham, Christie Anne. *The Education of the Southern Belle: Higher Education and Student Socialization in the Antebellum South*. New York: New York University Press, 1994.

Faust, Drew Gilpin. *The Creation of Confederate Nationalism: Ideology and Identity in the Civil War South*. Baton Rouge: Louisiana State University Press, 1988.

———. *Mothers of Invention: Women of the Slaveholding South in the American Civil War*. Chapel Hill: University of North Carolina Press, 1996.

Fehrenbacher, Don E. *The Slaveholding Republic: An Account of the United States Government's Relations to Slavery*. Completed and edited by Ward M. McAfee. Oxford: Oxford University Press, 2001.

Feimster, Crystal N. "Rape and Mutiny at Fort Jackson: Black Laundresses Testify in Civil War Louisiana." *Labor* 19, no. 1 (March 2022): 11–31.

Fellman, Michael. *Inside War: The Guerrilla Conflict in Missouri During the American Civil War*. Oxford: Oxford University Press, 1990.

Fields, Barbara J., and Karen E. Fields. *Racecraft: The Soul of Inequality in the Heart of American Life*. 2nd ed. New York: Verso, 2014.

Fields-Black, Edda L. *Combee: Harriet Tubman, The Combahee River Raid, and Black Freedom During the Civil War*. Oxford: Oxford University Press, 2024.

Floan, Howard R. *The South in Northern Eyes, 1831–1861*. New York: McGraw Hill, 1958.

Foner, Eric. *The Fiery Trial: Abraham Lincoln and American Slavery*. New York: W. W. Norton, 2010.

———. *Forever Free: The Story of Emancipation and Reconstruction*. New York: Alfred A. Knopf, 2005.

———. *Free Soil, Free Labor, Free Men: The Ideology of the Republican Party Before the Civil War*. Oxford: Oxford University Press, 1970.

Foote, Lorien. *The Gentlemen and the Roughs: Manhood, Honor, and Violence in the Union Army*. New York: New York University Press, 2010.

———. "Rethinking the Confederate Home Front." *Journal of the Civil War Era* 17, no. 3 (September 2017): 446–65.

———. *Rites of Retaliation: Civilizations, Soldiers, and Campaigns in the American Civil War*. Chapel Hill: University of North Carolina Press, 2021.

Ford, Lacy K. *Deliver Us from Evil: The Slavery Question in the Old South*. Oxford: Oxford University Press, 2009.

Foucault, Michel. *The History of Sexuality*, vol. 1: *An Introduction*. Translated by Alan Sheridan. New York: Vintage, 1978.

Fox-Genovese, Elizabeth. *Within the Plantation Household: Black and White Women of the Old South*. Chapel Hill: University of North Carolina Press, 1988.

Frank, Lisa Tendrich. *The Civilian War: Confederate Women and Union Soldiers During Sherman's March*. Baton Rouge: Louisiana State University Press, 2015.

Frank, Lisa Tendrich, and LeeAnn Whites, eds. *Household War: How Americans Lived and Fought the Civil War*. Athens: University of Georgia Press, 2020.

Frankel, Noralee. *Freedom's Women: Black Women and Families in Civil War Era Mississippi*. Bloomington: Indiana University Press, 1999.

Fritz, Karen E. *Voices in the Storm: Confederate Rhetoric, 1861–1865*. Denton: University of North Texas Press, 1999.

Fulton, DoVeanna S. *Speaking Power: Black Feminist Orality in Women's Narratives of Slavery*. Albany: State University of New York Press, 2006.

Gallagher, Gary. "Two Generals and a Valley: Philip H. Sheridan and Jubal A. Early in the Shenandoah." In Gallagher, *Shenandoah Valley Campaign of 1864*.

Gallagher, Gary, ed. *The Shenandoah Valley Campaign of 1864*. Chapel Hill: University of North Carolina Press, 2006.

Genovese, Eugene. *Roll, Jordan, Roll: The World the Slaves Made*. New York: Vintage, 1976.

Giesberg, Judith. *Army at Home: Women and the Civil War on the Northern Home Front*. Chapel Hill: University of North Carolina Press, 2009.

Glatthaar, Joseph T. *The March to the Sea and Beyond: Sherman's Troops in the Savannah and Carolinas Campaign*. New York: New York University Press, 1985.

Glymph, Thavolia. "Archives of a Different Sort: Marking the Battlefields of War." *Perspectives on History*. American Historical Association, May 7, 2024. https://www.historians.org/perspectives-article/archives-of-a-different-sort-marking-the-battlefields-of-war-may-2024/.

———. "Noncombatant Military Laborers in the Civil War." *OAH Magazine of History* 2 (2012): 25–29.

———. *Out of the House of Bondage: The Transformation of the Plantation Household*. Cambridge: Cambridge University Press, 2008.

———. *The Women's Fight: The Civil War's Battles for Home, Freedom, and Nation*. Chapel Hill: University of North Carolina Press, 2020.

Goodheart, Adam. *1861: The Civil War Awakening*. New York: Alfred A. Knopf, 2011.

Greenberg, Amy S. *Lady First: The World of First Lady Sarah Polk*. New York: Alfred A. Knopf, 2019.

———. *Manifest Manhood and the Antebellum American Empire*. Cambridge: Cambridge University Press, 2005.

Greenberg, Kenneth S. *Honor and Slavery*. Princeton, N.J.: Princeton University Press, 1997.

Grimsley, Mark. *The Hard Hand of War: Union Military Policy Toward Southern Civilians, 1861–1865*. Cambridge: Cambridge University Press, 1995.

Guild, June Purcell. *Black Laws of Virginia: A Summary of the Legislative Acts of Virginia Concerning Negroes from Earliest Times to the Present*. New York: Negro Universities Press, 1936.

Gullickson, Gay. "La Pétroleuse: Representing Revolution." *Feminist Studies* 17 (1991): 241–65.

Hahn, Steven. *A Nation Under Our Feet: Black Political Struggles in the Rural South from Slavery to the Great Migration*. Cambridge, Mass.: Belknap Press, 2003.

Halttunen, Karen. *Confidence Men and Painted Women: A Study of Middle-Class Culture in America, 1830–1870*. New Haven, Conn.: Yale University Press, 1982.

Harris, Leslie M. *In the Shadow of Slavery: African Americans in New York City, 1626–1863*. Chicago: University of Chicago Press, 2003.

Harris, Leslie M., and Daina Ramey Berry. "Slave Life in Savannah: Geographies of Autonomy and Control." In Harris and Berry, *Slavery and Freedom in Savannah*.

Harris, Leslie M., and Daina Ramey Berry, eds. *Slavery and Freedom in Savannah*. Athens: University of Georgia Press, 2014.

Hattaway, Herman, and Archer Jones. *How the North Won: A Military History of the Civil War*. Urbana: University of Illinois Press, 1983.

Hodes, Martha. *The Sea Captain's Wife: A True Story of Love, Race and War in the Nineteenth Century*. New York: W. W. Norton, 2006.

———. *White Women, Black Men: Illicit Sex in the Nineteenth-Century South*. New Haven, Conn.: Yale University Press, 1997.

Howard, Victor B. *Black Liberation in Kentucky: Emancipation and Freedom, 1862–1884*. Lexington: University Press of Kentucky, 1983.

Humez, Jean M. *Harriet Tubman: The Life and the Stories*. Madison: University of Wisconsin Press, 2003.

Hunter, Tera W. *Bound in Wedlock: Slave and Free Black Marriage in the Nineteenth Century*. Cambridge, Mass.: Belknap Press, 2017.

Hyde, Sarah L. *Schooling in the Antebellum South: The Rise of Public and Private Education in Louisiana, Mississippi, and Alabama*. Baton Rouge: Louisiana State University Press, 2016.

Inscoe, John C., and Gordon B. McKinney. *The Heart of Confederate Appalachia: Western North Carolina in the Civil War*. Chapel Hill: University of North Carolina Press, 2000.

Isenberg, Nancy. *Sex and Citizenship in Antebellum America*. Chapel Hill: University of North Carolina Press, 1998.

Jabour, Anya. *Scarlett's Sisters: Young Women in the Old South*. Chapel Hill: University of North Carolina Press, 2007.

Jeffry, Julie Roy. *Frontier Women: Civilizing the West? 1840–1880*. Rev. ed. New York: Hill & Wang, 1998.

Johnson, Whittington B. *Black Savannah: 1788–1864*. Fayetteville: University of Arkansas Press, 1996.

Jones, Jacqueline. *Labor of Love, Labor of Sorrow: Black Women, Work, and the Family, from Slavery to the Present*. Rev. ed. New York: Basic Books, 2010.

———. "Wartime Workers, Moneymakers: Black Labor in Civil War–Era Savannah." In Harris and Berry, *Slavery and Freedom in Savannah*.

Jones, Martha S. *Birthright Citizens: A History of Race and Rights in Antebellum America*. Cambridge: Cambridge University Press, 2018.

Jones-Rogers, Stephanie E. *They Were Her Property: White Women as Slave Owners in the American South*. New Haven, Conn.: Yale University Press, 2019.

Kasson, John F. *Rudeness and Civility: Manners in Nineteenth-Century Urban America*. New York: Noonday, 1991.

Kendi, Ibram X. *Stamped from the Beginning: The Definitive History of Racist Ideas in America*. New York: Nation Books, 2016.

Kerber, Linda K. *No Constitutional Right to Be Ladies: Women and the Obligations of Citizenship*. New York: Hill & Wang, 1999.

———. *Women of the Republic: Intellect and Ideology in Revolutionary America.* Chapel Hill: University of North Carolina Press, 1980.

Kimmel, Michael. *Manhood in America: A Cultural History.* New York: Free Press, 1996.

King, Wilma. "'Prematurely Knowing of Evil Things': The Sexual Abuse of African American Girls and Young Women in Slavery and Freedom." *Journal of African American History* 99, no. 3 (2014): 173–96.

Lande, Jonathan. *Freedom Soldiers: The Emancipation of Black Soldiers in Civil War Camps, Courts, and Prisons.* Oxford: Oxford University Press, 2024.

———. "Trials of Freedom: African American Deserters During the U.S. Civil War." *Journal of Southern History* 49, no. 3 (2016): 693–709.

Lang, Andrew. *In the Wake of War: Military Occupation, Emancipation, and Civil War America.* Baton Rouge: Louisiana State University Press, 2017.

Lewis, Jan. *The Pursuit of Happiness: Family and Values in Jefferson's Virginia.* Cambridge: Cambridge University Press, 1983.

Litwack, Leon. *North of Slavery: The Negro in the Free State, 1790–1860.* Chicago: University of Chicago Press, 1961.

Long, Alecia P. "(Mis)Remembering General Order No. 28: Benjamin Butler, the Woman Order, and Historical Memory." In Whites and Long, *Occupied Women.*

Lyons, Clare A. *Sex Among the Rabble: An Intimate History of Gender and Power in the Age of Revolution, Philadelphia, 1730–1830.* Chapel Hill: University of North Carolina Press, 2006.

Mackey, Robert R. *The Uncivil War: Irregular Warfare in the Upper South, 1861–1865.* Norman: University of Oklahoma Press, 2004.

Mammina, Laura. "Domesticity in Conflict: Union Soldiers, Southern Women, and Gender Roles during the American Civil War." In Bever et al., *American Discord.*

———. "'In the Midst of Fire and Blood': Union Soldiers, Unionist Women, Military Policy, and Intimate Space During the American Civil War." *Civil War History* 64, no. 2 (2018): 146–74.

Manning, Chandra. *Troubled Refuge: Struggling for Freedom in the Civil War.* New York: Vintage, 2017.

Mathisen, Erik. *The Loyal Republic: Traitors, Slaves, and the Remaking of Citizenship in Civil War America.* Chapel Hill: University of North Carolina Press, 2018.

McCurry, Stephanie. *Confederate Reckoning: Power and Politics in the Civil War South.* Cambridge, Mass.: Harvard University Press, 2010.

———. *Masters of Small Worlds: Yeoman Households, Gender Relations, and the Political Culture of the Antebellum South.* Oxford: Oxford University Press, 1997.

———. *Women's War: Fighting and Surviving the American Civil War.* Cambridge, Mass.: Harvard University Press, 2019.

McPherson, James. *Battle Cry of Freedom: The Civil War Era.* Oxford: Oxford University Press, 1988.

Miles, Tiya. "The Narrative of Nancy, a Cherokee Woman." *Frontiers: A Journal of Women Studies* 29, nos. 2/3 (2008): 59–80.

———. *Ties That Bind: The Story of an Afro-Cherokee Family in Slavery and Freedom.* Berkeley: University of California Press, 2005.

Mitchell, Reid. *Civil War Soldiers.* New York: Penguin, 1997.

———. *Vacant Chair: The Northern Soldier Leaves Home.* New York: Oxford University Press, 1995.

Morgan, Edmund. *American Slavery, American Freedom: The Ordeal of Colonial Virginia.* New York: W. W. Norton, 1975.

Morgan, Jennifer. *Laboring Women: Reproduction and Gender in New World Slavery.* Philadelphia: University of Pennsylvania Press, 2004.

Morris, Thomas D. *Southern Slavery and the Law, 1619–1860.* Chapel Hill: University of North Carolina Press, 1996.

Mortenson, Christopher R. *Politician in Uniform: General Lew Wallace and the Civil War.* Norman: University of Oklahoma Press, 2019.

Neely, Mark E. *The Civil War and the Limits of Destruction.* Cambridge, Mass.: Harvard University Press, 2007.

Nelson, Megan Kate. *Ruin Nation: Destruction and the American Civil War.* Athens: University of Georgia Press, 2012.

Oakes, James. *Freedom National: The Destruction of Slavery in the United States, 1861–1865.* New York: W. W. Norton, 2013.

Ott, Victoria. *Confederate Daughters: Coming of Age During the Civil War.* Carbondale: Southern Illinois University Press, 2008.

Penningroth, Dylan C. *The Claims of Kinfolk: African American Property and Community in the Nineteenth-Century South.* Chapel Hill: University of North Carolina Press, 2003.

Phillips, Jason. "A Brother's War?: Exploring Confederate Perceptions of the Enemy." In Sheehan-Dean, *View from the Ground.*

———. "The Grape Vine Telegraph: Rumors and Confederate Persistence." *Journal of Southern History* 72 (2006): 753–88.

Rable, George C. *Civil Wars: Women and the Crisis of Southern Nationalism.* Chicago: University of Illinois Press, 1989.

———. *God's Almost Chosen Peoples: A Religious History of the American Civil War.* Chapel Hill: University of North Carolina Press, 2010.

Rael, Patrick. *Black Identity and Black Protest in the Antebellum North.* Chapel Hill: University of North Carolina Press, 2002.

Ramold, Steven J. *Baring the Iron Hand: Discipline in the Union Army.* DeKalb: Northern Illinois University Press, 2010.

Robinson, Armstead L. *Bitter Fruits of Bondage: The Demise of Slavery and the Collapse of the Confederacy, 1861–1865.* Charlottesville: University of Virginia Press, 2005.

Romeo, Sharon. *Gender and the Jubilee: Black Freedom and the Reconstruction of Citizenship in Civil War Missouri.* Athens: University of Georgia Press, 2018.

Rose, Willie Lee. *Rehearsal for Reconstruction: The Port Royal Experiment.* Athens: Brown Thrasher Books, University of Georgia Press, 1999.

Rosen, Hannah. *Terror in the Heart of Freedom: Citizenship, Sexual Violence, and the Meaning of Race in the Postemancipation South.* Chapel Hill: University of North Carolina Press, 2009.

Rothman, Adam. *Slave Country: American Expansion and the Origins of the Deep South.* Cambridge, Mass.: Harvard University Press, 2005.

Rotundo, E. Anthony. *American Manhood: Transformations in Masculinity from the Revolution to the Modern Era.* New York: Basic Books, 1993.

Royster, Charles. *The Destructive War: William Tecumseh Sherman, Stonewall Jackson, and the Americans.* New York: Vintage, 1993.

Ruminski, Jarrett. *The Limits of Loyalty: Ordinary People in Civil War Mississippi.* Jackson: University Press of Mississippi, 2017.

Sacher, John M. *Confederate Conscription and the Struggle for Southern Soldiers.* Baton Rouge: Louisiana State University Press, 2021.

Samito, Christian G. *Becoming American Under Fire: Irish Americans, African Americans, and the Politics of Citizenship During the Civil War Era.* Ithaca, N.Y.: Cornell University Press, 2009.

Schwalm, Leslie. *Emancipation's Diaspora: Race and Reconstruction in the Upper Midwest.* Chapel Hill: University of North Carolina Press, 2009.

———. *A Hard Fight for We: Women's Transition from Slavery to Freedom in South Carolina.* Urbana: University of Illinois Press, 1997.

Scott, Anne Firor. *The Southern Lady: From Pedestal to Politics, 1830–1930.* Charlottesville: University Press of Virginia, 1995.

Sheehan-Dean, Aaron, ed. *The Calculus of Violence: How Americans Fought the Civil War.* Cambridge, Mass.: Harvard University Press, 2018.

———. *The View from the Ground: Experiences of Civil War Soldiers.* Lexington: University Press of Kentucky, 2007.

Siddali, Silvana R. *From Property to Person: Slavery and the Confiscation Acts, 1861–1862*. Baton Rouge: Louisiana State University Press, 2005.
Silber, Nina. *Gender and the Sectional Conflict*. Chapel Hill: University of North Carolina Press, 2008.
Smith, Bonnie G. *Ladies of the Leisure Class: The Bourgeoisies of Northern France in the Nineteenth Centuries*. Princeton, N.J.: Princeton University Press, 1981.
Sommerville, Diane Miller. *Rape and Race in the Nineteenth-Century South*. Chapel Hill: University of North Carolina Press, 2004.
Stansell, Christine. *City of Women: Sex and Class in New York, 1789–1860*. New York: Alfred A. Knopf, 1986.
Storey, Margaret M. *Loyalty and Loss: Alabama's Unionists in the Civil War and Reconstruction*. Baton Rouge: Louisiana State University Press, 2004.
Streater, Kristin L. "'She-Rebels' on the Supply Line: Gender Conventions in Civil War Kentucky." In Whites and Long, *Occupied Women*.
Sumler-Edmond, Janice L. "Free Black Life in Savannah." In Harris and Berry, *Slavery and Freedom in Savannah*.
Sutherland, Daniel E. *Savage Conflict: The Decisive Role of Guerrillas in the American Civil War*. Chapel Hill: University of North Carolina Press, 2009.
Taylor, Amy Murrell. *Embattled Freedom: Journeys Through the Civil War's Slave Refugee Camps*. Chapel Hill: University of North Carolina Press, 2018.
Teters, Kristopher A. *Practical Liberators: Union Officers in the Western Theater During the Civil War*. Chapel Hill: University of North Carolina Press, 2018.
Thomas, Emory M. *The Confederate Nation, 1861–1865*. New York: Harper & Row, 1979.
Thomas, William G. "Nothing Ought to Astonish Us: Confederate Civilians in the 1864 Shenandoah Valley Campaign." In Gallagher, *Shenandoah Valley Campaign of 1864*.
Thornton, J. Mills III. *Politics and Power in a Slave Society: Alabama, 1800–1860*. Baton Rouge: Louisiana State University Press, 1978.
Varon, Elizabeth R. *Armies of Deliverance: A New History of the Civil War*. Oxford: Oxford University Press, 2019.
———. *We Mean to Be Counted: White Women and Politics in Antebellum Virginia*. Chapel Hill: University of North Carolina Press, 1998.
Vogel, V. Jacques. *Free but Not Equal: The Midwest and the Negro During the Civil War*. Chicago: University of Chicago Press, 1967.
Vorenberg, Michael. *Final Freedom: The Civil War, the Abolition of Slavery, and the Thirteenth Amendment*. Cambridge: Cambridge University Press, 2001.
Walters, Ronald G. *American Reformers, 1815–1860*. New York: Hill & Wang, 1978.

Welcher, Frank J. *The Union Army, 1861–1865: Organization and Operations.* 2 vols. Bloomington: Indiana University Press, 1989.

Wells, Jonathan Daniel. *The Origins of the Southern Middle Class, 1800–1861.* Chapel Hill: University of North Carolina Press, 2004.

Welter, Barbara. "The Cult of True Womanhood: 1820–1860." *American Quarterly* 18, no. 2 (1966): 151–74.

White, Deborah G. *Ar'n't I a Woman? Female Slaves in the Plantation South.* New York: W. W. Norton, 1999.

White, Jonathan W. *Emancipation, the Union Army, and the Reelection of Abraham Lincoln.* Baton Rouge: Louisiana State University Press, 2014.

Whites, LeeAnn. *The Civil War as a Crisis in Gender: Augusta, Georgia, 1860–1890.* Athens: University of Georgia Press, 1995.

———. "'Corresponding with the Enemy': Mobilizing the Relational Field of Battle in St. Louis." In Whites and Long, *Occupied Women.*

———. *Gender Matters: Civil War, Reconstruction, and the Making of the New South.* New York: Palgrave Macmillan, 2005.

Whites, LeeAnn, and Alecia P. Long, eds. *Occupied Women: Gender, Military Occupation, and the American Civil War.* Baton Rouge: Louisiana State University Press, 2009.

Wiley, Bell Irvin. *The Life of Billy Yank: The Common Soldier of the Union.* Baton Rouge: Louisiana State University Press, 1952.

Witt, John Fabian. *Lincoln's Code: The Laws of War in American History.* New York: Free Press, 2012.

INDEX

Locators in italics indicate a figure.

UNCIVIL WARS

Weirding the War: Stories from the Civil War's Ragged Edges
edited by Stephen Berry

Ruin Nation: Destruction and the American Civil War
by Megan Kate Nelson

America's Corporal: James Tanner in War and Peace
by James Marten

The Blue, the Gray, and the Green: Toward an Environmental History of the Civil War
edited by Brian Allen Drake

Empty Sleeves: Amputation in the Civil War South
by Brian Craig Miller

Lens of War: Exploring Iconic Photographs of the Civil War
edited by J. Matthew Gallman and Gary W. Gallagher

The Slave-Trader's Letter-Book: Charles Lamar, the Wanderer, and Other Tales of the African Slave Trade
by Jim Jordan

Driven from Home: North Carolina's Civil War Refugee Crisis
by David Silkenat

The Ghosts of Guerrilla Memory: How Civil War Bushwhackers Became Gunslingers in the American West
by Matthew Christopher Hulbert

Beyond Freedom: Disrupting the History of Emancipation
edited by David W. Blight and Jim Downs

The Lost President: A. D. Smith and the Hidden History of Radical Democracy in Civil War America
by Ruth Dunley

Bodies in Blue: Disability in the Civil War North
by Sarah Handley-Cousins

Visions of Glory: The Civil War in Word and Image
edited by Kathleen Diffley and Benjamin Fagan

Household War: How Americans Lived and Fought the Civil War
edited by Lisa Tendrich Frank and LeeAnn Whites

Buying and Selling Civil War Memory in Gilded Age America
edited by James Marten and Caroline E. Janney

The War After the War: A New History of Reconstruction
by John Patrick Daly

The Families' Civil War: Black Soldiers and the Fight for Racial Justice
by Holly A. Pinheiro Jr.

Sand, Science, and the Civil War: Sedimentary Geology and Combat
by Scott Hippensteel

A Man by Any Other Name: William Clarke Quantrill and the Search for American Manhood
by Joseph M. Beilein Jr.

A Continuous State of War: Empire Building and Race Making in the Civil War–Era Gulf South
by Maria Angela Diaz

Between King Cotton and Queen Victoria: How Pirates, Smugglers, and Scoundrels Almost Saved the Confederacy
by Beau Cleland

Hard Women, Hard War: How Southern Women Shaped U.S. Policy During the Civil War
by Laura Mammina

www.ingramcontent.com/pod-product-compliance
Lightning Source LLC
LaVergne TN
LVHW040504011026
849280LV00024B/216
* 9 7 8 0 8 2 0 3 8 0 6 0 5 *